The
Last
Soldiers
of the
King

The Last Soldiers of the King

Wartime Italy, 1943–1945

Eugenio Corti

Translated by Manuela Arundel
Foreword by Carlo D'Este

Copyright © 2003 by
The Curators of the University of Missouri
University of Missouri Press, Columbia, Missouri 65201
Printed and bound in the United States of America
All rights reserved
5 4 3 2 1   07 06 05 04 03

Library of Congress Cataloging-in-Publication Data

Corti, Eugenio, 1921–
    [Ultimi sodati del re. English]
    The last soldiers of the King : wartime Italy, 1943–1945 / Eugenio Corti ; translated by
Manuela Arundel ; foreword by Carlo D'Este.
        p.   cm.
Includes bibliographical references and index.
    ISBN 0-8262-1491-6 (alk. paper)
        1. Corti, Eugenio, 1921– .   2. World War, 1939–1945—Personal narratives, Italian.
3. World War, 1939–1945—Campaigns—Italy.   4. Italy. Esercito. Corpo italiano di
liberazione—History.   5. World War, 1939–1945—Regimental histories—Italy.
6. Italy—History—Allied occupation, 1943–1947.   I. Title.
D763.I815.C67 A3 2003
940.54′1245′092—dc22

                                                                          2003017878

♾™ This paper meets the requirements of the
American National Standard for Permanence of Paper
for Printed Library Materials, Z39.48, 1984.

Designer: Kristie Lee
Typesetter: The Composing Room of Michigan, Inc.
Printer and binder: The Maple-Vail Book Manufacturing Group
Typefaces: Adobe Garamond and Benguiat

Publication of this book has been assisted by a generous contribution
from Eugene Davidson.

Contents

Foreword

Carlo D'Este

WITH THE PUBLICATION of *Few Returned* (University of Missouri Press, 1997), Eugenio Corti, one of Italy's most distinguished postwar writers, was first introduced to American readers through his poignant account of his experiences as an Italian soldier on the Russian Front in the winter of 1942–1943. As a young twenty-one-year-old lieutenant of artillery Corti was one of the 250,000 men of the Italian Eighth Army sent to Russia by Mussolini ostensibly to fight alongside his German ally, but in reality to be in a position to gain a measure of the plunder from an Axis-occupied Soviet Union. On the River Don the Italian force of 30,000 of which Corti was a member was surrounded by the Red Army and faced annihilation.

Few Returned recounted the appalling experience of these Italian soldiers during their breakout from encirclement and a forced retreat from Russia. Their near annihilation by the Red Army during the dreadful winter of 1942–1943 was an experience reminiscent of the conditions encountered during Napoleon's retreat from Moscow in 1812. Corti was one of only an estimated 4,000 soldiers out of the force of 30,000 to survive the ordeal of the retreat from the Don. Untold thousands were killed, and of the 50,000 to 60,000 Italian soldiers of the expeditionary force captured by the Red Army, only 10,300 were later repatriated. Mussolini's dreams of empire were shattered and his ill-fated Eighth Army had simply ceased to exist.

By the summer of 1943 the Allies had driven Axis forces from North Africa and with the July invasion of the island of Sicily were poised to bring the war to mainland Italy. With the backing of senior officers of the Italian Army, King Victor Emmanuel III acted in July to remove Mussolini from power, then placed him under house arrest in a resort in the mountains of the Abruzzi, where he remained until September when he was rescued at Hitler's orders by SS Lieutenant Colonel Otto Skorzeny.

The joyous celebrations after the fall of Mussolini were short-lived as

Italy soon became a battleground that would be fought over for the next twenty months, leaving most of the country devastated.

The disastrous war to which Mussolini had so willingly committed his nation in 1940 had come full cycle. A new Italian government headed by Field Marshal Pietro Badoglio informed Hitler that Mussolini had resigned voluntarily and pledged Italy would honor its commitment to Germany as an ally, even as it negotiated Italy's surrender to the Allies. The announcement of Italy's capitulation in early September 1943 was greeted with unbridled fury by Hitler, who condemned it as a betrayal and swore revenge. Henceforth Germany would treat its onetime ally as the enemy. What had once been an uneasy partnership had turned into a state of war. In rapid order a series of harsh reprisals were carried out. Italian Jews were rounded up and deported to Nazi death camps such as Auschwitz, thousands of Italians were taken as hostages and murdered, and a reign of terror was initiated not only throughout German-occupied Italy but also in other occupied states in the Mediterranean. Although conditions in the north were somewhat better, southern Italy was plunged into starvation and deprivation every bit as brutal as that of the nations conquered by Germany.

The surrender left the Italian Army virtually leaderless, and it all but disintegrated in the chaotic period that followed. What is less well known is that while some elements of the Italian Army remained loyal to fascism and continued to fight alongside their German ally, others switched sides and aligned themselves with the Allies after the British invaded southern Italy and the U.S. Fifth Army landed at Salerno on September 9, 1943. Those who did so were subject to immediate execution if captured by the vengeful Germans. As British historian Richard Lamb points out, "Hitler ordered that all Italian troops fighting against the Germans were to be treated as *francs-tireurs* and shot as they surrendered, in order to minimize Italian military co-operation with the Allies; his generals obeyed these criminal orders."[1] Some of the very worst atrocities were perpetrated against Italian soldiers captured in Italy, Greece, Yugoslavia, and the islands of the Aegean. An estimated six hundred thousand Italian soldiers were deported in cattle wagons to Hitler's slave labor camps in Germany where they became fodder for the German war machine.

After his escape from Russia in 1943, Eugenio Corti remained in the Italian Army and was one of those who switched sides, joining the fight along-

1. Richard Lamb, *War in Italy, 1943–1945* (New York: St. Martin's Press, 1994), 2.

side the British in the Abruzzi. *The Last Soldiers of the King* is Corti's account of his experiences during the remainder of the war.

The war in Italy was the longest military campaign fought by the Allies. From the time of the first landings in September 1943, the war in Italy lasted 602 days as the Allies fought some of the bitterest battles of World War II from Calabria to the foothills of the Alps. The cost in human misery was staggering. Allied casualties totaled 312,000, including 31,886 killed. German losses in Italy have never been fully affirmed but are cited as 435,646 (including more than 48,000 dead and more than 214,000 missing, most of whom have never been accounted for). The number of dead and homeless Italians can only be guessed.

The Last Soldiers of the King is one soldier's deeply personal account that depicts the war from the perspective of the average Italian soldier. As was the case in *Few Returned,* this book focuses not on high-level strategy or the wars of the generals, but what life was like at the sharp end of battle, and during those times when men fought boredom as well as the enemy and attempted to make sense of the chaos of war.

Corti's book is more than yet another war memoir; it is the story of life in wartime Italy, as reflected in his descriptions of a proud people forced to endure death, poverty, and the virtual destruction of their nation during the most oppressive period of Italian history.

Piedmont

•Milan

Bologna
•

Florence
•

Filottrano
•

The Marches

•Macerata

Istria

•Teramo

Abruzzi   •Chieti

•Rome

•Nettuno

Adriatic Sea

Molise

Sardinia

Tyrrhenian Sea

•Naples

•Bari

Puglia

Mediterranean Sea

Sicily

🌣 **Part One**

Lady, make a bridge between us and God, our Mary
show me in Him the things I attempt to narrate,
and my voice will be like a song,
as it tells of all
that I and my companions lived through in those years.

1

IN EARLY JUNE 1944, Italy was divided into two opposing halves: the north occupied by the Germans, the south by the British and Americans. On the Anglo-American front—and more precisely within the British Eighth Army—twenty thousand of us soldiers from the *Corpo Italiano di Liberazione* (a bitter appellation, more aspiration than name) had inserted ourselves.

We were lined up above Lanciano, in Abruzzi. From the observation post of my platoon, established in the attic of a country home, one could see, on the right side between the distant hills, a slight streak of sea. Sometimes, within the silence of the front, I scrutinized that brief, colorful streak with binoculars and tried to distinguish the outline of the waves, but the distance was too great. On the shore of that melancholy sea I had walked alongside Margherita during the summer of the previous year.

Ahead to the north were what would become our objectives during the bloody days of the advance: villages ruined by artillery, deserted under the sun. A series of long, hilly ridges sloped from the Apennines to the sea; each ridge allowed us to see only in part the crest and road of the next, in a scene of consecutive steps, always more faded in the distance. On the most distant ridge one could detect the city of Chieti, of which my binoculars distinguished few details: some city walls, perhaps house fronts, and bell tower tops, but nothing of the life that should have been thriving there.

We wanted the bloody days of the advance to arrive soon.

*

The Nembo Paratroopers Division (half of them a regular force from an ordinary division), to which my artillery regiment belonged, had come to the line shortly before, on March 30. Our group's commanding officer, a Sicilian major—gaunt and stubborn, nicknamed *Pelaformiche* because of his meticulousness—had taken us to the observation post on a half-track.[1]

Barely out of Lanciano we had passed an emplacement of heavy British guns; farther ahead was another one of light artillery, and then a few British camps around huge tanks. Still farther ahead was a large camp of Indian soldiers—maybe just withdrawn from the line—who had set up their low, ocher British tents on the back of a hill, around which they wandered or squatted.

Our halftrack driver had proceeded with caution because of notices on both sides of the road that warned of mines. Occasionally we passed a few farms, more or less in ruins; if they were inhabited the farmers greeted us joyfully, yelling words like: "Now that you are joining the line, the front will finally move. It hasn't moved since winter. Now it will really go forward."

The Abruzzese farmers didn't laugh at us. On the contrary, with simplicity, they expressed their faith, which had remained uncompromised in spite of the army's disgraceful collapse the previous fall.

We had only found our paratroopers again near the line; they were on the road in small units, waiting to go up.

Almost all of them were very young, conspicuously undisciplined. In khaki or grayish-green shorts, with bare arms and legs and small daggers on their hips, they all wore their berets pressed on their foreheads in a style of their own. We too, artillerymen of the Nembo, wore berets. We had distributed them in a hurry the previous week when, in order to complete the division, our regiment (small, with sixteen guns in all) had joined the two meager regiments of paratroopers arrived from Sardegna. On our heads, however, the same headgear lacked style and, rather than warlike, appeared tame and awkward. We realized this every time that we looked at the paratroopers.

Two of them had stopped us suddenly, holding out their arms. "Where are you going? The front line is just a few meters ahead."

The major had searched the map: "The Catabbi house . . . Tell me," he insisted, as though they weren't just as new to the area as he, "where is the Catabbi house? Isn't it farther ahead?"

The paratroopers had shrugged. "Who knows! But you can't go on ahead because there's barbed wire."

---

1. Translator's note: *Pelaformiche* is a term used to describe someone who is so meticulous as to remove hair from ants.

4

After some hesitation (out of habit he didn't trust what they were telling him) the major turned back to the last crossroad. Fortunately the hedges of oaks on the sides of the road hid us from the enemy.

"What a deployment!" muttered Sergeant Canèr, second-in-command of the platoon. "All those guns and tanks in the rear zone, and we almost cross the line without running into anyone."

"It's the British and American system," Major Pelaformiche explained, looking up from the topographical map, but keeping a pencil pointed at it. "The machinery in the rear zone fights the war; the line is only a protection in front."

The teetering halftrack had gone down a wooded valley and, climbing up the other side, had brought us at last to the shelter of a farm with a view, the Catabbi house, where we would put the observation post. There was already a British post, which would stay until new orders, undoubtedly because our arms must have appeared insufficient to the British command.

While we unloaded our gear, a salvo of minenwerfers came from the German line. The sounds passed over us, and three or four rockets exploded with some smoke between the trees, a hundred meters behind us.

After having repeated a few orders in great detail, as was his habit, the major again climbed onto the halftrack, which drove once more down the small valley road. Shortly we would learn that the minenwerfers had injured some of the paratroopers.

This is how it began once more.

*

I had asked the paratrooper sergeant major, whose platoon had lined up at the Catabbi house a few hours earlier, to show me the layout of the defenses. He seemed glad that an Italian officer was in the house to balance in some way the presence of those enigmatic British observers—courteous on the outside, tough on the inside—who sat apart on their own in the attic.

The paratroopers intervened immediately. "Look," one of them said to me, "where those filthy Indians slept."

"The stinkers!" another said. "The British said that they were from . . . where did they say they were from?"

"From Nepal," came the answer. "It must be a savage place. It can go to hell. Over there they have two kinds of soldiers: one brings back the head of his enemy from each battle, the other only brings back ears. In this post are those who bring back ears: maybe we'll happen to find a collection behind some rock. Filthy people!"

Indifferent to his companions' disquiet, an earnest paratrooper, as though in a hurry, offered me a bazooka (maybe just handed out along with the submachine guns, with which all were armed) and placed in my hand a rocket. "Lieutenant, somebody told me that it's enough to pass through a tank. Do you know anything about bazookas?"

The matter should have interested everyone, as the men were new to the weapon; in spite of this, the others barely let him finish.

"Tanks, not on your life!"

"Not on your life will it go through."

"That thing isn't enough even to go through your . . ."

With this vulgar remark the sergeant major—short and stout with a protruding jaw—positioned his small mustache into a hint of disapproval of me, as he did whenever we heard swearing (which, unfortunately, happened all the time). He was southern, and would have liked for his men to be better behaved. In the following days, however, becoming used to our presence, he would no longer worry about etiquette.

The house inherited from the Indians contained rudimentary apertures by the windows facing the enemy and reinforced with small bags of sand, as well as other even more rudimentary foxholes on both sides of the house, behind bushes; the platoon—small, because of use in air-drops—was without heavy machine guns and had just three light guns.

Within a couple of days I realized that the paratroopers—assault troops—were inept at keeping watch. During their watches they looked around bored, scratched their heads, chewed on blades of grass. What would they have done had we stayed there for months? On the second day, the sergeant major had a tantrum, forbidding them to sit on the edges of gun pits to smoke, chat, or wander around between the house and the outbuildings, which probably would have sufficed for the Germans, with their deadly 120−mm mortars positioned about half a kilometer away, to detect the presence of troops in the house and demolish it.

The entire area inherited from the Indians was organized by strong-points. In the battalion sector (the sixteenth, the only one in the Nembo made up of recruits) it followed a road along the ridge of a hill. There were farms and other houses—each with its stables—on the side of the road, situated a few hundred meters from one another, and in each house was a platoon. The street was full of weeds, since no one had used it in months; patches of red poppies, resembling flowers on the dresses of peasant women long ago, grew there, amidst the strange smell of the dead grass (which in my memory became the smell of Abruzzi).

2

THE DAYS HAD BEGUN to pass—always un-
changing—with starry nights. We never heard the songs of birds nor the
song of peasant women among the olive trees, which were untended, or in
the golden wheat that the sun, faithful to its role, slowly ripened. The silence held all. When sunny afternoons gave the impression that silence
came from the sultry weather, one would listen in vain for the staccato of
regional accents from men in the fields, or the cluck of some hen.

During those hours, whoever wasn't on duty got away from the heat and
flies by lying in the shade on his bed. My platoon occupied a partly ruined
little house, adjacent to the farm. In one of its rooms, only barely fitting,
were my cot and, on some planks, the bed of Canèr; against the wall and
at our feet were packs and optical instruments, shovels and picks covered
with dirt, and two submachine guns with cartridge clips next to them.

Canèr, a Trevisan, a gigantic fellow of few words, usually slept; I kept my
eyes on the ceiling. Each time I became attracted to the sequence of small,
thick wooden beams, carefully arranged above larger beams; these, however, brought me back to the family of farmers that had once lived here.
Where were they now? Roaming who knows where, like all peasant families—how many thousands?—who had to evacuate this strip of land between the Adriatic and the Tyrrhenian Sea, where the front had pressed for
too long, indeed, since December. Who knew where the residents of this
little house had taken refuge . . . Certainly, every day they must have
thought about the black hearth in the kitchen, where the packs of soldiers
now lay in a pile.

And what had become of my family? Since the days of the armistice—
nine months ago now!—I hadn't had any news, just as my family knew
nothing of me.

Better not to think of it. Otherwise I came back to the suffering of my
father and mother—as my brothers had described it—when a year and a

7

half earlier our divisions on the Russian front had been broken and I, as now, hadn't sent news . . .

Who knew how much my father must have had to work, there in the north, occupied by the Germans, to keep his employees' jobs, thousands of them . . . Well, I could not think of it. I could not even think about my friends who died on the Russian front. And about those missing, even more numerous. Not one of them, for all I knew, had yet written . . . And among them was my dearest friend, Zoilo Zorzi: who knew if at that instant he was alive, or if they had killed him in the moment of capture along with all the others?

Indeed I could not ask myself these questions. I could not let myself be paralyzed by such thoughts, if I wanted—so far as was within my power—to do something useful, for myself and for the others, for my people who, especially in the southern regions, incomprehensibly succeeded in surviving under the conditions . . . All kinds of rumors were going around in this regard. There was talk that prostitution in Naples and everywhere was spreading in a frenzy; that gangs of children (so-called *Sciuscià*)[2] whose parents were not able to care for them survived by stealing from the Allies. My country had been reduced to this. And there were other causes of anxiety, different but not any less urgent, particularly the absence, so evident, of legitimate authority (that poor king, Badoglio the head of government, the ministers) to confront the problems with which Italy was struggling.

Enough.

Next to me Sergeant Canèr continued to sleep, maybe dreaming about his Treviso or the engineering classes at the University of Padova, of which on rare occasion he talked. Enough melancholy!

I tried to relax, to think of something else, and I twisted and turned on my cot.

In any case it wasn't up to me, up to us soldiers, to resolve the enormous problems into which Italy had sunk: we didn't have the slightest means. Our purpose simply was to fight, to support those (able or not, welcome or not) who were at the head of the nation. We were soldiers; we had to behave like soldiers. And in fact we did so, with goodwill and even, when possible, with good cheer: after all, we were young men. In spite of the disorder, at barely more than twenty years of age we had our lives ahead of us . . . With this thought Margherita came to mind: I saw her again, her beau-

2. Shoeshines.

tiful hair, the forehead that shaped her profile, her eyes, so far from my memory.

*

An artilleryman opened the broken door: "It's your turn at the post, lieutenant."

I got up with a gesture (one that for years afterward, I would miss). I buckled the leather belt that held my gun and, amidst the smell of dead grass, reached the farmhouse. I went up the wooden ladder to the attic; here Lance Corporal Freddi, from the Parmese Mountains, a carpenter in civilian life, was preparing to give me his place. From the beams of the roof between the roof tiles, the British officer on duty greeted me courteously in French. I hoisted myself to his side, in the heat of the tiles and sandbags. The enemy line appeared deserted, its few houses destroyed.

"News?"

"None." The officer wiped the sweat from his face.

We looked carefully through binoculars at the enemy territory, separated from ours by the gorge of a hill where an entire village, Crecchio, was hidden from us. Everything—the ruined village, the streets, the remains of farms, the countryside here and there covered with poppies—was without movement. We exchanged a few remarks in French.

At times, my eyes lingered upon the ruins of a small house with the remains of a once lovely red roof, where one night we had detected a dim light: "Not even there, by any chance, some movement?"

"Not even there."

Within a few days the officers gave us the first news of the Allied landing in France, then of the Americans' entry into Rome; the Red Army had crossed the Polish and Romanian borders and was about to enter the heart of Europe. It seemed that the war, at least against the Germans, would not last much longer. The question, another of the tragic, terrible problems that troubled us in those days, was whether, once Germany had been overcome, the Soviet troops would halt.

Among these officers was Maugham Brown, from Cape Town, a cordial fellow with a tuft of brown hair at his forehead who had given up the rank of captain in the South African Artillery to become a lieutenant in the British Army: "In order to meet new people," he explained to me. I believe that it was for this reason that he had volunteered. Now, however, he had had more than enough of war.

"By now the only thing that seems sensible," he told me several times, "is to find a girl who can understand me, and to marry her." Due to our slight familiarity with French, the two of us only discussed the essentials. This didn't stop us from playful speech, common in those disheartening days, when something almost wasn't worth discussing if we couldn't laugh about it.

Maugham Brown listened to me, astounded, his pipe bowl in one hand, when one afternoon, passing from a playful tone to serious, I shared my experiences of the Bolshevik world. The British lack of sensitivity in the face of the danger that threatened Europe dismayed me. They said, "If the Russian Army is as powerful as you say, and should invade the Continent, we'll have to let them." "How could we offer resistance?" asked Maugham Brown. "Our forces have been taken over by the navy."

"That's good for us Continentals," I answered, not realizing at the time that the British, although their troops moved forward, weren't winning the war after all. I wasn't aware that by now their strength was weak compared with the Americans. Not even these remaining officers realized that power had shifted in the world.

3

AFTER THE TAKING of Rome—June 5, 1944—our sector seemed to revive. The British artillery continued, like before, to bombard the opposing line with unexpected force, which pushed the Germans farther inland; but German fire from the bottom of the hills began to increase and shells fell around us several times with deafening roars. We spent nights in a state of alarm.

After one such night, at dawn Maugham Brown and I were sleepily scrutinizing the front from the observation post—behind us Canèr, seated on a crate, yawned—when we heard from the ground floor unexpected noise and unfamiliar voices. All three of us turned toward the ladder, where, shortly after, the bespectacled face of Major Pelaformiche appeared and, behind, that of the commander of our artillery regiment, Lieutenant Colonel Leonardo Giaccone, who had by his side an important-looking British colonel; other superior officers, British and our own, followed the others.

"We must," Giaccone announced (with the touch of solemnity he used in important moments), "conduct and observe the Italian artillery fire." Hence, a sort of test. Maugham Brown and I lay down, freeing the aperture between the roof tiles where three or four ranking officers took position.

Second Lieutenant Antonio Moroni, with whom after the armistice I had walked south from dawn to dusk for four long weeks to reach German-free territory, had also entered the attic, following an unknown colonel of nondescript appearance. He came up to me. "What in the devil have they done with you?" I asked him softly, warmly shaking his hand. "You're no longer in the battery?"

"Please don't mention it," he muttered, disgusted. "Now I am at the order of commander . . ." He named a type of command I'd never heard before.

"What did you say?"

"They discovered," he explained, still softly, "that by organizing themselves both in the Italian and British manner, there's a way of bringing in some of the superior officers who do nothing near the regiment's command. Imagine: to justify their presence!"

"I understand. But, really, what do you and your colonel do?"

"Nothing. We have nothing to do, so we do nothing . . ."

"Ah, right."

"Aside from rubbing his stomach once in a while and saying: 'I once again *feel like a little Napoleone*: who would have thought, the armistice?'"

"And what else does he do?"

"Nothing, I told you. But let's understand each other, all things considered he's a good devil."

"Indeed."

"Do you think that we Italians will succeed in making the British and Americans lose the war too?" Sergeant Canèr, having followed the conversation, whispered behind us, thoughtfully looking at his fingernails.

Meanwhile they were calling the artillery registration on telephones, and the name of the observation post was uttered and even yelled out often: that name was Margherita.

Antonio looked at me: "They asked you to give the post a woman's name, right?"

"Well, according to the British system . . ."

"And without a doubt you gave it that name."

"Yes."

"It's your style."

"Thank you," I said uncertainly.

"It's your style to be so foolish."

I didn't deny it.

Having shaken his head, he turned his attention to the British. He was from an aristocratic Bergamese family, and had light-colored hair and eyes, a rosy face, and a build—at just over twenty years old—already verging on heavy; he had been a good companion in the long trek to the south.

"By the way," I told him, "I have a little surprise for you."

"A surprise? What?"

"Now, don't be impatient."

"Come on," he burst out, "what surprise?"

"Would you like to see again the little house of Petroro?"

"Why? Can you see it from here?"

I nodded.

But right at that moment he was called and sent off with an order.

Meanwhile Colonel Giaccone had started the firing. Giaccone enjoyed the reputation of being a very bright man: having been the chief of staff of the Centauro Division in Libya and Tunisia, he was (so I had heard) one of the most esteemed "brains" of the Italian general staff. Now he had to be satisfied with commanding a regiment of barely sixteen guns.

After each of his orders came the shriek of our shells—like an unfurling of stiff paper—which, passing high above us, went over the enemy line. The British colonel silently observed through binoculars, at Giaccone's side.

I removed myself as much as possible from the group, to a corner of the attic where, in front of a small round window, a sizable siege telescope was positioned on its tripod. From the small window the view stretched to the right toward the Apennines, dominated by the huge clear massif of the Maiella. One could see the distant village of Petroro at its foot; there Antonio and I had taken our longest rest during the journey from German-occupied Italy to where our army was reestablishing itself. I again focused the powerful telescope on that tiny place.

I located, thanks to the small church by its side, our hosts' blurred house. Once the front passed through, maybe we would be able to find some news there of my family and that of Antonio. But did that house still have residents?

In the attic, the loud talk, created almost exclusively by our visiting compatriots, not by the British, kept increasing. Of course they all realized its uselessness but, as it was, they couldn't help it. The British, however, succeeded in controlling themselves, and even proved more reserved than usual; in some of the older men I noticed that their air of unhappiness, which wasn't unusual among them, was accentuated.

Maugham Brown winked at me several times from behind Giaccone and the British colonel, indicating the two bores in front of him. He didn't seem to notice the noise, probably ignored it tactfully.

*

At noon the small group of intruders went back the same way they had come, answering the concern that had distressed Antonio's "little Napoleone": having to arrive late at the dinner table.

As they were about to leave the attic, another man with the rank of "first captain," with a shaved head and an eyeglass who until then had remained aside, wanted to take a look through a now unattended observation aperture.

He called me immediately: "The observer," he said, becoming animated, "where is the designated observer?"

"Here I am, captain." I moved myself quickly to his place between the beams.

He indicated—with courtesy, I must say—a fence post fixed in a field: "There. You see there? It's a German soldier. Do you see him?"

"Are you talking about that . . . thing, in that field? No, captain, that's a fence post. I've known it for a while by sight."

"But no, but no," he said, and shook his head, irritated by my lack of usefulness.

He left without insisting; maybe he was afraid to be left behind. Reaching the first steps of the ladder that went down from the attic, he turned around, his eyeglass shining: "I count on coming back here," he said with a smile, "and soon. See you again, then."

I rubbed my face. "Lucky that the British didn't witness that scene," was my first thought.

Only an Italian second lieutenant, Bergna from Monza, and hence almost my countryman, observer of a group of horse-drawn 75s who had come to the line just the day before, remained in the attic.

"My God, what a strange individual!" he exclaimed. "He's . . . he's in your command?"

"Yes, but attached," I pointed out. "Before today I'd only seen him a couple of times, in passing."

"How can someone . . . like that find himself with troops?"

"Because he's recommended by politicians. The usual story."

"Do you know by what person he's recommended?"

"No, I don't know. The fact remains that the War Ministry assigned him to the regiment, even if he's past—did you notice?—the age limit."

Bergna nodded.

"Why do they do these kinds of things?"

"Do you know that in Naples, Benedetto Croce succeeded in posting bills on the walls calling people to arms? That he attempted to gather his own army, or rather politicians, separate from the regular army?"

"Yes, I heard something of it."

"Right. At this rate, anyone, like Croce and anti-Fascist parties, even the Sicilian separatists, for example, could call people to arms. Or, I don't know, the Mafia? After all they too have been persecuted by fascism, haven't they?"

"Sure, and even the others. What do they call them? The Camora," Bergna said.

"Those—I'd say—you can be sure that they'd gather more recruits in Naples than Benedetto."

We burst out laughing.

"But," he said, disapprovingly, "we shouldn't laugh at this kind of disaster."

"Do you understand why the ministry sends this sort of individual to the front once in a while? It's a concession, a sop. To avoid worse trouble." It was my turn to shake my head. "Who knows what might be going on now, back there."

In the meantime Bergna had pulled himself up to the peephole: "He was Piedmontese, right," he wanted to know, "the old man?"

"Yes. And from nobility; at least according to his name."

"What charge does he have?"

"None. At the regiment's command they nicknamed him Ancestor— and they all consider him a source of entertainment. Well, if you're staying, I'm going down for the rations." I descended from the attic.

"To what have we been reduced . . . " he concluded, as he shifted his attention outside.

Reaching the bottom of the wooden ladder, I turned around. "It doesn't matter. You'll see that we'll make it anyway," I said.

*

As a positive result of our firing test, the British cleared out of the post within a few hours. Maugham Brown brought their visit to an end. "Goodbye, friend," he said, holding out his large hand; it was his turn to be at the bottom of the ladder. "I really hope that when we see each other again this damned war will be over." If I had met him a year before, I thought, my task would have been to kill him . . . What an absurdity! I felt at that moment the familiar regret of partings particular to the front, becoming strangers again after having shared, even for a brief period, the hardships known by whoever faces combat. I tried to tell him this jokingly, but my French became tangled.

I would never again see Maugham Brown, nor the other British officers of the observation post. From that day until the end of August, the end of our time at the front, we would have nothing more to do with the British. We would not even meet them.

4

THE EVENING OF that same day I was with some artillerymen in the courtyard outside the farmhouse. Sitting on the grass, we conversed in melancholy voices.

Suddenly we heard the growing roar of an engine in our zone; it was on the road that led to the post. The sound of tires echoed among the rocks as it came up the hill.

It turned out to be a truck of the regiment's command. Even the enemy must have been listening; firing instructions must have been passing along the telephone lines. The truck stopped with a lurch near us.

"The platoon lieutenant? Where is the platoon lieutenant?" asked the Ancestor, stumbling down and almost tumbling into me. "In the dark, I can't see well," he explained; a German submachine gun hung from one of his shoulders, getting in his way. He regained his balance with my help and, having organized gun and eyeglass, announced smilingly, "Fellows, I've come to spend a night with you. I too want to participate in life on the front!" Seeing my scowling face, he added, "With the commanding colonel's consent: this is his submachine gun. He lent it to me."

"Fine, you'll experience life on the front right away. In two, at most three minutes, you'll begin to experience it. Can I send back the truck?"

"Sure. But why . . . in two or three minutes?"

"You'll find out why."

I turned to the driver. "You idiot, coming to the line by making as much noise as possible, leave." I raised my voice. "Leave!"

Frightened, his face dumb like a rabbit—without a doubt they had placed at the Ancestor's disposal the dumbest driver of the command—he turned the truck around and left in a great hurry.

I took the old man by his arm and led him toward the post, amidst the looks of the artillerymen and of a few paratroopers who had in the meantime come out of the farmhouse. Meanwhile I was sending Colonel Giaccone my blessings; if he was truly so clever, I told myself, this time he had lost a golden opportunity to prove it. The Ancestor stumbled and, stuttering, asked that I explain my remarks. I felt compassion for him and his age. Clearly, this strange captain, incapable of being a captain or even simply a soldier, driven for whatever reason to go to war, was a pleasant person, courteous, too insensitive to military life to know what to do.

In the attic—after having taken away the submachine gun so that he wouldn't fire into the window—I made him sit on a crate in the corner best protected by the sandbags. I entrusted him to Second Lieutenant Bergna, who was on duty: "Keep that captain on that case. Don't let him move a finger, and as for yourself, try to be lucky, because in a little while you'll really need it."

I went down the ladder to the other telephone.

I wasn't yet on the ground when the first German shells arrived; they were heavy mortars, probably 120–mm.

Silence. Then two long explosions. The shells were deafening, like tremendous pots breaking on the ground, filling the night air with violence.

The ladder got cut in two, and soon a succession of explosions surrounded the post; almost immediately artillery joined the mortars.

I had gotten in touch with the colonel. Giaccone laughed at my protests: "Ah, he came to you, the little old man? I imagine that he wants to earn himself a decoration to become ambassador or minister . . ." And since I insisted: "Well, listen, that type of man shouldn't be enjoyed only by the regiment's command: we should all enjoy him, all right? A lot of incoming fire? Who knows if one doesn't arrive in his size . . ." until the voice faded, interrupted by the fire that fell on the road behind the post, along which ran the telephone line. The phone failed, and the post was isolated.

A shell hit the center of the farmhouse wall that faced the enemy exactly in the middle of a submachine-gun nest, where the sergeant major and two men were. We saw them come out of a cloud of dust, shaking it off, all three white with plaster, fortunately unharmed, the sergeant major angry and waving the submachine gun, its barrel bent.

Since the shelling didn't show signs of diminishing, I ordered my men to enter a dugout that I had had them dig behind the house during the previous days. I invited the paratroopers who weren't in the foxholes to join us. We stayed there together for a long time, amidst the explosions and whistling sounds that continuously tore through the darkness, while the earth shook and dirt fell on our helmets. I had had that dugout built with a sense that the paratroopers' recklessness—certainly not ours—would get us into trouble.

"Too bad," the sergeant major exclaimed, still covered with plaster, "that the Germans don't see war as a game, like that captain of yours."

"Another nation of fools like ours," Canèr offered, "doesn't exist in the world."

After a while I felt I had to interrupt: "Come on, try to be good." I added, "If you're good, I promise that I'll take you all to see the colonel die, when he dies."

The firing lasted for hours; it ceased around one o'clock. We went out to check the telephone lines; some stretches were reduced to fragments that we couldn't repair, and had to replace. I put the men to work right away.

When I went back up to the observation post, I found the Ancestor still seated on his crate.

"He wasn't afraid. Strange," Second Lieutenant Bergna whispered to me, trying not to laugh. "Only at one point, he put the British helmet on his head without straps, the one they gave us to wash our feet in. Then, when the house was hit, he stuffed half his jacket in the telephone mouthpiece: 'So that the Germans don't hear it if it rings,' he explained to me. What a character, damn!"

I placed my arm under one of the Ancestor's and stood him on his feet. "Come, captain. I'll take you to the group's command nearby; even there you'll still be on the front. We don't have anywhere for you to sleep here."

"But no, but no . . ." he said, stumbling down the ladder. "I'll stay awake until morning. You know, in the other war I too was on patrol."

"Come. Meanwhile, we'll inspect the telephone line."

"Can we see the captain face to face?" the paratroopers said when we went by them on the ground floor. "Thank him, at least?"

Instead, when we went down the road he took to pitying us.

"Poor fellows, what a life of danger you have! And at the end of the war no one will even say thank-you."

I was about to remark that, after all, ambassadorial and ministerial appointments are quite few, but I succeeded in restraining myself.

We passed the artillerymen at work along the telephone line; a bit farther ahead artillerymen of the platoon, out on their own (I had left them near the group's command because they weren't needed at the post), met up with the workers and joined in repairing the line.

The Ancestor began laughing softly.

"What's funny, captain?"

"You said you'll see, in two, at most three minutes, you will experience life on the front. It was true! You felt it in your blood, you did!" Meanwhile he leaned on my arm, because he couldn't see and, if he let go, he would have ended up outside the road on the mines, defenseless as a child. Strange old man, fallen from who knows where in a world that isn't his . . . In such a world we walked under the immense night sky that embraces so many such different creatures.

*

The group's headquarters was at Villa Consalvi: two or three houses a few hundred meters right of the Catabbi house, still on the front line, stables and silent pigsties preceding them, as well as a group of leafy oaks, under whose silence our trucks were parked. Pumpkin vines covered the pigsties, while in the vegetable garden plants overflowed into the road, especially lettuce, high and flowery blue; the place was wonderfully rural.

We entered, pushing aside a blanket used as a door, into a room that was the command of Major Pelaformiche. The major was there, seated at his desk.

Without wasting time I entrusted to him the Ancestor as "discharge," I said laughingly, and since I was already there I took the opportunity to request equipment that hadn't been sent to me. His face oddly tense, the major stared at me without speaking. This worried me. I had heard soldiers say that having taken on too much work (in theory—distrustful as he was of everyone—all the command's work), he couldn't finish it, and so once in a while lost his temper. I arrived at a time when the roar of the explosions hadn't allowed him to sleep. He turned on me; his mouth seemed to want to bite me.

"I will rid myself of you," he shouted. "You must leave the Second Group, do you understand? Do you understand? You must leave!" He was obsessed. When I had been transferred to the Second Group of the regiment from the First, it was "as punishment," the major—commander of the Second—had told me, and I hadn't been able to take it. In truth my transfer hadn't occurred as punishment, and I had not been too concerned with that outburst. When he realized that this time too his words didn't impress me, he resorted to insult. "Do you know why you are here?" he yelled. "Only because you were afraid—do you understand? Afraid to stay at your post," and, in his anger, not succeeding in finding other words, he turned to repeating them, still shouting.

Two officers had arrived: Second Lieutenants Provera and Canèr. The latter, the brother of my sergeant, was a survivor like me of the encirclement at the Russian front and, therefore, instinctively sympathetic. They realized immediately what was happening. Provera signaled for me to be patient and walked out of the room; Canèr stayed to show me his friendship and possibly to support me.

Meanwhile: "Afraid?" I tried to interrupt the major. "Afraid?" Until he suddenly let me speak: "Fear under attack is normal, it's simply a matter of controlling it. And we've been on the line too short a time not to control it. Besides—even if I was a total idiot—I remind you that I came to the front voluntarily . . ." The rest of the conversation was pointless—when I left the observation post, the German fire had stopped.

He shook his head no; it was a waste of his time, I must necessarily—according to him—be a coward. I realized that only if I had admitted to this would he have calmed down, after which, obviously, he would have taken care to discharge me for contemptible action.

Then came my turn to let myself lose my temper. "All right," I exclaimed, and I too raised my voice. "It means that I'll pray to God to watch over my fragile . . . you understand?" I emphasized: "fragile nerves."

"Consider yourself under arrest," the major shouted, leaping to his feet, and continued to insult me.

Behind him Second Lieutenant Canèr, increasingly incapable of holding himself back, had begun walking up and down the room, dimly outlined by a lantern on the desk; I saw him gradually fill with rage, like a bull (he was not as tall as his sergeant brother but he was equally robust).

Unexpectedly, the Ancestor rose to his feet.

"I can't permit that this artillery lieutenant be treated like this, he who is the prototype of the Italian officer," he said, pointing at me.

"You wretch," I thought, clenching my teeth (even if that unexpected definition pleased me after all): "You wretch, what are you trying to do?"

"Yes," he continued, "the prototype," and not knowing me at all, he sang my praises.

The major didn't interrupt him, maybe because he considered him an important person; on the other hand, objectively, the Ancestor proved to be an uncommon speaker, even if maybe a bit archaic. He finished by shaking my hand, knowing nothing of military discipline.

I looked the major in the eye. "I've seen some pretty strange things tonight," I said. Saluting, I about-faced and went out. I didn't thank Canèr, not even with a sign, hoping to spare him the wrath of the major; I felt that unfortunately, with his friendly conduct toward me, he was already becoming involved on his own.

*

I walked back on the dirt road in silence; not even a barking dog could be heard, and only the fireflies moved here and there among the oaks' dark trunks. My irritation gave way to unease: "In any case, what a miserable people we are! These farces: the bombardment provoked by our recklessness, and that scene among those few of us who, in some way, would have to initiate the rebirth of the nation."

At the bottom of the road, where crouched men were testing the telephone line, two soldiers rose out of the darkness: I recognized Lance Corporal Freddi and Artilleryman Sciera, a reserved character with red hair from my mother's hometown in the plains of Lombardy.

"The line works, lieutenant," Freddi said when I was near them; I could barely see his keen, good face.

"All right. Thank you."

Both of them were staring at me. In spite of the darkness they must have noticed my unease and sensed that something unpleasant had happened.

"Lieutenant, it's only military life," I seem to remember Freddi saying; Sciera, as usual, said nothing.

They followed me step by step toward the post, Freddi with the line-testing machine, its leather holder hanging from his shoulder.

I thought about the men in high places: the politicians and their endless quarrels, the military commanders who didn't seem to have learned any wisdom from terrible lessons . . . Thank goodness that there were also these others, these simple people who carried their share with goodwill, and without chatter or foolishness; here was the salt of the earth.

5

THE GOOD TIMES were over.

Strangely, after the British stopped their retaliatory fire, the enemy seemed to become nervous; now more often the German shelling broke the stillness of the camps, and the telephones were busy day and night. With the firing, with no actions on our part, we began losing track of time—as happens at the front—and an episode that maybe occurred the previous day seemed long ago.

Until one night, to our surprise, the enemy no longer fired.

In the morning, from the post, its sector appeared as always to be without even the slightest movement. Was it possible that the Germans, threatened by Anglo-American outflanking in the Tyrrhenian sector, had left? (The Allied front in Italy was held between the Tyrrhenian and the Adriatic by the American Fifth Army on the left, the British Eighth Army on the right; the British were for the most part concentrated to the west of the Apennines, and it was there that the armored and air forces, American and British, were concentrated.)

During lunch, seated in a circle in our small house on our rolled-up cots, we talked about the silence. Maybe we could enter the devastated towns ahead of us without loss? Or else the enemy was setting a trap?

Artilleryman B., with a beret on his unkempt hair (he was a poor fellow, mildly alcoholic, with more than one hundred days of service), was standing as always against a wall, waiting to return the soup container and the bread bag to the kitchen of Villa Consalvi. When the telephone rang, he bent down to pick it up.

"They want you," he said to me, handing me the receiver.

"Wake up," the major shouted at the other end of the line, as soon as he heard me. Evidently I was still in his disfavor.

"Yes," I answered.

"Dismantle everything, and get ready to join the Sixteenth Battalion here at Villa Consalvi. You'll move forward with the paratroopers. Is that clear? Prepare the distribution of excess equipment."

"Yes, sir."

Shortly after, as we feverishly prepared ourselves, came—still by telephone—the counter-order, then new orders, and finally the definitive counter-order.

The rays of the sunset that day painted red the wooden arrow inscribed *Osservatorio Margherita* which Lance Corporal Freddi had nailed to the trunk of an oak not far from the Catabbi house, in an area where the access road forked. I went to take a look to remember it as much as possible. "By tomorrow," I daydreamed, "the Margherita Observatory will become a memory, and memories will certainly be important for us, young and old soldiers, who will find ourselves out of place in everyday life."

6

AT FIRST LIGHT of the following day we joined the Sixteenth Battalion, which was carrying shells. The Sixteenth was waiting to leave Villa Consalvi, which until then had held its command as well as ours.

The paratroopers of the Catabbi house, already organized, welcomed us with teasing remarks: "Hey, look who's coming: the artillerymen on foot . . ."

"Good, you're right not to travel sitting down."

"A little walking will be good for your figures."

Several paratroopers looked toward us.

"And airplanes? Where are your airplanes?" an artilleryman tried to stand up to them.

My orderly Morandi, a Piedmontese mountaineer, pointed to mules present amid the columns: "There are the airplanes," he said.

At first glance it was clear that the loads on those mules weren't uniform: the drivers had not only ignored the art of making them compact but also had not distributed them for balance. To make up for it, several drivers covered their loads with canvas, to camouflage them from friends and enemies. (The mules, the only ones in the paratroopers' line-up to realize the level of disorder, seemed thin; some had their ears pushed back and their teeth exposed, actually snarling at so much ignorance.) I realized that these troops—to whom the mules had just been distributed—were to be used again for an unsuitable task.

Now it was the artillerymen who were laughing: "Hey, tell us, why don't you put barbed wire around the mules' loads?" they asked.

Several drivers began cursing.

"You will be next to me," the commander of the battalion, Major Vittorio Pellagatta, said curtly. "Get your men's heads straight." He was a character with a grim profile, dark skin, with a head as strong as an ox. He was giving orders to the three officers of his company who faced him with respect; in them one still noticed some of the paratroopers' style, only more refined.

We got in line where the major had ordered and remained waiting.

I realized that it would be one of those same old dawn departures, enlivened by the jibes of soldiers who if by chance said a witty remark then repeated it with impertinence. All of this stirred many memories . . . Below us, on the side of the sea, the barely risen sun projected its light, painting gold the damp roofs of Villa Consalvi; the lettuce plants with their blue flowers from the untilled vegetable gardens overflowed toward us. In the morning light, these colors appeared enchanting.

*

On Major Pellagatta's order we began the march, organizing ourselves in a line to reduce the danger of mines.

Here we were, advancing to kill, and it was certain that several of us would be killed (some probably in the course of that same day). Many times we did this. The reasons that had motivated us at the beginning of the war had lessened: it was absurd to consider our reasons sufficient for what we had done! Many had died, but the circle that formed our attitude could not be broken.

Reaching the road beyond Villa Consalvi, which until the previous day had represented the front for us, and then two small rows of barbed wire full of poppies, we slowly went down into the valley between our line and that of the Germans. Here, even more so than at the Margherita Observatory, one could smell the grass, a smell typical of unkempt places that's difficult to describe, like sheep and honey, which—I said this already—I associate from those days to my memory of Abruzzi.

Each of us tried to place his feet exactly in the footsteps of the one in front of him. The previous afternoon, without encountering resistance, men of a preceding company had marked some stretches of the grassy descent into paths, crossing the strips of land most heavily mined, with the help of long thin streamers of white cloth (maybe British bandages) tied to riddled branches. Once in a while behind us, shouts and laughs exploded when a mule's load overturned.

At the bottom of the valley, near the ruins of the town of Crecchio—which I saw for the first time—we went around a medieval castle with heavy walls damaged everywhere by artillery, but still firmly standing. (In that edifice the king of Italy had made his only stop, of about an hour, during his strenuous journey from Rome to Pescara right after the armistice, but we ignored it.)

Groups of Indian soldiers were in a clearing a little beyond the castle; I recognized them as Gurkhas from the single patch of hair at the center of their shaved heads. These were the Nepalese ear choppers that Maugham Brown had described to me; they were short in stature, with dark, unsmiling faces. They answered yes to every question, opening mouths full of teeth. "They resemble more Siberian Russians than the other Indians," I noted.

"You know that you're a bunch of rascals?" the paratroopers asked them, drawing a crowd. "How would you like it if other people cut your ears off?"

"Yes," the Nepalese answered, without understanding.

"What would they do with them then? Make broth?"

"Yes."

"Or a necklace for your British commanders?"

"Yes, yes."

To bring an end to this farce the few British noncommissioned officers among the Gurkhas came forward and, politely, relayed to us that farther ahead, in the German zone, the danger of mines was still great.

Shortly after, we passed foxholes while climbing up along a road on the opposite slope of the valley, infrequent and well dug in the ground, carefully camouflaged with branches that were now rotten. Wherever there had been houses there now were piles of wreckage.

At the end of the hill, the company that preceded us the previous day was waiting for us. Its paratroopers were also in single file, halted near a cemetery; they had one dead, two wounded, and a mule dead because of mines. The wall of the small cemetery of Canosa Sannita, which on our maps had been "objective 301," was demolished in several places by grenades; tombs were torn open, stone crosses and marble statues broken or chipped. In front, three or four surviving cypresses stood against the sky, arms slanting toward the earth. The stretchers with the two wounded were in their shade.

"Do you want to see them?" the stretcher bearer asked Major Pellagatta, and without waiting raised an edge of cloth, revealing a swollen head with a frightening mask of clotted blood.

"He doesn't open his eyes because they are full of splinters," the stretcher bearer explained. A few flies rushed down on those big, closed eyes, and he chased them off: "He's not dead yet," he grumbled to himself and to the flies. The wounded man didn't give any signs of movement. He seemed so dead that not even his chest moved.

The company's commander, appearing promptly, made his report to the major. He warned that in the nearby town even the handles of the few doors left standing were mined: "The wire bedsprings are mined, anything that could interest a soldier is mined."

"Spread the word," the major said to one of his officers, "even if it will be of little use, because until everyone realizes it on their own, they won't be convinced. Pigheaded men."

The word spread along the long winding line of the battalion, halted behind us up the hill.

Again, we went forward slowly, avoiding the mines, where two pieces of wood in the shape of a cross had been.

Among the piles of wreckage in the country town of Canosa only a few recognizable places remained. The poppy's flashy red flowers and, even more numerous here, the golden yellow of the mullein, grew everywhere, in the streets, on top of ruins, even on the foundations of walls. Only on the most recent piles of debris had they not yet grown.

A dead mule lay at the main crossroad. Already swollen, it had one of its back legs pointed up; one would have thought it was painted wood. We passed near it, unaware of walking on anti-tank mines, one of which exploded under the next mule. The head of the column had in fact just left the village when the force of the mine knocked us down from behind and then moved quickly among the hills, with a long trail of echoes, always farther off in the distance. Some men near me burst out with profanities. This reminded me that I had not yet finished my morning prayers, which had been interrupted several times: I began again, and since some soldier might be dead I dedicated them to him. If he was dead, I thought, now he perhaps saw inside our hearts, to see if we, as his officers and companions, had helped him. Indeed, even if he had not died, he had sinned and therefore separated himself from the grace of God, and so could not immediately receive full life from God. Like a part of a vine, he must suffer: men should be one with God, unless not part of him they remain writhing, like the tail torn off from a lizard.

We continued to advance slowly, still in a line, our eyes fastened on the earth. By now it was hot, and sweat was on our foreheads; the spirits of our dead companions, I thought, continued perhaps to walk with us, their arms around the shoulders of each of us, one after another, accepting on the palms of their extended hands the gift of our brotherly prayers.

*

On our lunch break the order was given to sit on the ground in the road; we did this, leaning the barrels of the submachine guns across our legs or chests. The sun blazed on the green stretch of the wooded hills, upon the unripe wheat, upon us, lying carefully inside the womb of the earth.

"Will there be many dead from the mines, lieutenant?" my orderly Morandi asked, seated a step from me, his blond head sweaty under his helmet. "From Canosa on, several exploded."

"We'll only find out tonight the number of dead."

"It's because the paratroopers aren't suited for these types of marches," Morandi said. "They get tired staying in a single line."

"Stinking destiny!" Sergeant Canèr intervened. "Before the armistice we fought with gasoline bottles against tanks. Now that we're with the most equipped army in the world, we're missing the few magnetic mine detectors that we had before."

"Mine detectors?" observed another artilleryman of the battalion, Bertolini, from Parma, who sat just ahead. "We're even missing clothes to wear. Can't you see?" He nodded toward the paratroopers, who offered the most inconceivable medley of uniforms: colonial khaki shirts or jackets on top of grayish-green trousers, long jackets on top of short pants; the worst of it was that this wardrobe was partly torn.

"*Nuèter ac pensema mei* (we never think about this), *ma sema ardusì c'me di sercòn* (but we are reduced to beggars)," Bertolini concluded.

"Beh, *col che cont* (well, what counts)," his countryman Freddi objected, inclined to see the positive in things: "*l'è ca sema vivv* (is that we are alive)."

There was a pause.

"Alive, yes, but . . ." Canèr resumed, shaking his head: "Did you see the condition that those poor wretches have been reduced to?" He alluded to the few civilians, four in all, that we had met so far. Having been in the zone evacuated by the Germans, those civilians had risked their lives, hiding in order not to abandon the little they owned; peasants usually do such things. The first group (a small family made up of a man, a pregnant woman, and a small boy) had appeared from a hole in Canosa. They had given the major a mangled account of the Germans' insolence, part of which probably they had suffered and part of which they had heard told;

28

the woman, as though dazed, lamented having lost a younger son during the course of the winter because of the hardship. Before resuming the march, some paratroopers had offered them their ration of bread; the six parallel, dirty hands reached out to take it.

Afterwards, as we marched, several others had sought to offer bread and cans. At one point the woman, having let everything fall to the ground, had pulled her black apron over her head: her pregnant belly seemed even more swollen above her thin legs.

And the old woman we had met shortly after, outside of the village, had come running toward us from a farmhouse in ruins shaded by a walnut tree. "English? Are you English?" she stuttered.

"We're Italian," we raced to answer her: "All Italians."

The old Abruzzese woman had recognized us from our appearance and features—I think—more than from our answers.

"Oh, sons!" she cried at one point, raising her arms, "Oh, bless you! Long live Italy, long live Italy, long live Italy!" She kept shouting like this, her arms raised to the sky.

Coming to a stop, we looked at her, moved.

"We were right to take up arms again," a paratrooper officer whispered, turning halfway, "if only to shorten these sufferings."

We asked a few questions. Having found her on her farm, the Germans had beaten her already ill legs with the butts of their rifles, so she could not leave; she was almost dying of hunger. When the column again began to march, bread and cans had begun to pile in front of her.

We were distracted from these experiences by paratroopers who, examining the ground, were leaving the place where the battalion had stopped. In a field were cherry trees loaded with fruit, and it was the red of those cherries between the leaves that had attracted them.

Arriving at the closest tree, one of them began—with bravado—to hoist himself between the branches. He hadn't yet gotten into the branches when an explosion occurred. The man fell to the ground screaming. The Germans had attached grenades to the branches of cherry trees . . .

After the man was taken away, another paratrooper arrogantly wanted to try again. While we artillerymen looked on incredulously, his attempt concluded in the same dramatic fashion. Afterwards, in spite of the shouts of their officers, still others attempted it, with incredible recklessness: they tested each branch before reaching for it. Grenades exploded and others were wounded. All this was senseless. Under those circumstances I realized the extraordinary possibilities that such soldiers offered during combat, and made a mental note of it.

That night the sad count of the battalion's losses due to grenades and mines was five men dead, eight wounded, and four mules dead. The other battalions which like us were without mine detectors advanced on a parallel route and had greater losses. In one explosion, an armored vehicle and all five occupants were blown up.

Resuming the march, we arrived during late afternoon at a handful of houses named *Madonna della Neve*,[3] where the order to halt for the night reached us by radio. The place got its name from a small church, empty of pews and every ornament, with remnants of a fire and refuse on the floor. In its center the enemy had shot a large painted plaster saint whose arms stretched in a gesture of love and—maybe on their way out—smashed his face with the butts of their guns. At first, he was almost laughable, then he seemed tragic, increasingly tragic, motionless in that solitary gesture of love, his face reduced to straw and plaster.

Before sunset the Fifteenth Battalion (the other battalion of that paratroopers' regiment) with a few armored vehicles converged at *Madonna della Neve,* as well as the Fourth Group of horse-drawn artillery, to which Second Lieutenant Bergna belonged.

The men divided up to sleep inside and around the little church and beneath the rows of vines and the hedges.

3. Madonna of the Snow.

7

THE FOLLOWING MORNING I joined the
groups of paratroopers who watched with embarrassment (which in any
case didn't last long) the measured movements with which the artillerymen
of the group with horses tended their mules, tied in orderly circles under
the trees.

Those two types of soldiers, the paratrooper and the mountain artilleryman, seemed to belong to two different nations . . . While I observed the
artillerymen I discovered that some differed considerably from others: not
only by their uniforms, which were newer, but also, if I can say so, because
they seemed less complete as men. My fellow townsman Second Lieutenant
Bergna—who, seeing me, had come up amicably—asked that I explain
why.

"That's easy," I answered him. "Those with the new uniforms aren't cav-
alrymen. They're ordinary recruits that we received as reserves in Puglia." I
shook my head: "A real cavalry group today, in Italy, is impossible to find."

Once again there was the sense that everything in Italy was collapsing
. . . Nevertheless, here we were, the soldiers of the small *Corpo di Liberazione* who, with all our shortcomings, had somehow or other begun marching and were inaugurating the recovery.

We began the advance in early afternoon, continuing to cross the green
country without inhabitants. Some of the houses that we passed, isolated
or in groups, had only walls left to them: there was not a piece of furniture
in the rooms, not a door, and even shutters were rare. The Germans had
pillaged everything, to use as shelter, and fire in the winter, and maybe even
as packing on the ammunition trains that returned to Germany.

At the crossing of the Foro River we met the first two of their prisoners.
In gray uniforms and gray service caps with visors, they held themselves by
tightly clasping the backs of two paratroopers' motorcycles, who recklessly

pushed on, in the direction opposite ours, their machines jerking on the stony road.

"They're the squads that set the mines," the paratroopers began explaining. "Now they're taking us to clear the mines."

In the rushing river lay the remains of an arched bridge, surrounded by bubbling water. The men—still in single file—entered the water up to their knees and, after having crossed, went up the opposite bank. Anti-tank mines lay at the bottom of the river, near the ruins, producing bubbles. The men crossed without harm, as though they were rocks, but when behind us the first of the cars of the Fifteenth Battalion began to ford, it was thrown up in the air inside a mass of foaming water. A shoe with its foot inside became embedded between a fender and the hood of the following car.

Little by little the day began to grow dark around us, announcing the night of the second day of our advance.

The sun was setting when, leaving the valley between the hills, we found ourselves in front of the town of Villamagna, with its houses tightly together on a ridge. It was like a herd that from a distance might seem crouched for the night in the dark, peaceful air, but that close up was found to be lifeless . . . One could make out a few ruins, but above all the silence and lack of life was striking. Such abandonment, at that hour, cut to the heart, so that our conversation stopped.

Suddenly in the evening air the toll of a bell sounded. It became incessant. Perhaps in reaction to that sense of desertion, some paratroopers had climbed up to the bell tower to ring the alarm.

How will we forget that sound? We were giving ourselves our own welcome.

We entered the town's streets, accompanied by the voice of the bell. The men found quarters quickly; the platoon settled in the neat cellar of a villa that the battalion's command had taken over.

We found a civilian inside the villa, the elderly owner, who—glad of our arrival—came down to sleep with us on the hay.

Realizing that, like everyone, I was without a blanket, he opened one of his large blankets under the uncertain light of a candle that he had lit. "Sleeping in shirt-sleeves brings rheumatism, lieutenant. If you'd like to take advantage of it . . . this one is even enough for more than two."

I accepted, smiling, uncertainly.

"Well, there might be a few fleas."

"Accept," Canèr said, who had taken a spot on the hay in a corner. He raised his head: "Don't forget the aches that you caught in Russia."

"Right, the blanket," my orderly, Morandi, added. "Accept it, since these men are glaring at me because I didn't bring one for you . . ." And with a less intelligible voice: "It'll turn out that I'll become responsible for the rheumatism you caught in Russia."

A few of the men began laughing; I thanked the old man, who then took his place on the hay next to me and stretched out his big blanket over both of us.

Minutes went by; one could already hear breathing from sleepers.

There was a question that I'd been asking myself for a while: "Where did they end up," I asked the civilian, "all the people from this area?"

"What," he answered, "you don't know? They went to Chieti, under the bishop's protection."

"The bishop's protection?" I said in surprise.

"Sure. Who else can one get protection from at this point?"

"It seems like we've gone back to the days of barbaric invasions," Canèr muttered from his corner.

It was the first time that we came across this phenomenon of medieval proportions.

"But who's to say barbarians still respect bishops," Canèr added, after a pause. "Did you see how it went in Cassino . . . Who knows how many monks and refugees died in February, in the bombardment of that monastery?"

"It's the third time that Monte Cassino was destroyed," I said after a while.

"The third time?" the old man asked, amazed. Our voices sounded sleepy.

"Yes." I counted: "First the Goths leveled it, fifteen hundred years ago; then the Saracens, one thousand years ago; now these others."

"Well, the monks will rebuild it again," the old Abruzzese concluded.

*

The following day, June 11, the battalion entered Chieti.

It was Sunday, the Day of the Lord, and the statue of the town on top of its hill caught me while I prayed, as if I had a smiling answer from God.

Rumors began: "The motorcycle company has been in the town for a day."

"A day or two?"

"Since the day before yesterday: it captured a German rearguard at the station."

This was true. But the circulation of fanciful news wasn't missing either: "They say that many landings have occurred."

"Where?"

"In Livorno and Ancona."

"Really? Then the war is ending . . ."

"What landings? How can you believe such rubbish?"

"They've landed, I'm telling you."

We rejoiced at a pleasant and bright drizzle that began to fall.

As we passed along the asphalt road, we saw packages of TNT near the holes where they should have been deposited. Their yellow powder filled the puddles. Evidently, the paratroopers' advance guard had surprised some German detonation squads.

We came across groups of civilians descending toward the countryside, loaded with belongings; they barely greeted us, each anxious to see what he had left.

Before passing among the houses the Sixteenth Battalion came to a halt and organized into columns. Behind us the Fifteenth did the same. Afterward we advanced at an even pace, forcing our way through the growing crowd; the people cheered, shouted, broke out in unexpected applause.

Our steps resounded on the asphalt. "Italians! All Italians! They're our soldiers, and they've arrived first!" People shouted in enthusiasm, threw us a few flowers, tried to touch our uniforms.

"See," I told myself, "we were right to put this stump of an army back on its feet! Too bad that Antonio isn't here, after all that walking we did together to join the army."

While I marched, deeply moved, the long days of my journey in the mountains with him came into my mind: the mercilessness of the sun and of God, all the hardships since the day when, with the armistice, Italy fell to its knees.

🌿 Part Two

1

I'LL RECOUNT BRIEFLY the days of our humiliation. When on the evening of September 8, 1943, the radio announcement of the armistice came, as it did in all of Italy, Antonio Moroni and I were in the same battery in Nettuno, near Rome.

The exultation of the Italian soldiers blended with that of quite a few Germans; at dawn of the following day, however, the Germans attacked all Italian barracks and bases.

It must not have been a big undertaking, because with the first attack, and actually even without attacks, our army in Nettuno, and in the rest of Italy as well, dissolved itself into an immense swarm of disarmed men, each on his way toward his home. It has been suggested, contrary to what was generally believed then and is still believed now, that our army would not have been able to withstand the Germans in Italy. If in fact we were far superior in numbers, their regular divisions, after the recent influx of new units from other lands, had become more numerous, whereas the men in Italy's gray-green uniforms were in depots, in surveillance squads, in posts, in all useless territorial commands, in unmovable units designated as coastal divisions. In short, they were not fighting troops. The greater part of the Italians in Italy's service were almost solely to satisfy the pride of our dictator, and would not have been worth much compared to regular divisions.

The Germans were stronger, even if at first a few of their units retreated as though fleeing toward the north, even if small was the number that achieved the disintegration (not the surrender) of large Italian forces: the Germans' large forces had been kept wisely in reserve.

The disgraceful collapse of the Italian army was due to that position of inferiority, ignored by most; the forces were defeated because one by one the men who were a part of them were no longer prepared to risk their lives in a war that was by now judged senseless, but instead waited only for the opportunity to return home.

On the evening of September 9, Moroni and I went up from Nettuno to our barracks, to see how things were.

We were filled with remorse for not having participated in its defense, but when at dawn sixty or seventy Germans attacked it, opening fire with a pair of anti-aircraft guns placed in front of its gates, the two of us, like many other officers, were in our houses, sleeping.

In the afternoon civilians, especially women, looted the abandoned barracks. They were joined in swarms by people of the town and countryside, almost as though they had been called. Seizing everything within their reach, they had made all kinds of bundles for themselves, which they had taken away on their shoulders, or on their heads, or under their arms, or dragging behind them in the dust.

Those dark Latin women, who until the previous day had been so solemn, balancing copper amphorae on their heads, moving slowly around their musical fountains, had lost all dignity.

One of them, overloaded with goods, had had one of her bundles fall to the ground and hadn't moved from her spot but cried out in an angry yet plaintive voice for help. And it was only a bundle of tent pegs, as I happened to see, which would have been useless to her. In any case, it was better for that equipment to end up in the hands of civilians than with the Germans, who without a doubt would return in the following days.

A deep silence welcomed us now. Near the fallen gate the small house of the Life Guards was reduced to a pile of debris. The Germans, after some shooting, had blown it up with the Italian weapons stacked inside, following a truce.

The moon beat down silently on the oaks of the wide courtyard and on the buildings destroyed by the anti-aircraft guns. We realized that not a living soul had remained in the barracks. The few souls of the dead yes, maybe, crying, next to the dark stain of blood in which that morning he had poured out its life, the pitiful end of our arms and of our dignity.

Under a row of oaks was a well-aligned battery of heavy anti-aircraft guns, so essential to us, that the Germans' allies had given us too late and in too small a quantity. We touched the steel of the breech blocks, the imprints of the hammer blows with which the Germans had nailed them.

While we wandered, a shadow emerged from one of the buildings and came in front of us. We stopped.

The shadow also stopped. After having scrutinized us with head leaning forward, it raised its hand to its forehead in a military salute; from the shape of the uniform I realized that it was an old noncommissioned officer; I vaguely caught sight of his gray hair.

"I am the paymaster, officers. There's still money in the pay box and therefore I can't abandon it. But I've been left without orders . . . What is happening in Italy? Give me some orders."

"You want orders?" we answered, as pity for him and for us clutched at our throats. "Listen: do you know the proclamation of the armistice? In short, it says that we must not hand over our things to anyone. Here is an order then, of which we assume responsibility: take away the funds that are in the case, and look after them. When in a few days the situation clears up, you'll deliver them to the authorities. First jot down our names."

Because we hadn't given him an evasive answer, the paymaster listened to us, stunned, trying to see our faces with his head pushed forward. Little by little, however, his head was retracted.

"Yes, sir," he murmured softly, finally.

"Good," I said, "these are our names." I repeated them several times. "You will take them down."

He agreed: "Yes, of course." But he did not obey. Undoubtedly he had remained quiet, watching over the funds in his custody, waiting for who knows what orders that would allow him to be in accord with regulations. He had respected regulations his whole life; they had been his guide and his boundary, and his pride had been in respecting them. Now he could not admit that regulations had vanished and become nothing. In truth the paymaster wasn't waiting for orders; he wandered around looking for the meaning of his life, which had slipped out of his hands and turned into smoke.

*

Three days later, on the afternoon of September 12, even in Nettuno, the Germans had brought an end to the disorder that had followed the armistice. After having convened all Italian officers at a given time in the small palace of the command for a "clarifying report," they had taken away their pistols, then, shouting and even kicking them, had pushed them outside, toward the crowded trucks.

Many had fallen into their hands, since many officers remained in the city four days after the armistice. As for me, knowing the Germans, I not only had not let myself be deceived but also up until the last minute had tried to stop the few colleagues with whom I was acquainted from being brought down (I had come to Nettuno from Bolzano only a week before). I had followed some of them, arguing, up to the door of the palace, on the sides of which two German sentries mounted guard. I had succeeded in grasping the wrist of the lieutenant commander of my battery, to keep him from going inside; finally, nodding his head indulgently, he asked me to release his wrist, and had entered last of all. (The memory of this little episode, as I learned later, would distress him above all else during his harsh year and a half in a German prison.)

On that occasion I saw with my own eyes the kind of blindness that strikes men, as they lose even the most ordinary capacity for discernment that could dissuade them from following an already formed opinion. The Gospel says it well: "they would not even believe in the resurrected dead."

When the old general in command of the district, who had guaranteed the Germans' deceit, groped his way, dazed, toward the cab of one of the trucks, he was stopped by a heavy-set German sentry and pushed with kicks to the back of the truck, along with the others.

Men of proven worth, who would have been difficult to capture on the battlefield by anyone, were among the many taken in so miserably by the deceit.

2 THE ONLY ONE to listen had been Antonio Moroni. The following day, at first light, Antonio and I set out to reach the mountains of Abruzzi.

German columns, camouflaged in yellow and brown, were halted in the small city, mostly along the sea route colored by the morning sun. One of them, in tanks, arrived noisily from the north and passed near us, headed probably toward Salerno and the Western forces that had landed.

We both wore plain civilian clothes acquired the previous night; nevertheless, when we saw from afar a German roadblock in the distance, we left the road and went around it by crossing yards and vegetable gardens damp with dew.

It broke our hearts to see what was happening and what was about to happen. We no longer felt any sense of relief from the armistice now that the Germans had resorted to their usual behavior. "Maybe shortly they'll begin behaving like in Poland, like in Russia . . . As soon as they feel sure of themselves, they'll begin massacres."

"The army came undone on its own! How we'll regret it . . . It makes you crazy to think of it!"

Around Nettuno the fields were almost entirely covered by vineyards. We entered a sandy path between the vines, familiar to us, with concern in our hearts and at times dismay, because an unarmed nation in the hands of armed barbarians is a frightening prospect.

"We agree, in any case, that we're not returning to our homes in Lombardy," I said at last. "We won't idly endure the Germans' violence and involve our families in retaliations. Therefore . . ."

"All right. But I'll tell you again that I'd prefer to wait for the British in Rome," Antonio said, in one of his last attempts, "rather than with your friends in the mountains of Abruzzi. It's easier to disguise oneself near people than in the mountains."

"I don't trust the crowd of the city. Even less so after the looting we saw . . . Sure, the British will be in Rome in a week, at the most two. But in the meantime? Who can predict what the Germans will do? And the Fascists even?"

"The Fascists?" said Antonio: "Well, they got out of the way on their own . . ."

"In any case, in Rome we could find ourselves involved in some way. In the mountains, on the other hand, we'll always be free, and we can always trust the Abruzzese mountaineers, even if—actually especially if—we have to fight. Because, I'll tell you again, in the Julia Division they not only proved to be good soldiers, but also as good as the best German soldiers."

"I don't think that in Italy there will be time for a partisan war," Antonio said, displeased. "I'll agree to come to Abruzzi only because you were so right yesterday, regarding the German trap."

"After all, who knows if we Italians will ever fight a partisan war . . ." I turned toward him. "It suits mostly uncivilized people, since it's reduced to terrorist and anti-terrorist retaliations. Luckily, like you said, there won't even be time for it, because by this winter the war in Italy will be over."

But it didn't end that winter, nor the next, and partisan warfare occurred everywhere; even if for the most part, because of the innate benevolence of our people, it was kept within the limits of ordinary warfare.

As for the Germans, they didn't avenge themselves for the armistice—a very considerable fact. They preferred to return reluctant Fascists to power, through whom they could exploit what Italian resources remained. Undoubtedly this prevented millions of deaths. In the end they treated us like their other Latin enemies, the French and Belgians, for example, and not— as I expected—in the incomparably barbaric way that they treated Slavic nations, the Russians, Poles, and Yugoslavs. Everything, it must be said, was based on the paradoxical classification of people established by their racist theories.

We reached two of the straw huts among the vineyards, where after leaving the barrack Antonio and I had gathered as many of our soldiers as we had been able to find.

Realizing that our army did not prevail anywhere in Italy and that all hope of recovery was lost, we had allowed them to return home or to fol-

low us to Abruzzi; they had all chosen to return home, setting out immediately.

"There really isn't anyone any more," Antonio murmured. The silence
of the place seemed strangely troublesome.

"All right. Instead of leading them in the defense of the barracks, we gathered them afterwards, waiting for the occasion—imagine how improba-
ble—to reconquer the city . . ."

"Remember—when was it? the day before yesterday? three days ago?
how it seems so long ago!—the excitement at the news that a column of
Bersaglieri was marching from Rome to Nettuno?" Antonio said. "What
strange rumors, though, spread in a time of chaos!"

"Would you believe me if I told you that many, many of those that I saw
die in war died clinging to one hope, to false news, small or big? These are
things we don't realize during normal times. But that's enough, let's go."

"Yes, it's useless to linger, let's go."

Beyond the vineyards the fields stretched out, spotted here and there by
groves of pines, laced by long wooden fences faded by the rain.

We entered; every familiar place disappeared.

*

After a few hours' walk from Nettuno we crossed an almost new asphalt
road that stretched east-west, straight as far as the eye could see. It was traveled by swarms of soldiers headed in both directions; they walked sweating
under the sun, due to the fact that the branches of the young pines flank-
ing the road cast only small ragged shadows.

We found smaller roads ahead, traveled similarly. In those days, all of
Italy's roads presented a similar spectacle. More than the sacking of our military buildings, or the trains of prisoners the Germans sent to Germany,
that immense swarm of men who limped toward home gave the sense of
our decay, the symbol of our defeat. Under the Roman sky we were forced
to become part of it. (But who in Italy then didn't move about haunted by
their thoughts, soldiers on long roads, all others inside the brief concentric
walks of their daily lives?)

A few kilometers before Cisterna we reached an area that recently had
been transformed into valuable land. We entered, step by step, passing
identical, sparse farmhouses. Far ahead of us, beyond the yellow stretches
of stubble, the golden roof of the small city's bell tower sparkled blinding-

ly under the sun. The air quivered in an incessant vertical sway from the great heat; the voice of cicadas could be heard above everything, like the singing of a queen gone mad.

Having eaten in the shade of a farmhouse and drawn bad water from the well (without anyone from the house showing his face), we resumed our journey, and in midafternoon we reached Via Appia. As we crossed, a column of our Fiat 626 trucks, in the hands of German soldiers, arrived, rumbling with a roar well known to me for having had it as a companion the previous year during the long advance on the Russian front. Hearing it again was painful. The drivers and escorts seated at the windows, grasping submachine guns, exulted in their loot. The distinctive sound of the engines lashed at the Italian soldiers walking in both directions, forcing them even more to the edges of the road.

"Thank goodness they don't swerve to run them down for fun," I said to Antonio, "like they sometimes did to columns of Russian prisoners."

The farmers informed us that in this area the Germans had rounded up scattered soldiers and taken them to remove the ruins of Frascati (headquarters, as we would later learn, of the German command in Italy) brutally bombarded by the Allies the day of the armistice, with two thousand dead.

In the evening we stopped at a farm not far from Velletri, having traveled forty kilometers. We improvised beds on boards with mattresses and sheets.

3

ALREADY ON THE following day, September 14, the land began to be hilly.

Near Valmontone we crossed another large road, the Casilina. A German soldier who patrolled it slowly on a heavy motorcycle, staring at us with eyes glittering with contempt, carried an American helmet hanging from the handlebar, almost like a trophy tied to a horse saddle. Behind him a column, too long for its end to be visible, was arriving from the north. We left the road quickly and entered a large forest on the other side.

We crossed it and stopped there, away from all noise. Even that day it was very hot. After eating the rest of what we had brought from Nettuno, we stretched out on the grass.

In our hearts we continued to ask what was happening in Italy. What was the fate of my brother in the army in Puglia, and of Antonio's in Piedmont? What were the people in our homes thinking of us, almost a week since the armistice? And what were the men of our two armies scattered in the Balkans going through? But above all: what would happen next? Yes, what would happen? What would be the fate of our people?

"Lord," I exclaimed to myself, closing my eyes, "help us in a disaster too big to anticipate!"

The peaceful countryside around us tried, with its customary drone of insects, to give us the illusion that nothing had occurred, and nothing was happening. But our minds returned to harsh reality.

It was under those circumstances that, for the first time since we had been on our journey, the memory of Margherita came to me. I had met her five months earlier during sick leave after the Russian front, on the occasion of a Catholic student conference near the Oropa church. Margherita was a beautiful young woman of seventeen with no interest in the discussions of the conference, happy to stroll alone down the long balconies of the church—kept clean by the mountain air—while others debated in the halls. I too, in those days, wasn't able to find any interest in abstractions and debates: at the time, there were too many pressing troubles in Italy (they would materialize shortly with the fall of fascism, and the armistice), which—along with the distress I held inside for so many cruelly lost companions—consumed me. Margherita's beauty had attracted me. Later, in August (only a month ago), finding myself near Riccione where her family had a villa, I had gone to pay her a visit, and we had walked for more than an hour on the shore of the "tireless" sea. Both times, an extraordinary comfort had come from this young woman: deaths and troubles and prospects of tragedies were not all that existed on earth, after all!

The memory of her came to me now unexpectedly, as if making its way with difficulty between the branches of the trees, along with some of the sun's rays. I remembered with amazement the purity of her profile; her hair, delightful on the nape of her neck; and her eyes, which at that moment I imagined sad like stars when at first night they observe a soldier's solitude from above.

I ended by speaking of her to Antonio, who out of courtesy appeared interested.

Once we resumed our journey, I thought about how no one would be able to keep me from thinking of her again—chastely—if it could be of comfort, among so many causes for anxiety. Provided that my thoughts were pure, I told myself, why not? In fact—my imagination began to run away from me—the thought of her would elevate me; Margherita, who I barely knew, would be able perhaps even to become for me a kind of Beatrice . . .

*

During late afternoon we passed through a village before beginning our ascent of a barren hill, on top of which another village appeared; a small village, where we intended to spend the night.

At the end of that second day we were increasingly amazed at the misery and crudeness of the dwellings. In the streets children played in front of filthy stone huts. Here and there some melancholic donkey walked around, and one could see shabby furnishings through the doors, while taller and older houses, typical of central Italy, frequent in this area, seemed empty of everything but their onetime grandeur.

For us, such misery near Rome was a discovery.

"Who would have imagined that such poor places existed," Antonio said several times, "so close to the capital?"

Some would blame fascism, according to the behavior established after July 25; however, such misery, with plain evidence, was attributable instead to the temporal power of the church, which I thought (and still think today) had been in its time absolutely necessary, so that the Catholic Church would not become in the course of history the *instrumentum regni* of any ruler, Orthodox and Protestant. But still, here it was, and it was evident that it still produced great difficulties.

While the sun was setting, we slowly traveled the last stretch of the long climb toward R. among rust-colored walnut trees, whose poor nuts the barefooted children, here and there, beat down with long poles.

We entered the village as it was getting dark; we proceeded more slowly because of my blistered feet in the used shoes I had bought in a hurry in Nettuno. The people in this out-of-the-way place watched us from the thresholds of their huts with long inquisitive looks; a few old women, knitting needles between their fingers, watched us with eyes full of curiosity.

Having located the house of the parish priest, we climbed its few steps and confidently explained our situation; if he could help us find food and lodging we had the necessary money.

He listened to us, saddened, without speaking, and we thought it was maybe for the state of Italy, reflected in us. But when we suggested to him that he keep our officer rank quiet, to avoid German detection, we saw that he became troubled. "A German column is encamped a few kilometers below the village," he exclaimed. And he looked at one of us, then the other, distressed, passing a hand through his short hair, damp with sweat: the man was a coward.

"This is a poor village," he began repeating. "It's a poor, small village," and he didn't respond to us in any other way.

He called his ill sister, and to her too he said, without explaining anything, that it was a poor, small village, and she repeated it to us, looking at us with resentment. The poverty in this place mirrored the spiritual poverty.

When the priest realized that, in spite of everything, we had no intent of leaving, at the height of his fear he sent his sister to call his friend, the mayor, at least to share in the trouble that on this day providence had bestowed upon him, the small parish priest of a small village.

The mayor was a gray-haired man, as fearful as the priest, and the regional accent in his voice (from which at times he seemed to want to draw courage) contrasted greatly with the meaning of his words. He differed from the priest in that while the latter insisted on the poverty of the village, he emphasized the insolence of the Germans, who were the type not even to stop in front of a mayor.

The result was that, without dinner and irritated by the talk of those two trembling men, we left the room which nonetheless had been provided for us, and began to walk in the dark. We headed toward the large town, C., on the side of a hill farther north, which we had seen at sunset.

*

A slight moon lent its light to the first dew that clung like a cool-scented cloak to the stones of our path and to the scarce, delicately milk-colored vegetation. Small, shabby fields appeared, here and there, in that untamed light, at times only irregular patches of land between rocks, planted with wheat; only bristly stubble remained. In some areas, even the smallest squares of only a few meters had been cultivated.

As we walked we commented—at first mockingly—on the attitude of the parish priest and the mayor, "small men," and chuckled at the resentful attitude of the parish priest's sister. Then we spoke of other things. Our voices were becoming more disconnected as we proceeded. Finally, we were almost forgetful of what we said, because the late hour and the moonlight and the many kilometers made us weary. I found myself daydreaming that Margherita was walking along with us and, at times, I wondered if it wasn't she who moved, brushed the leaves on the edge of the path. It was with such a suggestion that a peaceful joy absurdly entered my heart.

We came to C. toward midnight. It didn't seem a village as poor as the previous ones: here the taller houses of central Italy, where a sense of endurance lingers, seemed in the moonlight sufficiently well-kept, and maybe some monumental place also existed somewhere. A nice asphalted street went through the middle of town; the slit of a window above a tavern gave out the only light.

We knocked. "Individual soldiers?" The host welcomed us. "Come in." He made us sit at a table. "There's always a meal ready for you: the people offer it to you. We're not rich, but we do what we can. My God, though, so many of you are going to your homes in the south!"

He stayed to watch us eat, along with some late-arriving customers. Then he lit a lantern and took us to a barn where other soldiers already slept. "You seem to me people who were brought up well," he said. "If this suits you . . . We don't have anything else."

Taking advantage of his lantern, we prepared our holes in the hay, where we lay down using our jackets as blankets.

"Hey, 'well brought-up person,'" I said to Antonio once the host had left. "This isn't exactly like at your house, huh?" By some of his remarks, I had realized that his house in Upper Bergamo must be very beautiful, as well as very old.

"Well, let's make do," he said jovially.

That second day we had traveled another forty kilometers; we felt a noticeable fatigue in our legs.

4

THE NEXT DAY the other soldiers sheltered in the barn, around fifteen of them, woke up before we did, talking loudly, almost all speaking Sicilian. Some of them were those young men who grow up badly because of poverty, often illiterate; the Sicilian recruits, unsuited for war and everything else, who in attack and retreat our army had left behind dead on every front.

Even these men now must have felt lost, not really able to find the road that would have taken them home. Therefore they appeared to be importunely playful toward more experienced companions and slapped their backs, to touch their support with their hands, to feel that it was there; to avoid feeling, once again, rejected.

We started our journey, washing up after them in a fountain of the monument that rose in the square.

We walked that entire day, first on the asphalt road that passed through the town, then along roads of interior Lazio that were not asphalt and, therefore, were dusty, although some were wonderfully shaded by large oaks, until a way to Abruzzi was shown to us near Gerano. An intelligent boy, pointing to the first of the Apennines, the foot of which we had reached by now, said, "Beyond this mountain is the valley of Aniene; going back up the river to its source, you'll arrive at a mountain higher than this one. At school they taught me that on the other side is the province of Abruzzi."

"Do you know if there are any big villages on the Aniene?"

"Yes, there's Subiaco."

I thought that we would be able to find a map, and began climbing the mountain again with vigor.

Above, in front of us, a country woman in the white and black dress of those parts with barely visible colorful stitching had hurried up from a field to our path and was waiting for us, her bare feet on the rocks. But what was in her heart must have hurt more than rocks.

When we were close she asked: "Where are you coming from, my sons?" We stopped. "From Nettuno," we answered.

"Have you met someone down there coming from Greece? Do you know what happened to Mama's boys who are in Greece?" she asked and, without waiting for our answer, burst into tears.

We didn't reach Subiaco. As we crossed the mountain the darkness caught up with us in the middle of vineyards; after a few useless attempts to proceed in the dark we knocked on the door of a small farmhouse.

Two women opened it, one old and one young; upon learning that we were soldiers, they let us in. I was struck by some of the items on the walls of that small house, maybe old and maybe not. I pointed them out to Antonio; in any case the house was very poor. The women made us sit at a rough table and immediately placed warm food in front of us. "Now I'll prepare somewhere for you to sleep," the younger one said briefly, adding, "My husband is also a soldier, and is away. May God help him and, like you, may He bring him home too."

Shortly after, while we finished eating, we heard her whisper in the next room to the other woman: "We have some milk left: we can drink that."

We looked at each other. "Can you believe it?" Antonio said.

I nodded: "They gave us their dinner." I pondered for a moment. "Well, it balances out the sacking of the Nettuno barracks."

"People like this make taking action, continuing to fight, worthwhile," Antonio murmured with unusual force.

We lay down on large bags of corn leaves; in the kitchen the two women had begun saying the rosary softly, so as not to disturb us.

After some hesitation we too decided to recite it. From that night on, following the example of those two country women, we would preface our individual prayers with the rosary, our communal prayer; like, after all, we did when we were home.

5 SUBIACO (a small city whose name neither of us really knew back then) is at the intersection of two valleys. It consists of a few ancient convents on cliffs supported by retaining walls, and alleys rising past the arches of medieval stone houses, and a beautiful bridge, also arched, above a narrow river, the Aniene, whose waters at the time were wonderfully clear. Harmony hung on all those walls like a nest of swallows.

When the small city appeared—below us—we stopped to look at it with admiration; then we hastened toward its streets. "It's not like having to cross a modern city, is it, where one curses the highway?" Antonio noted. "These medieval cities seem to have a soul: we meet them like we meet people." Maybe he was thinking about Upper Bergamo, his city.

We crossed Subiaco at a good pace, from one end to the other, and headed toward the largest convent, Santa Scolastica, which, we learned, had been founded by Saint Benedict a millennium and a half before.

"Surely back then it wasn't so impressive," I observed as we walked. "Maybe not much more than a cave, who knows . . . But with the passing of centuries and millennia it grew without ever betraying its early days." To think of this gave me peace and confidence, like thinking of the Catholic Church: when the clamor of modern times will become a brief stroke of silence in the panorama of the past, she—in spite of all the pain she endures and will continue to endure—will increase in size and power.

The entrance to the convent was by a small wrought-iron gate. We rang the rusted bell; a monk in a white and black frock came to open the door. "What do you want?" he asked.

"If possible, to speak with a teacher or superior. Better yet if he's Abruzzese."

The monk made a gesture of approval and, without asking anything else, led us through a cobbled courtyard and showed us to a large, plain room.

We sat on a bench and waited.

Through an open window, the sun's long rays fell on the floor, reminding me of the heavy silence of some summer study days before the war.

After quite some time a bishop—without a doubt the abbot—entered the room, and we stood up. He guided us to a lone table. In a paternal manner, he invited us to take seats, and sat across from us.

"How can I be of service, gentlemen?" he asked.

"We are two officers," I explained, "who intend to reach the town of Pretoro on the Maiella, on foot. We came to this convent in search of a map, and also—if you can provide it—advice on which way to follow."

I was astonished at the dignity of the man seated at the wretched table before us. "Although great, it's not only the dignity that's characteristic of church leaders," I told myself. "There's also something else, not easy to define . . ." Something that oddly reminded me of biblical and Greek kings who were shepherds. It was, we would discover shortly, the natural dignity among the elderly shepherds and peasants who followed Abruzzi's patriarchal customs.

"Yes, I can give you a map of suitable scale," the abbot answered, "and also some suggestions on the roads to follow, because I am from Abruzzi, a native of those very mountains." He fell silent in thought, as a shadow of regret passed over his eyes, thinking of his ancient land during those times of decay and shame.

"Do you intend to follow the roads or keep to the mountain?" he asked.

"The mountain, if possible."

"We're halfway through September," the abbot considered. "The shepherds should have left the pastures by now. Only 'cocciari'[1] should remain on the mountains." He smiled. "Clay pot makers. They're poor people with good hearts, like everybody in that region. Without a doubt they'll help you if necessary. Keep that in mind."

After leaving the premises, he returned again with a small folder. He opened it, chose a small map, removed it and offered it to us. Then, while showing it, he wrote an itinerary on a white sheet of paper.

He stood up, and we wished to kiss his bishop's ring, but he prevented us from it and shook our hands. "Poor men," he said, "how I pity you! You who are so young pay today for the ills committed mostly by others. Remember, however, that the mystery of reversibility is remarkable, and perhaps one day you most of all will find grace from the suffering of others."

---

1. Slang term used to signify potters.

He then raised a hand to bless us, like a king: "Never hate anyone: maybe the German who dies trying to hurt you, dies also for you."

When we left the courtyard, the monk doorkeeper brought us back to the fine dust of the road without a word. No visitor surprised him: for a thousand years, his brothers had opened the door to emperors at the height of their splendor, to fugitive kings, to people in despair, to assassins, to saints. Clearly, anyone can be in need of a monastery. And we too left the monastery comforted.

We stopped once again on the road that descended to the flat land, for a long look this time, drinking in medieval Subiaco and the walls that sustain its monasteries.

Influenced by my education in school, which, like everything in contemporary culture, was shaped by the destructive spirit of the Enlightenment—the philosophy that has found a way of rendering everything suspect—I felt an unsettling prejudice toward quite a few of the realities that made up contemporary Italy. But when I happened to encounter one of its most ancient sites, intact in an isolated place, like on that day, I found it to be unexpectedly consistent with my spirit: I felt as though I was collecting an inheritance from our forefathers, and I collected it with spontaneity and gratitude, like something prepared for me that had been missing for too long. So, with this insight, in those days of disintegration, my spirit affirmed itself, and nourished itself, and built itself.

6 WITH REGRET, we left the city and entered the wooded valley of the Aniene. From the start it proved to be deserted, with no voice other than the clear river.

It was hot that day also—the fourth of our journey. The sky was a beautiful, uniform blue.

The white, small road ran parallel to the river, only a few meters removed from it. We took a ten-minute break every hour, as in army marches, sitting on the bank in the shade of alders whose white roots lay in the river. The bank was dressed in musk—the entire green riverbed was woven with solid musk.

At times we listened curiously to the river's endless whisper, because we remembered (we had completed high school recently) Ovid's Latin verses, and the long tales that the deity of the Aniene used to tell him. After Subiaco and the Christian middle ages, here we had been transported, almost instantly, to a classic valley. What an extraordinary wealth of scenes, I told myself, was our Italy!

The Italy that was now reduced, defenseless, to a battlefield between foreign armies . . . Why had it come to this? What had thrown us into such a state? Would there be a future for our people? These were enormous problems, but even if our preparation was modest (nothing more than that of high school students) we had a mind to confront them, not to elude them. Our quest was clearer to us that day than in previous days, and reached its height. For hours, in fact, Antonio and I stretched our young intellects, striving to find the depth and reasons of things. While we reasoned, the river's ancient whisper—sometimes it seemed almost as though it was participating—blended with our voices.

Leaving the valley of the Aniene, by now reduced to a stream, during late afternoon, we traveled a deserted, uphill road between woods and fields that bordered some poor miners' villages.

We entered Filettino in darkness, the village of Marshal Graziani, who would soon become the commander of the armed forces of the Fascist Republic. According to the custom of dictators, the name of an illustrious citizen had been combined with the name of the village, and both names now appeared precariously side by side, in smooth writing, on the coarse walls.

The residents weren't any different from any others in that area; as a matter of fact a carpenter lodged us and gave us dinner. In his shop among his work tools he brought out for us armfuls of clean hay. We lay down to sleep in the beech-scented air.

7

WE BEGAN WALKING again at first light. Barely out of the village we met a British prisoner who undoubtedly had escaped from the nearby prison camp of Sulmona. At the armistice the guards had let all the Allied prisoners escape so they wouldn't end up in German hands. We would soon learn that there were now several thousand of them on the mountains or in dwellings, all provided for by our civilians.

We observed with curiosity his unfamiliar khaki uniform and the strange square mess kit (which one day would also become ours) that he held in his hand, full of steaming tea collected from some house. Then we began climbing up a very steep Apennine ridge covered with large beeches, below which the earth—clean of flies and all decayed matter—was blanketed with small curled-up leaves. It took us several hours to reach its crest, where we were able to see many other near and far peaks, boundless stone waves swelling up to the sky, resembling the waves of the sea.

We couldn't discern any flatlands, only mountains and tremendous rock ridges, and stone precipices that woods assaulted from below, so that Italy didn't seem to be a land of people but of giant unknown spirits that fed on air and morning light.

We allowed ourselves a break of barely half an hour, then we began our descent. We were in the land of Abruzzi; although we couldn't express how, we felt that our surroundings had been transformed.

*

Perhaps it was because the two small villages, nested intimately down below in the valley along its silent roads, offered a different view from the ones we had encountered. Toward the end of the descent, when we met the first people, we were surprised by the difference in their language and in their features, and even more in their spirit, at such a short distance from Lazio.

We reached the bottom of the valley after noon. In the fields a young woman sang a long song in a melodious voice; the melody spread beyond the cultivated rows and lost itself in the reflection of the sun on the stubble, absorbed by the monotonous concert of the cicada.

Reaching the source of the singing—invisible to us—we stopped on the path to listen, and it reminded me of the wide-open windows of my house, its stone windowsills from which the song of my busy sisters poured out on sunny days: the shrill voice of Angela, and the sweet voice of Pina. Perhaps now the windows were shut on their sad sills ... When the beautiful singing died out and the chorus of envious cicadas doubled, we headed to the closest farmhouse, small with a wooden porch and fronted by almond trees. "*The guest comes from Jove,*" we used to say in the old days, and also, as Christianity prescribes, "*host the pilgrims.*" These principles are deeply rooted in the spirit of the Abruzzese: we were welcomed as though sent by God. After all, who could say that we weren't?

One of the house's sons—there were two, both returned a few days before—chased and, by throwing a stick, killed the rooster of the modest henhouse, then quickly prepared it for cooking. The mother, postponing all other chores, dedicated herself to kneading a portion of wheat flour; the pleasant sight of genuine pasta appeared between the active hands of the countrywoman.

There was also the father, with his hairy arms, who invited us to sit facing him on wooden stools. He spoke to us with gravity. "Don't get discouraged, fellows, about today's state of affairs," he said, more or less. "Don't be among those who say 'by now it's over for us Italians.' I only know the story from what I hear at church sermons, but I know that throughout time our people have been tested in every way and have always passed the test. We mustn't let ourselves be taken over by the kind of discouragement that threatens the farmer when, full of debts, he has a bad crop. He wants to abandon the small field that his father left him: but if he is tenacious and persists like a man, the good times return. I'm telling you because I've experienced it." And afterwards, touched by his wisdom, we agreed: "How can we consider ourselves finished," he exclaimed, his hands on his knees, his head stretched out forward, looking in our eyes, "if each of us feels his own heart full of strength?"

His two sons spoke impulsively, sharing with us their travel experience. "Take the train," they said. "Don't be afraid. The Germans only make roundups in the big stations, not in secondary ones. One of the two reported, "I came from Trieste. Up there the Germans have captured all the officers and also many soldiers and are deporting them to Germany. But near the Po they're preparing some trenches in a big hurry. That's a sign, I think, that the British will soon be at the Po."

Their father added, "You'll rest in my house for as many days as you want."

Shortly after, the mother called us to the table and placed a steaming plate in front of us. While we ate, she was the last one to speak, from her stool against the wall, below religious paintings; with instinctive delicacy, she only spoke of everyday things, of small matters that wouldn't remind us of our circumstances. The comfort that came from her was matched by the smell arising from the bread.

After eating, we lay down to sleep in an airy hayloft, where the sons used to rest during hot hours.

I wonder why in school no one had told us about this place, about the existence of people such as these. Apparently the classical and Homeric world in our books that we thought had faded millennia ago hadn't disappeared. I was beginning to make one of the most wonderful discoveries of my life.

"We were in charge of soldiers like this, and look to what we've been reduced," I said to Antonio before we dozed off.

"In any case, it wasn't conceivable that people like this would contribute to Nazism's victory," he observed.

"Look to what point we have been driven!" I murmured.

8

IN THE FOLLOWING days we continued our journey, from dawn to dusk, interrupted only by hourly halts, like in marches. In such a mountainous region, the distance we traveled each day was much shorter than the forty kilometers of the first days. We received the same royal reception as our first day everywhere we went in Abruzzi.

The peasants with whom we stayed gave us food, places to sleep, and even their razors for shaving. We almost never succeeded in getting them to accept money in exchange; during our entire journey we lived off their hospitality. Everywhere we introduced ourselves as simple soldiers—rumors of money rewards for officers were going around—and the people of the nation opened their souls to us, without reticence or fear of being misunderstood.

The third day after our entry into Abruzzi we climbed the main ridge of the Apennines, the middle one. We were in the national park and at the foot of tremendous beeches with twisted trunks; many rocks seemed recently overturned, by bears in search of larvae. It was one of the most demanding and wearing ascents.

According to our small map the mountain reached two thousand meters. Its high watershed emerged powerfully from the woods and was surrounded by a few pastures. When we were near the top and weary, two large shepherd's dogs came running and howling at us. To defend ourselves we took up rocks; fortunately, the shepherd was nearby and with shouts and pebbles chased away his dogs.

He led us hastily to his stone hut in a small valley. "You'll eat with me," he said, "then you'll stay here to rest." Seeing that it was Sunday, we decided to accept.

It was almost noon, and smoke rose in the sky from the roof of the hut. That smoke was like the song of a bird with ashen wings.

We observed the shepherd as he prepared the meal: bread with oil and salt, the poorest meal of poor southern people.

With almost ritualistic movements he removed from the fire a pot of boiling saltwater and poured it into a copper kettle. He had arranged some slices of bread inside the kettle; he soaked the bread, drained the water, and sparingly distributed a little olive oil. The food was ready.

A few steps away the two white dogs attentively observed the preparation; when they saw it was ready they came forward and the shepherd poured part of the bread in two bowls for them, but without oil.

He offered us two small apples, one for each of us, which seemed to be wild.

"Is this always your meal?" we asked while we ate.

"Always," he answered.

"You vary it sometimes," I said.

He looked at us, surprised and smiling. "Well, once in a while I also eat some cheese."

We stayed the entire afternoon conversing with him, while the sheep grazed nearby. Among other things he explained why his dogs' collars were full of metal spikes and their ears mutilated: they had to endure duels with wolves, who always aimed at the throat and lacerated the dogs' ears. His life consisted of such hardships, which were necessities, not objects of satisfaction. He seemed to enjoy reflecting or, maybe more appropriately, meditating.

The cold of the night brought us inside the stone hut. The ugly Abruzzese sheep had been herded, with our help, inside a hemp net fence.

We slept on small, concave tree-trunk beds filled with leaves.

Throughout the night the dogs whimpered or barked softly, waking us, since we weren't used to it. "What is it? Maybe some bear in the vicinity?" I asked once, hearing that the shepherd was awake.

"No," he answered, "the dogs sigh when they dream."

Once in a while the sleepless stone plates that covered the hut sighed, under the stronger power of the nocturnal breeze.

"Hear it?" I said to Margherita. "Even things cry . . . everything on the earth seems to be suffering!"

"But am I not in your heart?" she answered. "So there's also joy and love on earth."

*

At dawn, taking leave of the shepherd, we began our descent along a rugged path.

Before reaching the bottom of the valley, we encountered, as we had been told we would, a man with two mules who was bringing up provisions to the hut. We were following one of the lowest buttresses of the mountain through the ruins of a village, Lecce dei Marsi, abandoned centuries ago. Only the stones of the ancient dwellings remained, in the middle of which small trees and bushes grew. At the sound of the mules a large black bird came out of a roofless house with a cry of protest; one would have thought him the owner of the house. Immediately a flock of migrating birds rose from the cliff below and settled on the trees' highest branches; I remember that this was in the fall, in spite of the heat. Soon the days of rain would begin . . .

The bishop-abbot of Subiaco had told us, as he handed us the map, that we wouldn't find any shepherds on the mountains, since by now they would all be traveling toward winter pastures, but would meet only "cocciari," patient makers of clay pots. Yet because of the war that raged in the lower areas leading to the plains of Puglia and to winter pastures, the shepherds were forced to extend their mountain stay.

9

THE EVENING OF the following day we saw a slow-moving train, overloaded with soldiers, almost all in civilian clothes, who filled the cars up to the roofs and also rode on the cow catchers in front. This convinced us to take a train.

By now we were close to the midpoint of our journey, and we were tired. We reached the closest station and took the next train, which was almost empty. Shortly after, as it was beginning to get dark, the train was stopped in the station of Sulmona—I wondered by whom—and we were notified that it would not go any farther. So we joined the people who camped with their few belongings among the ruins of the station, demolished by aerial bombings.

Seated on a sidewalk with our backs against the remains of a wall, we waited for a train to leave in the direction of Pescara. The time passed under the light of dirty lamps hanging from a long, thin wire. Sometimes the lamps would sway, pushed by a breeze; the distinctive smell of burnt things was in the air.

Of all the many thoughts on my mind, one surpassed all others, and, with the slow succession of the hours, began to hammer at me. It was a line by Ovid: "*Sulmo patria mihi fuit, celeber gelidissimis undis . . .*"[2] I said it to Antonio to free myself of it, but it wouldn't leave me: "*Sulmo . . . Sulmo . . . Sulmo . . .*"

Maybe the phrase was *est,* not *fuit:*[3] I tried to remember, and little by little my doubt began to torment me.

Every so often I opened my eyes. A small woman with a black scarf covering her head and tied below her chin sat almost in front of me. She addressed us suddenly: "Sons, is it true that in Sulmona there are as many Germans as in Pescara?"

2. "Sulmona was my birthplace, surrounded by very cold waves."
3. *Is,* not *was.*

She didn't seem to be a peasant; impassive peasant women let the hours pass in silence.

"We don't know. We arrived when it was dark, and we haven't left the station. But it's possible that there are fewer—Sulmona is less important than Pescara."

"I've been here seven hours," the small woman said. "Seven hours!"

Next to her, sitting on bundles tied at the corners, were two girls, undoubtedly her relatives, who sighed at those words. They were somewhat disheveled, their faces dirty; in their shyness, they never looked at us. Once in a while one of them stirred the black dirt of the sidewalk with the toe of her torn shoe. The woman studied them and said, "Several times, it's seemed like a train was about to leave, and we ran to it with the others, but then it didn't leave."

We didn't comment, and the woman became silent. In a short while, however, she began again: "The day before yesterday a woman from Pescara came to my village. Do you know what she told me? That in that train station there was a train full of provisions, and the Germans invited the people to come take them: 'Take it, Italians, take it,' they said, 'anyway these are your things; don't be afraid, Italians.' Then, when a crowd formed around the train, they shot them with machine guns. So many dead, my sons. There were so many dead."

"Do you hear this? They're starting with the slaughter," I whispered, looking at Antonio.

He made a sign to mean, "Who knows if it's true . . ."

After a while the woman began again: "You're Italian with that speech?"

"Yes, Italians like you; we're Lombards."

"Well, yes, you're certainly Italian," she agreed, after having observed us better, "with those clothes," and grew silent again.

Time crawled under the yellowish lamps. Once in a while one could hear some child crying; then someone nearby, woman or man, intervened in the same benevolent Abruzzese accent to comfort it or try to get it to sleep. The Latin phrase had returned to hammer at me: "*Sulmo . . . Sulmo . . . est* or *fuit? . . . est* or *fuit?*" "My goodness," I mumbled to myself: "this is like a twitch inside my head . . . A twitch that wears the brain!"

Antonio was huddled within himself, his head low.

"They really messed it up, this station?" I said to him, to exchange a few words.

"Mess it up?" he answered in a bad mood: I realized that he wanted to contradict me, even without reason. He was as tense as I, but succeeded in controlling himself. "It's better to fight the war on the front, like soldiers," he said softly. "I was just thinking. At least you don't have to see children and women suffer. Soldiers are the strongest part of the population: if there's a weight to carry, it's up to them."

"We're not the strongest part," I objected, absurdly offended by his sensitiveness. "Women are stronger with these types of things."

He didn't answer.

"We were right not to go to Rome," I pressed. "We shouldn't have come here either, in the midst of these people. These are times when we should stay clear of people." I felt an increasing, senseless resentment toward him, for having suggested Rome.

The irritation was increasing inside of him, but he didn't strike back. Well, he could go to hell! But that damned expression, that cursed expression . . . "Let's try to keep calm, and if possible to think this over," I protested to myself. "Think it over? Not on your life. It can all go to hell! In any case, let's stay calm, all right? Stay calm!"

More time went by.

"You're angry, aren't you, Antonio? Today too we made some kilometers, at least thirty, on top of all the others, and we can't sleep."

He stayed silent.

"I'm going to start singing," I said.

"Knock it off," he said.

"I want to sing," I said, "to get rid of your anger."

We were left with no one around us, because once in a while someone would get up to stretch, so all three of the women near us had left suddenly with their bundles, in an awkward procession.

"I sing badly," I said. "Once in college they put me by mistake with the singers, then they stopped the chorus one by one until they singled me out and pulled me out. But I'll sing anyway."

"Stop it," Antonio repeated, with his head between his bent shoulders, hands hanging between his knees.

I sang and repeated all the excerpts of popular songs that I knew. It seemed to me that my out-of-tune singing lasted perhaps half an hour. When I fell silent Antonio grumbled, "Here's the connection."

"What connection? What are you saying?"

"The connection. You're your usual stubborn self. You think you're the only one who can read the map."

With the tip of my foot I hit his shoe: "Wake up, you're dreaming."

He raised his head and looked at me. "I must have been talking in my dream," he said.

"You were dreaming. Our nerves aren't worth a thing."

"I hate you," he said.

It seemed like a train was about to leave. We stood up hastily and rushed with the others, knocking into people to pass them. It was a false alarm. Wandering up and down the station in search of a place to sleep, we went to lie down in a stock car stopped on a dead-end track, but the bottom of the wagon was so foul that we were forced to leave.

We went back to sitting on a sidewalk among the ruins. Occasionally, the phrase would begin pounding my weary brain. Finally, I turned to prayer. Why hadn't I done this before? I probably had told myself that I was too tired, that for God we must reserve our best moments, not feeble ones. There's a demon inside us, detached from us, that leads his own fight.

As always happened when I prayed, I felt that I was part of something much larger, not limited by human affairs but on the contrary surpassing man, so that, thanks to it, even the affairs of man appeared bearable. I was ashamed of my behavior. Was my nervous strength still so slight? I had been on the verge of delirium, as I sometimes had been during sick leave, right after I had come back from the Russian front.

As of tomorrow, I promised, I would be friendlier to Antonio, to make him forgive me. "Like a child? So be it."

10

IN THE COOL MORNING we came down from the train at the foot of the enormous, clear massif of the Maiella, which the train had rounded at first light.

All around us were large hills covered with bright gold stubble. We started to climb toward the town of Pretoro, in our hearts hoping to find my companion-in-arms Virgilio De Marinis, on whose hospitality we were counting.

We walked slowly on the knolls among serene old olive trees. The events of the night seemed distant. Suddenly, we saw from a knoll a streak of sea: "The Adriatic! Look, we're in sight of the Adriatic!" we said, pointing to it.

On the shore of that sea, in Riccione, I had walked in Margherita's company . . . Now I began to dream that Margherita walked with us . . . the sky-blue of the fleur-de-lis, which in that area had escaped the scythe, made me think of her feet among the stubble . . . Gradually, I came to see the girl with such force that it seemed as though she were present. I greeted her youthful face joyfully: her beautiful curly hair, unparalleled in this world, I told myself; her deep gray eyes.

Antonio kept quiet, absorbed in the peace that came from this place. Inside my heart I talked with Margherita and spoke kind words to her; "Skylark," I called her, and playfully, "second Melisenda" . . . (That hour too, like all of life's, has passed, has gone forever. Youth, love of love, hills covered in the enchanting Abruzzese gold of back then, Margherita my skylark . . . how distant you are today from me who remembers!)

Pretoro, a town of small houses, rose on the first peak of the imposing mountain. At its entrance an old bridge defied the passage of time and arched over a torrent that plunged from the mountain, yet gentle olive branches brushed against windows here and there. The house of my former fellow soldier Virgilio, modest and similar to the others, was in the center of town near the church. We were finally able to rest, take a bath, and eat to satiety. And be at peace!

But in those days there could only be the semblance of peace, much like the cruel semblance of the sun on our columns' retreat ten months earlier from the Russian winter had made the nostalgia of a little warmth more acute in the heart of each soldier.

Peace, which one felt to be customary and ancient in that house, was broken during those days. One of Virgilio's brothers, an infantry lieutenant, was in Greece. There had been no news from him; Virgilio, his other brother, and his sister, who were also present, deliberately spoke of it with careless optimism in front of the almost blind old aunt they regarded as a mother. At times the old woman cried in silence; she always sat in the same corner with a statuelike face, the calm color of the fire waving in the chimney.

There were many well-chosen books in the house and, after not having been able to read for so long, I shut myself off and read poetry for hours. I savored Petrarch as I never had before: I compared ingenuously his relationship with Laura to my growing relationship with Margherita and rejoiced. During those hours of reading I let my mind wander to the point where the surrounding world no longer touched me.

But at times an internal voice urged me on: "Don't you feel the selfishness of this placid thirst-quenching at a time when everyone is in distress?" Eventually, I stopped reading so that, within each hour, I could experience everyone's life.

Perhaps the best time, without remorse, was when Filomena, the active sister, placed bread on the table. Even before sitting down, Antonio and I took the big round loaf and, holding it against our chest like peasants do— we had learned it from them—used a knife to cut long white slices, bordered brown, fragrant, a blessing from God.

"There's one going to Milan that'll return within a month," Virgilio told us one day. "If you want, you can send letters home and have an answer."

"We'll surely take advantage of it."

"We'll also ask for clothes and underclothes. Because who knows when the British will arrive."

Radio Rome, upon which we waited, impatiently, for decisive news, had at first announced the draft of five, then fifteen, classes to establish workers units that would serve the Germans. The town crier wandered the streets blowing a bugle to notify the villages and shouted the announcement: the crier, a figure that we had believed buried in the past.

For its part Radio London gave news that the Italian army was reorganizing in Puglia by orders of the king, joined fortunately by the head of the government and principal ministers.

On this side of the front, which by now split Italy in two, the Germans were putting the Fascists back in power; on the other side the legitimate authorities were trying, not any less miserably, to resettle themselves under foreign protection.

A few days after the announcement, German units quartered themselves in a few towns below Pretoro; many of the young men included in the draft classes set off for the mountains.

It was September 29. In order not to expose our hosts to the danger of German retaliation, both of us decided to reach Puglia. We had to do it right away, while the front was moving. In spite of the news to the contrary transmitted—incorrectly—by Radio London, my experience taught me that we would be able to cross.

"Stay with us," the De Marinis said. "Don't worry about retaliation. We'll share our fate like brothers."

"Stay," the old, half-blind woman repeated from her corner, raising a hand that held the rosary.

But we had decided, and we took our leave.

Our respite in Pretoro had lasted six days. After a few hours of travel, it was as if we had never stopped. Only now in place of the shoes that had blistered my feet I wore Virgilio's comfortable sandals, which according to Antonio gave me a fittingly pastoral look.

11

LEAVING ABRUZZI with regret, we entered the coarse Molise, a land of a different, older roughness. Here the men, who seemed more indolent than the Abruzzese, did nothing in town, but sat on the thresholds of their stone houses with small windows.

"Aren't you worried about the draft of classes?"

"In the province of Campobasso there aren't any drafts; at this point we're too close to the front."

"The British are coming."

"They're already in Termoli."

"They're already in Vasto . . ."

We consulted the new map, given to us by Virgilio. Before leaving Pretoro, we had also listened to the radio one last time: we knew, therefore, that the British could not be very close. But all these people waiting here almost convinced us.

On the mountain of Capracotta, covered by an immense forest of firs, we almost ran into a group of New Zealanders, former prisoners, sitting in a circle on the ground. When they saw us they leaped to their feet and took flight in a clinking of mess kits. It was our turn to turn back with pounding hearts when we saw the color of their uniforms and heard that sound; we began looking for them with intense curiosity.

A decrepit structure, vaguely resembling a small church, stood among the firs. It was the home of an old-fashioned "hermit"; we noticed that smoke came from the ridge of its roof. The former prisoners' base must have been there, where they had taken refuge. Entering, we tried to reassure them; I asserted, first in Italian, then in French, that it was useless for them to give me a demonstration on how to escape because I was already good at it on my own. They didn't seem to understand a single word. Pointing to the map, we showed them the closest spot, according to the radio, where

70

their troops had arrived. They looked in silence, both at us and the map: it seemed that they didn't understand this either. They all had an appearance that was both dignified and unimpressive, so that we were surprised when one of them, thanking us for the news in a language that was incomprehensible to us, used a tone that nonetheless seemed condescending.

"What manners . . ." I mumbled.

"If it's to cover up the impression their flight left, it seems excessive," Antonio said. "But maybe it's just that they don't trust anyone, and everyone they meet worries them."

"All things considered, they're more in need than we are," I concluded. We left the place perplexed.

*

In Pretoro we had been told that since Capracotta (built on the highest and most exposed mountain) was a vacation place, we would be able to find some hotels where we could rest.

As a vacation spot it had, incongruously for those times, a multicolored, carefree appearance. But not for much longer: the Germans would include it in their band of scorched earth across their winter lines, and within a few months not one stone would remain standing. But one, two, three hotel keepers (who back then accommodated many evacuees, and who therefore, in spite of everything, had good business) refused to host us like regular guests, or even to speak to us. The last hotel keeper—almost frightened when he saw us, a reminder of an unpleasant reality—tried to scold us. We quickly changed his mind, but: "The peasants are better," we decided. "This stupid place has nothing to do with us." That fashionable location was similar to a cheerful face painted on an advertising poster that continues to smile even when the paper begins to tear and goes to pieces, mocking as well as foolish and tragic in itself.

We went down to the lowest, nontourist part of town, where the small Molisan houses were like everywhere else.

We were placed in a kitchen, where we lay down to sleep on the floor. Unfortunately, it was filthy. Flies covered the walls and ceilings and fell on our faces by the dozens as we tried to sleep; fleas also attacked us and, more repugnant, bed bugs with their painful stings. Once in a while a pig grunted nearby. "It must be because the bugs are keeping him from sleeping too, poor animal."

We did not find the situation amusing that night. We became irritated and managed to quarrel over the tugs one or the other gave the filthy blanket when the bugs tormented him.

We succeeded in falling asleep only because we very much needed to, but at dawn we sought as soon as possible the fresh mountain air, like a cleansing, leaving behind the inhospitable village among the firs.

Seventy-five silver American four-engined aircraft (we counted them), high and untouchable in the bright sky, passed in long formation above us, headed north; the valley became filled with their thunder.

Where would they bomb?

German anti-aircraft fire came from a knoll. We could imagine the angry faces of German artillerymen in the smoke of the small clouds that dissolved, too low, impotent. But where would those airplanes bomb?

At length that morning we had to fight ourselves and convince each other to continue the journey. Indeed, it seemed to foretell that not a few months but years of difficult circumstances would separate us from our homes once we joined the front.

12

TOWARD EVENING, near the village of Pietrabbondante, we reached the first sheep track marked on our map, a long grassy area between woods and cultivation. Conforming to every portion of the land, its irregular green ribbon ascended a hill, beyond which I imagined it plunged into a valley and then climbed back up, on and on like the ribbon of a memory that travels through the landscape of time.

We intended to complete the rest of our journey on those grassy and solitary paths, where shepherds since time immemorial (perhaps three thousand years) had migrated from the Apennines to the pastures of Puglia, kept green in the winter by the warmth of the sea. We thought (correctly) that the Germans would not watch over the sheep tracks, because they presented difficulties for automobiles and because the Germans were not a nation old enough to understand such roads. In fact, until we reached the front we would not leave the delightful roads of the shepherds, except for brief exits. The sheep paths were unfailingly respected, we discovered, by all other roads, which passed over the shepherd roads on bridges.

We weren't the only ones to travel on them. We came across southern soldiers walking toward their homes, officers who were faithful to their oaths or their needs, civilians from the politically compromised north. We never joined with anyone for more than a few hours, in order not to increase the difficulties of eating and sleeping.

It rained at intervals. Our footwear would slide on the grass, marking it with furrows of mud. Still we felt comforted by the reception of the peasants with whom we took our rest.

*

I remember a night of hard rain and wind when we arrived in Ripalimosani, inside a gorge covered by large patches of fog. We couldn't see the town, except when it appeared below like a handful of gravel thrown on the lower part of a slope, with each small stone a house. We entered in the dark, with a boy pushing forward two sheep and returning in a hurry as our guide.

Soaked, we knocked at the first house.

They opened the door; dinner was interrupted. The mother, a country woman, heated some water and poured it inside two copper basins, inviting us first to wash our muddy feet. Then the women prepared a new dinner, almost solemnly, that was placed on the table in a single large plate, around which the family sat with us.

"Just think," the peasants said while eating, "here there's never been war, never, and within days we'll be in the middle of it."

"What will happen?" the women murmured, troubled. "May the Virgin Mary help us!"

"If my house is destroyed," argued the head of the family, Pietro de Bartolomeis, "how will I be able to rebuild it? It's cost me my whole life's work." Once an emigrant to Argentina, he knew the world and treated us strangers with a sort of fellowship.

"Is it true that there's never been war in these parts? Even the elders say so."

"There hasn't been in many years," I ventured. "But inhabited areas that never experienced war don't exist. It's just that through the centuries we end up generally by forgetting. Fortunately."

"Not here where we live, never, they say."

And yet this land, I remembered vaguely, had been among the principal theaters of the Gothic wars, frightening wars that had depopulated Italy. But why speak of it? Who remembers the Gothic wars any more? The same rule for art holds true for wars and for every other event: the size of the event or of the work doesn't count as much as the universality it contains. That's how everyone happens to know, for example, the Termopili, and no one remembers the Gothic wars.

"You don't look like simple soldiers," the head of the family observed. "Are you maybe . . . noncommissioned officers?"

He meant officers with ranks, but we preferred to take his words literally: "Yes, we're corporals."

"And in civilian life what work do you do?"

"Clerical workers."

The peasants nodded, expressing their appreciation.

"There's nothing savage in these mouths, in these faces gathered around food," I noted, while eating. "Good health instead and, especially in the women, a native civility . . ."

"What can we do, Lord, with the war that is about to come?" one of the women repeated. She was asking herself, but ended by looking at us questioningly, as if we, having come from elsewhere, were able to suggest something.

"We can only hope that the front won't stop here and passes quickly. Then, you'll see, the danger won't be great."

"May the Virgin Mary help us."

"May the Virgin Mary help you, like you helped us."

"You are good, soldier," the mother said to me. "The Virgin Mary will bring you home."

At the end of dinner Antonio and I lay down to sleep on quilts and blankets stretched out on the brick floor of the kitchen.

In the unexpected silence, the singing of a hearth cricket suddenly rose (I was hearing it for the first time in my life) a couple of meters from our heads, perhaps expressing satisfaction that the weather had cleared up outside and the rain was lifting. That small voice, which trembled and constantly filled the darkness of the house, was similar for us to when a silly woman in church unpredictably begins singing next to you with a reserved voice, and the satisfaction at the sound of her voice sometimes follows the first reaction of embarrassment.

"What a land of ours!" Antonio said, after having listened at length, so that I thought he had fallen asleep. "What contrasts! I think of the women who sacked the barracks in Nettuno and the two who fasted in order to give us their dinner. And those two little cowards, the parish priest and the mayor of R.; and at the opposite end the bishop-abbot of Subiaco, and that meditative shepherd on the Apennines . . ."

"But even back home in Lombardy," he added after a pause. "I'm thinking of the details that I hadn't thought about until now because I was raised there. I understand when you say that the essence of your experience among soldiers showed you that there isn't one human accomplishment or flaw, for which a man is a man and not something else, that is lacking among us."

We fell asleep with these thoughts while from the hearth the cricket continued singing, as far as he was concerned doing his small part.

13

PASSING THE CAPITAL of Molise, Campobasso, at a distance along the sheep track, we noticed many more German cars on the roads. We even saw encampments in the woods and groups of armored cars. We happened to see two German sentries near our sheep track who, with their rifles under their arms, were forcing civilians (possibly military men who fell into their hands) to dig holes at the bottom of a road bridge, in order to mine it.

The sky was patrolled by British airplanes, flying at a very low altitude over each road; their machine-gun fire and shells followed us from dawn to dusk. Our daily pace had returned to forty kilometers. We were suspicious of those we saw traveling the sheep tracks.

As we approached the Fortore River, which separated Molise from Puglia with its large gravelly shore, we began to hear the guns: the front was close. Here the peasants stayed quietly on their farms and silently placed food in front of us as soon as we stopped, almost as though it was their duty, so much did they share our worry.

We stayed for the night in a barn six or seven kilometers from the river. The hooded headlights of the German trucks, in continuous transit, shone through a grating of giant reeds that closed off our shelter. The lights began in a corner, opened like a fan inside the walls, and disappeared, absorbed by the darkness. We wondered how we would be able to cross the front, with its dangers and possible obstacles.

*

The next day we studied the situation from a terrace on the edge of the town of Gambatesa, which from a steep hill dominates the valley of Fortore.

In the countryside below we saw German guns open fire—small toys whose barrels recoiled with each shot, and clouds of smoke. Occasional British fire struck the precipices above Fortore; then a few explosions on the shore raised fountains of water and pebbles, with clouds of smoke. Suddenly a British plane discovered a German gun below us and attacked it with a cluster of shells, but the gun wasn't hit, so it continued firing with an added fury.

The residents made uncertain trips between the village and caves in the ground nearby. Women who had children stayed in those damp caves. They held the children in their arms or by the hand, and once in a while questioned the parish priest and the mayor, the miserable authorities of the place: "Will they also fire on the village? When will this torment end?" The priest and the mayor stretched out their arms, and wandered with troubled faces among the people.

Since a German command was in Gambatesa (probably a battalion) we decided to spend the night far from the town, in an isolated farmhouse on the opposite hill, dominated by the side of the river and the long bridge that crossed it with thirteen arches.

Even on that out-of-the-way farm the peasants welcomed us in a friendly spirit. Strange conversations, however, transpired between them at night during dinner, and later in front of the fireplace; some of them, even the very young, thought back to the distant details of their lives, almost as though they felt on the verge of losing them.

*

The next morning two or three of the bridge's arches were missing: that was precisely what we had been waiting for. Antonio, having gone outside, noticed it first: "The Germans have evacuated the Puglian shore," he announced. "We'll have to hurry."

"I'll finish shaving and we'll go."

"Who are they?" I heard him ask a moment later, his voice worried.

I promptly went to look. A strange procession of staggering men, lifting their shoes with difficulty from the mud, was coming from the rear zone toward the farm. There were twenty of them.

At first we didn't make out their weapons. "They could be former British prisoners," I suggested, perplexed. "See, they have our gray-green coats on top of their colonial uniforms."

But it was a German platoon that was coming to take position where we were.

As it stopped in front of the farm, three or four soldiers—tall and massive figures they seemed, although they were actually adolescents—left the line and, with movements that seemed habitual, entered the kitchen and took possession of all the bread, without giving the peasants a glance.

Antonio found himself in the midst of them. Truly noble and irreproachable, he didn't betray his own feelings. When a German rudely ordered him to pass some bread that was on a dough tray, he picked it up calmly and passed it. Should the occasion arise, I realized, he would have gotten himself killed without losing composure.

"What are you doing? Are you distributing presents to the people like the old sovereigns?" I asked him in a low voice, amused despite everything.

The officer commanding the platoon, perspiring and with his submachine gun hanging on his chest, left the house to study the edge of the threshing floor toward the Fortore River.

"The German command must have set its eyes on this farm from Gambatesa like we did yesterday . . ."

At this point they would keep us to dig trenches. Probably they would realize that we weren't peasants; maybe even that we weren't from the area. Especially Antonio, blond, with his rosy face in the midst of all these dark people; after all, it was readily apparent that I too wasn't a Molisan peasant. Maybe we had gotten ourselves into some real trouble.

But providence (I thank it with a shiver, even today, so many years later!) sent three British planes flying in tight circles above us. "*Flieger alarm,*" sounded a voice; without breaking order, the platoon moved toward a group of trees on the edge of the threshing floor. Pretending to fear the airplanes—with gestures that we hoped seemed southern—we both headed in the opposite direction toward a straw stack, then, almost without stopping, toward a tree somewhat farther ahead; finally we moved down to the river, placing between us and the Germans a nearby rise of land.

I can't say for certain that someone fired at us, because, as happens in such situations, we weren't sure. Possibly it was simply stray bullets that whistled around us among the fruit trees.

After crossing the shore and shallow swamp water through grass higher than us, we were welcomed by green slopes that climbed toward two towns, Celenza and Carlantino.

"It was child's play," Antonio commented.

"Everything seems that way in war when it all ends well."

"All right. Then you can add this one to your heroic deeds," he said, laughing.

A ruffled woman, who was running who knows where alone around the countryside, warned us, shouting, "Six or seven Germans are still in Carlantino."

In Celenza, civilians had already been killed by mines. (We learned this in front of an isolated farmhouse, from whose door even an old monsignor, with a red brimmed hat and a very southern face, terrified, driven from who knows where with the front's advance, appeared with others when we arrived). As we looked up toward the town, small clouds of shells broke overhead, exploding above its little houses.

We entered a wooded gorge between Celenza and Carlantino populated only by sheep without shepherds. After a few hours of walking, it led us inside the British rear zone.

That was the twenty-second day since our departure from Nettuno.

14

IN THE AFTERNOON we appeared near Castelnuovo della Daunia, a town notably different from Molisan ones, almost Arabic in appearance. Here were the first British soldiers. They were stretched out in the grass next to crawler tanks with treads (the carriers, unknown to us then); they answered our curious looks with yawns.

A motorcyclist had stopped in the square and was surrounded by a small group of peasants. We too approached to observe him; he went inexplicably from pose to spineless pose, his face shining with grease, his hair too long under his large helmet. He joked with the people with languid gestures that appeared affectionate.

"This one," Antonio said, shaking his head, "seems to come directly from shallow waters."

"I'm curious to look at British soldiers more closely," I murmured as we were leaving. "They're winning the war, all right, but the slowness with which they advance leaves me puzzled. Surely we'll have to wait, see a lot of them, before forming an opinion."

We waited indeed and, after having seen many, I continued waiting; those who gradually passed under my nose seemed like civilians instead of soldiers. This impression (I record it here, bizarre as it is) would increase in the following weeks, from their truck convoys with strangely square contours to their extensive and peaceful parking areas, even to the ammunition gathered everywhere without protection that made one think of piles of merchandise.

*

The next day, and the following ones, my first thought upon waking in the morning was that now no one would think to hunt us down. Each time a sense of relief came. I wondered if the British and Americans realized that behind their lines one could feel a respect for men.

It felt like this whenever one saw notices where occupation troops threatened fines and at most jail for offenses that on the other side were invariably punished with death. We would no longer hear talk of executions and more executions, and this fear—which makes man nothing more than beast—would no longer hang over us. The principle of civility, determined throughout the course of centuries, did not survive only in the closed spaces of our souls! Here it was, in a world where principles still regulated ordinary life ... I remember, as I lingered in front of those notices, how I thanked God from the bottom of my heart more than once.

Later we became used to these things, so as almost not to notice them. Nonetheless we felt humiliated that strangers were in charge of our home. But it always happens like this: when an individual or a people is helped in finding or finding again the fullness of his own human condition, he does not accept limitations, even when they are set by whoever has helped him. He feels entitled to that condition by the single fact that he is a man.

*

Two days after crossing the lines we arrived in Bari on a train; since the Germans had actually left a good part of Puglia without any time for destruction, a few trains still worked.

It was night, and the badly lit streets of the city, washed out by a sudden squall, were flooded with British and American soldiers. Many Italian women walked by their sides; some even embraced the soldiers openly, almost as though they wanted to prostitute all their people as well as themselves. Did anyone rebel? No one. I noticed that many of the foreigners, probably just landed, had an air of exultation.

Slowed more by what we saw around us than by our fatigue and the sores on Antonio's feet, we eventually reached the Italian officers' mess. From there we were sent to the command's stopping place, surprisingly in the city's general hospital. The previous day, in Lucera, shortly after coming upon the British, we had discovered the first Italian stopping place (isolated evidence, whatever the reason for the officer to establish it, of our readiness to recover: only someone like me, who had just seen other people overtaken by war, would be able to understand it). There we had given false names. "The teaching of Ulysses wasn't only literature for us, was it?" Antonio had said, laughing; in Bari we would do the same thing. We intended, in fact, to keep our freedom until we were certain that the reviving army was free, and not mercenaries at the service of foreigners.

The window for "passing officers" was closed, but since the shutters revealed light, we knocked. An angry lieutenant colonel with gray hair opened it. "Who are you? What do you want?" he asked us rudely. We explained: we had arrived after a journey that had lasted about a month, from the area of Rome; we had just arrived, on the train.

Only this last detail seemed to interest him; he made a show of checking his watch. "The train arrived half an hour ago," he said angrily.

"Indeed. But since at the station we learned that the officers' mess is still operating in Bari, seeing the time, we went there immediately. From there, they sent us here."

"Ah!" he began to scream. "At the mess! You went to the mess, and here's a lieutenant colonel, I said a lieu-ten-ant-ker-nel"—he pronounced the syllables as though he exulted at the idea of so much rank, then ended by being angry with us because in truth he no longer was worth a thing— "should wait at your convenience!" We listened to him, astonished.

"Please, colonel, sir, give us lodging vouchers," I said when his outburst was finished. "The city is full of British and Americans, and without vouchers we won't be able to find anywhere to sleep."

"Vouchers too?" he shouted. "After what I've told you, you have the nerve to ask me for vouchers too!" and he slammed down the window, hard, leaving us in the dark.

We stayed there without speaking or moving, two young men facing troubles that were too great to confront.

"I can't make this into a joke," I finally murmured.

"Let's go," Antonio said. He took me by the arm and led me outside. "Forgive me if I talk to you about Russia again," I said while we left the hospital, and I burst out in tense laughter. "Do you know how I was welcomed at a mess for artillery after I broke out of the encirclement? There were maybe a thousand of us left out of the whole corps. The town was Gorlovka. Well, I and a certain Antonini had arrived at that mess walking in the snow at a snail's pace, stopping every few meters, we were in such bad shape. When we finally went in, a lieutenant colonel assaulted us because, he said, 'we dared to present ourselves at mess in that state.' Do you understand? It was an outburst even longer than this one, which we had to put up with standing at attention, while the rear zone officers, seated at their tables, looked at us, surprised. Maybe I was ridiculous also because, while I feverishly stood at attention, one of my legs was shaking. Now this other nice welcome!" I paused. "I really think that idiots like us, fools like us who intend on never deserting, should get used to this kind of welcome."

Antonio stopped. In the middle of the flow of foreigners and women who walked openly on their arms, he held his hand out to me solemnly. "What do you think? In the Italian army there aren't only rear zone lieutenant colonels," he said. And I shook his hand with infinite gratitude, because at least he didn't betray, didn't shout, didn't reproach me even in his thoughts, for having convinced him to cross the lines.

Afterwards we had an unrewarding discussion with the captain directing the mess. "This hotel has been requisitioned especially for idiots like us," I tenaciously answered his arguments. "We learned from the attendants that there is room; therefore, even without vouchers, we won't be stopped from both eating and sleeping here." The man was no genius (how could he have been—a captain who is director of the mess?). Furthermore, we realized, he assigned much importance to superiors, so that, narrow-mindedly but without malice, he even tried to take advantage of our situation. "Couldn't you go back to the colonel of the stopping place and explain to him that without vouchers the captain of the mess gives absolutely nothing?" Finally he yielded.

In the course of the night a well-trained squad of bed bugs took revenge on us for the lieutenant colonel and for the captain. "Let's not speak badly of bed bugs," Antonio announced, who held out better than me against adversity. "After all we must be understanding; like helps like."

"So be it. Meanwhile I won't present myself to the army again until I have money in my pocket."

"We could go to Lucania," he suggested. "I have some friends in Potenza who would put us up for sure, for a week or even two."

"Good," I agreed. "First, though, I have to make some inquiries around Brindisi, if I can find my brother, Achille. You know he was in that area at the armistice."

"All right," said Antonio.

15

WE LEFT BARI the following morning by train. At twenty years of age, a few hours of sleep are enough to pick you back up. From my window I studied with interest this landscape unknown to me, the plains that stretched as far as the eye could see, in which were nestled villages of one-story Arab houses with flat or round roofs. Close up, the sun-baked houses were often poor and dirty. The men of the region no longer displayed the simplicity of the Abruzzese and Molisan, but instead showed a disposition marked by astuteness and a harsh way of thinking that was not ours.

We learned, after being sent around from town to town, that my brother was in Manduria, near Taranto, continuing his cadet officer's course.

Long lines of black African soldiers, seated quietly on the sidewalks, were at the Manduria station, which our train reached as it was becoming dark. "Look, their legacy of humiliation follows them here too," I thought, "leaving them lined up and mute in the dark." They came from nearby air force fields, we learned, and weren't waiting for any trains. Who knows, perhaps the thought of an impossible return to America, to Africa, was pulling them here during their evening hours of freedom.

The headquarters of the officers' course was in the city's elementary school. I asked an elderly officer who had just come out of the building for permission to see my brother; he quietly looked both of us up and down, since we had introduced ourselves as officers but were dressed almost like shepherds, and cast his eyes on the sandals on my feet. "The Reveille has already sounded," he said finally. "You'll see your brother tomorrow."

Moving away from the entrance, we waited for the elderly man to leave—which he did after looking at us out of the corner of his eye several times—then we headed toward a group of officers who were our age. While I was still talking, one of them pulled away from the group and went inside the school; shortly after, Achille's silhouette appeared on the threshold. When he turned his head I saw his profile against the inside light. We ran to meet each other. "I was waiting for you," he said simply. His personality wasn't emotional, but firm and naturally modest, so different from mine! He stretched out his hand, but I hugged him.

"Come sleep at our place," Lieutenant Angelo Boletti, a Brescian, commander of Achille's battery, yelled out to Antonio and me. "We're reduced to dogs, but we'll make room for you in the kennel."

"No, thank you," I answered him impulsively, not wanting to be occupied with anything else at that moment but with meeting my brother. Achille looked at me and shook his head, smiling; he hadn't changed.

We began walking in the darkness side by side, two brothers. Our distant home came back to us among the shadows of unfamiliar houses. Our mother's smile, tested by anxiety (so much worry, with ten children in her life); our father, much loved; our eight brothers and sisters, all younger than us; while we were talking it seemed at times as though I could breathe in the atmosphere full of life that was in our home.

"We mustn't worry about our folks," I said. "The others will undoubtedly help them. You'll see, they'll protect them."

"Don't worry about our folks," said Achille. "They know how to defend themselves even on their own."

Our youngest sister, Maria, was nine years old; when we went back on leave, we enjoyed lifting her up high, happy and screaming in our outstretched arms: "You're an officer, but Achille is stronger," Maria shouted.

"Now she's sleeping under the eyes of God," said Achille, moved.

Antonio, who had immediately begun searching, had found a place to sleep. The three of us ate in a tavern where they served meat, surprising because provisions had run out after the Americans acquired everything with their *am-lire* (money of the occupation). Only later was it discovered that it was dog meat the restaurant served.

Achille said the rosary with us that night.

16

THE NEXT DAY we left for Lucania.

Not a single window along the short Ionian coast opened onto the sea (wonderfully classic that day, of a beautiful, flawless turquoise color): every small window, every door, was closed with thick wire fencing, a pointless defense against malaria. At that calm hour even the trees on the shore, disquieting to look at, seemed to flee from the beauty of the sea with their arms extended motionless toward the interior. Sibari kept coming back to my mind, its spoiled delights . . . The retaliation, perhaps? In any case, there was so much history even here, so many things undone forever . . .

The train took us from the coast, trudging toward Potenza between the interior mountains, arid at first, of sterile white clay, then rocky and covered with woods.

Little men with dark faces walked on the streets with their heads bent, although their features were not foreign, but ours. Villages of huts took up protective positions on the summits, where defense was easier; defense, it seemed, against everything.

In this region I could rest, reconsider my life, renew my strength.

Thanks to an unexpected invitation from the family of one of my former fellow soldiers, I had left Antonio and the city of Potenza for a brief stay in a village in the mountains.

It was an isolated village like few others in Italy: neither modern nor medieval, timeless, outside events of this century. In the evening around the fire they told of a British motorcyclist who, lost, arrived perhaps twenty kilometers from the village, then turned his motorcycle around and left. They had seen nothing else of the war. No one ever spoke of the countless incidents that had occurred on various fronts, nor of bombings that had destroyed or half destroyed many Italian cities; if the war was discussed at all it was only to complain that it continued to take sons, while they were at their strongest, away from the family's eternal struggle to provide food. Around the fire they spoke mostly, and more congenially, of other things: of bandits, whose wide cave I was taken to visit on the edge of the inhabited area, kept orderly as though they had disappeared not long ago, but could return at any moment. Or of wolves who during winter nights came down from the mountains and, at the entrance of the village, howled their terrible hunger in a way that aroused both fear and pity. It seemed at times, by the way people expressed themselves, that the fate of men and wolves was one and the same, both bound by the curse of having to obtain each day a livelihood in a world so inexorably lacking in resources.

Such a wearying condition induced many into a sort of melancholic immobility. Not everyone, though. A young woman lived in the house where I was a guest in whom this condition managed instead to be a cause of sorrow, of compassion for men and for their Savior, Christ crucified, from whom men, withdrawn into themselves, do not bother to accept salvation.

Never again in my lifetime would I meet someone who perceived such human tragedy as clearly as she did. As soon as she was of age, she told me, she would leave her father's house to become a nun. "Fire," she tried to explain to me with disjointed words, "consumes us all."

Sometimes, returning from praying in the town's ugly church, her forehead covered by a black veil that made her seem even whiter, her face was transformed. "Brother," she urged, "why are we so slow to follow God's path?" "Little brother," she said, "I've spoken with my Savior: He is falling under our burden, our sweet Christ is falling under the burden of the sins of the world." She nodded. "Why are we so idle? I want to suffer with Him. I want to sacrifice myself for men with Him, poor little men."

I felt coarse and heavy in front of her, not only when she spoke in that manner but also when she solicitously bustled about the low-roofed house with her sleeves rolled up, or prepared bread and plates of brown chestnuts. I still felt the weight of our long journey among the mountains, and of the terrible war at the Russian front; besides, I wondered what other troubles the future held. I found it reasonable to lie on my bed resting for hours, even during the day. But that soldierlike way of gathering rest seemed brutish to her. She reprimanded me several times: "Move. Why do you spend your time in idleness?"

One day, when I was in a bad mood, I answered her harshly: "If you want to know," I said, "I don't like your Bourbon church in the least, with those painted cardboard saints fitted with real beards. In fact, it offends my faith, especially all the tinsel attached to their garments. Don't tell me that it's an expression of the peasants' ingenuous faith; it's superstition, a leftover of paganism."

"Yes," she answered, nodding, humiliated. "Yes, a leftover of paganism . . . it's true. Poor peasants! But tell me: are you sure that there are no leftovers of paganism in the great art of the cathedrals that you love?" I remained speechless. "Don't trouble yourself," she added at once, compassionately, "this is in our fate: we'll never succeed in completely transforming the Earthly City into the Heavenly City."

"What do you know, you, a girl whose mouth is still stained with mother's milk, of Earthly City and Heavenly City?" I retorted rudely.

As I was saying such words I remembered where the Gospel says, "*I have concealed these things from cultured and intelligent people in order to reveal them to the children*" . . . After all, many times, when they were true believers, I had encountered an extraordinary perception of Truth in uneducated people, most of all in my Brianza.[4]

"All right, forgive my rudeness," I said after a pause to the girl from Luciana, who no longer spoke but looked at me, mortified.

She answered, lighting up again with a smile that seemed to come from her spirit, almost without her body's participation, as though made of light, different even from my mother's smile. "In these few days that you are with us, agree to exhort yourself again and again in the fight to build the Kingdom down here, little brother."

"Why do you insist on calling me brother? You know almost nothing of me."

"Wasn't the crusader who fought for the Kingdom perhaps brother of the monk?"

"But what do you know of what I am or will be?"

"Our sweet Christ has shown it to me," she answered. "I have seen it in Him." After such a surprising affirmation she continued talking of my future, with timid spontaneity, like when a swallow twitters softly, motionless on a wire.

Then and there, touched by what she was saying, I ended in serious reflection, trying to outline some decisions. Later, being a modern man ("What kind of talk is that?") convinced by physics, convinced by chemistry and by other sciences, the wonder from new thoughts lessened, I would gradually set aside, then almost forget, her words. I didn't share them with Antonio, nor with others. After all, what words would I have used to

4. Brianza is the author's birthplace.

tell them? I knew well that supernatural interventions repeat themselves in the life of every man and of every community. But we do not receive them entirely as such. Not only are we no longer capable of understanding supernatural manifestations and their clamorous witnesses (for instance, that German peasant woman who for thirty-six years lived without eating or drinking, her only communion with Christ—never, in any century, was there a testimony so extraordinary; or that humble Italian friar with the stigmata), but we no longer recognize even natural sublimity. How do we regard, for instance, those six Italian sailors—true and proper Homeric heroes—who alone engaged an entire fleet drawn up for battle? Penetrating between British ships, they sank (with six men!) two of the battleships that held the sea; hence our superiority in the Mediterranean returned for several months. We have seen, with our own eyes, mythological heroes becoming history, but as far as we're concerned we prefer to hold them to the same standards as charlatans or little more. As far as the witnesses of the supernatural, if ever we take them into consideration we confusedly try to fit them into some clinical category and give up before succeeding. And it is a good thing that neither our attention nor our means of communication remains on them, because what else could we obtain but controversy? How do geese do it? All that is unusual for them is merely reason for the same cackling.

In modern times, we've essentially taken from the definitive sciences acquired from the ancients that God is only with us rationally; thus we lose a large part of God, of ourselves, and of the world.

After a week's stay in the village outside of time, I returned, as we had agreed, to Potenza with Antonio.

17

IN MID-OCTOBER the legitimate Italian government declared war on Germany. We presented ourselves then, using our real names, to the garrison command of Potenza.

We were sent from there to Guagnano in Puglia, to a "reorganization camp" for artillery. In such "camps" (usually requisitional school buildings) were gathered all the soldiers who presented themselves to fight again, those picked up by the navy on the Balkan coasts, and finally those who were stopped by the *carabinieri* on the road or in railroad stations after crossing the lines toward home. Everyone would have to be put back into uniform, but because of the scarcity of uniforms even sentries guarding cantonments were often in civilian clothes, with their bandoleers and submachine guns on top of jackets creased from sleeping on hay. It reminded me of photographs of Spanish soldiers of some years ago.

It became clear that by no means was the Italian army being reconstituted: only a fraction still existed, which the Germans had left almost undisturbed when withdrawing from Puglia, and even this, with the passing days, tended to disintegrate. As for the Allies, they seemed to wish for it to dissolve.

The colonel in command of the camp gave us an advance on our pay and a leave of two days in order for us to buy uniforms in nearby Lecce, although he knew that we wouldn't be able to buy them there.

In the city's two clothing stores they looked at us arrogantly: uniforms? A few pieces of fabric remained, from which uniforms would have to be custom-made, of course, at the tailor's shop. Was this above our means? They didn't know what to do about it; they were reorganizing themselves for the Allies and for their own civilians.

"We've become a nuisance even to those who until yesterday lived off the army's business," Antonio commented.

The main streets of Lecce were swarming with American pilots in leather jackets, some with pictures of half-naked women painted in bright colors on the back. We wandered at length around the city without achieving anything. Many years later I would greatly appreciate Lecce for the *forma mentis* of its people and for the beauty of certain neighborhoods, but on that day I wasn't able to see anything besides misery.

At the command's headquarters where we asked permission to pick up a uniform from the military depot, the officers on duty didn't even pay any attention to us.

Soldiers hardly answered from their stools when addressed, and if one didn't appear forceful they didn't answer at all. They made it clear that in some way they were all in agreement or, better yet, were accomplices: they had the impudence of those who safely anticipate each objection. Some even seemed to want to provoke complaints as a pastime; this intention was obvious in some types who looked like cowards on account of their vaguely scornful eyes and bristly napes, motionless and confident. Not that in their cowardice they weren't ready to back down if they realized that the anger of their questioners could constitute an immediate danger. In our territorial commands this state of affairs was latent even before the armistice, and probably before the war, but now it had become more pronounced, at least at places such as Lecce.

"This rabble who's never fought," a young infantry lieutenant complained to us, after having left an office slamming the door, "they surely wouldn't want to do more work now when it's necessary than the amount they did before; on the contrary!"

The two of us obtained only—and as though it was a favor—a voucher to sleep in the "lodgings for passing officers."

Those lodgings consisted of assortments of rooms crammed with bunks.

One had to pick up, after written receipt, a mattress and blankets stacked in a room on the ground floor. We climbed filthy stairs in the dark with these on our shoulders.

"Why isn't there any light?"

"Because the 'guests' steal the lightbulbs," the guards, all scoundrels, answered.

We dressed in the dark. Bathrooms didn't exist (who knows, maybe the employees had locked the doors, or nailed them shut, to save themselves the work of cleaning them).

The next morning, while Antonio and I lingered on our bunks burdened by the prospect of another day of futile wandering, we were startled by the insolent shouts of a guard in the hall. "Mattresses," he had begun shouting. "Officers, remember to bring the mattresses downstairs." He was laughing.

Blood rushed to my head. "Oh, no! I'm going to take this one and throw it down the stairs . . ." But in the next bunk a second lieutenant burst out laughing. "Do you hear him?" he said to his neighbor. "He's right, by God, otherwise some officer would steal the mattress for sure."

"Bah, Italian officers!" the other answered with disdain. "Why, I ask myself, do they insist on keeping together this parody of an army? With soldiers who at this point walk around dressed ridiculously . . . What about subsistence? It's reduced us to starving, and each day skimps on more of its few supplies."

"It's those pigs in the government, beginning with Badoglio, who don't want to understand. Making all those poor devils rot in their quarters, while their families need help . . ."

One could tell from their way of speaking that they both lived on the other side of the lines.

"After all, why should we continue to fight? And then on which side, if the Allies consider us defeated? And who's going to give us ammunition for our weapons?"

"The Sicilians sure understand! Do you know that they're breaking off from Italy? In my unit they've already all deserted."

"Ah! I didn't know . . . I think they're doing the right thing!"

"Mattresses," the shouting from the hall resumed. "Officers, remember to bring the mattresses downstairs."

The two officers laughed again.

"Antonio," I said, heedless to the fact that they were listening. The saliva in my mouth seemed like bile. "This fragment of an army . . . with this kind of mob, against an army like the Germans'!"

"Forget it," he interrupted.

The two officers pretended not to have heard. That morning I felt an acute discomfort like perhaps never before; I sensed my too-young age. It seemed as though my spirit wasn't sufficiently developed for the enormity of the things against which we had to fight.

Suddenly, Margherita came to mind: her eyes looked at me as though frightened. So even I, even those few of us who until then seemed prepared to do all we could, were throwing in the towel? In that case, what would become of Italy, especially of those most defenseless, beginning with the women? After Margherita, I also remembered Zorzi, my dearest friend. In the dreadful valley of Arbuzov he had broken off from our small group and asked the colonel to be added to one of the platoons that was returning to the fight. As he was leaving for the last time, Zorzi had turned toward me with an embarrassed farewell; he seemed to be asking forgiveness for the lesson in generosity that he was giving me in spite of himself . . .

Margherita, Zorzi, indeed . . . I was ashamed for having begun to give up; we simply had to continue behaving like men, that was all. The discomfort remained and was deep enough to border on anguish.

Without wasting more time we returned to the reorganization camp of Guagnano and received permission from the colonel to pick up two soldiers' uniforms from the depot. A soldier who was a tailor mended them as well as he could.

*

The evening of that same day, in the starving officers' mess hall we met Second Lieutenants Antonio Castelli and Giovanni Guatelli, with whom we would be bound by fate for the rest of the war. Castelli introduced himself according to the rules—he bowed and very formally shook our hands—and we bowed with as much formality in our half-military uniforms. He was Bergamese, and his fellow townsman Antonio Moroni asked him, "Are you by any chance the Castelli who won the university's ski championship the year before the war?"

"Thereabouts," the new Antonio answered.

He came from a ship that had sunk near Crete; almost all his men had died in the sinking of the ship. He was older than us, skinny, thinning at the temples, with long arms and legs, and had somewhat of a refined style, especially his shirt with, unbelievably enough, a collar from the latest fashion.

We enjoyed lingering with him a while. He told me that for a few years he attended the same university as me, the *Università Catollica di Milano.* "But," he said, "the rector expelled me, and I had to graduate from the state university."

"That rector, Father Gemelli," I explained to Moroni, "before having been a famous friar was a famous Red agitator. But whether agitator or friar, he's always been arrogant and violent."

"The Kingdom of Heaven tolerates violence, huh?" he said, amused, visibly glad to have met someone who was civil, above all his fellow townsman.

"Not violent in that sense," I answered, welcoming the opportunity to talk for once about something besides military life and troubles. "You should have seen him during a student scuffle: with the excuse of reestablishing order he was more than happy to enter the fray and, huge as he is, knock down a student with each punch."

"Yes," Castelli said, "exactly. What a strange man! He reminded me of those artist-engineers of the Renaissance who spent their time bending horseshoes with their hands or swimming across the Po River while wearing armor. Tell me, can you imagine big Gemelli splashing about in the Po, wearing armor?"

"I'm afraid that now he really has to wear armor," I answered. "Do you know that last year he injured his back?"

Castelli became serious. "No, I didn't know that. His back? I'm sorry to hear it. During his airplane experiments, I imagine." He explained to Moroni, "In order to study aviation psychology he got his pilot's license when he was seventy years old."

"Not at all. It happened in an ordinary car accident."

"Well, I'm sorry."

"It means," I announced, with the recklessness of youth, "that now, since he's bound to a wheelchair, he'll finally be able to be a friar. But why did he expel you?"

"Do you remember that other friar, the much larger one, made of plaster, at the entrance of the library?" Castelli asked.

"Do you mean Savonarola?"

"Right. Once while I was talking with my girlfriend I took out of her purse some lipstick and began painting the nails on the statue's feet. Just a little pedicure for its big feet, you understand? Big Gemelli got on me for that one. I can't tell you the scene: he got angry with me as though I wasn't painting the nails of Savonarola but his own."

"You should have thrown a horseshoe into his hands, or the girl's purse," Moroni ventured. "Who knows, maybe he would have taken out his anger on that and wouldn't have expelled you."

We laughed. It seemed as though we were back in Milan, very far from this pitiful mess hall: three students wasting time, chatting in the halls of the university.

Guatelli had been in Puglia for several months: at the time of my first appointment we had worked for a few weeks in the same depot in Cremona. He was from Parma. The antithesis of Castelli, who, although having attended the *Università Cattolica,* wasn't a believer, Guatelli was very religious, young, stocky and strong, with a pale, ascetic face. He spent every Friday fasting because, endowed with exuberant virility, fasting helped him control himself. It isn't rhetorical to say that individuals like him prevented us from losing hope in our future.

So we finished that day, begun with so much grief, with real comfort, because we had met two companions-in-arms.

The next morning Castelli put his limited wardrobe at our disposal. Guatelli owned two pairs of boots. "If you have two tunics, give one to whoever doesn't have one," he said, and threw a pair into my arms.

18

THE WEEKS BEGAN to pass, one after the other.

Life in Italy during that time was exhausting: we weren't living, we were dragging ourselves along day after day, waiting for a solution. Meanwhile, only rumor was passing from one region to the next, and the only thing that was clear was that two opposing armies fought over our territory. Within the general discomfort, each one of us had his own private, acute suffering: for a family member or a friend killed in the war or from whom there was no news, for a house that had been destroyed or abandoned, for lost employment. For everyone the future was uncertain.

Disintegration and hunger prevailed in the reorganization camps. We weren't given anything substantial by the Allies. Some days, we had only as much as two rations of biscuits for each soldier, one of which, being spoiled, had to be wiped clean of worms and webs and redistributed—after boiling—as a soup with a lot of water. There was a shortage of uniforms for soldiers who were continually redrafted by governmental notices or picked up by our navy (what was left of it) on the Balkan coasts. For a few weeks I was commander of the battery, and in spite of my previous severity toward myself and others I managed to falsify the roster for "intangible provisions" and agreed—in exchange for flour for rations—that the battery's only truck be put on the black market on civilians' behalf. This was an experience of first importance for me, even among the most important of my life: I realized that man was free—in certain situations—only as to whether he will accept the things that he must do regardless; man is free only in his moral choices.

At Guagnano desertions occurred almost daily, and poverty caused thefts and theft attempts. We learned about the Germans slaughtering our garrison on the Ionian Sea, which, relying on the help of the Italian or Allied navies, had refused to surrender their weapons. Many officers had been shot, while others were tied by the dozen and thrown into the sea from ships; on the Greek island of Cephalonia there were thousands killed in battle and more than five thousand shot after our surrender. So this confirmed another conviction: that even if Italian armed forces had resisted, the fate of our soldiers and countless civilians would have been the same, not a bit different.

On the roads of Puglia, after the peasants passed with their multicolored carts pulled by mules or beautiful Arabian horses at dawn to work in the dry fields, American air corps trucks went by quickly, continuously, loaded with ocher-colored bombs or loud pilots who went to the city to dull their senses.

Since there were many airfields in the region, the autumn sky was always filled with airplanes leaving or arriving, like a slow flock of swamp birds.

*

Winter came.

The rain fell on the torn hills of Salento extending into the sea, and on the fields of dirt and crushed stone where wheat grows, as tenacious of life as man.

We came and went in our light colonial uniforms, without coats, hands in our pockets, along the streets of Guagnano adorned with oleander trees, among the small Arabic houses, under the trickle of the rain. In my memory of those days, even Margherita's hair was soaked with rain, like the delicate leafy fronds of the oleander, her face wet with raindrops, like someone who is crying but doesn't want to show it.

The Anglo-American advance had stopped in the mountains of Campania and Abruzzi. The Allies were wisely waiting—though they would not admit it—until the Nazis and Bolsheviks proceeded to destroy one another. The armies in Italy had passed inland or withdrawn into the houses along the front, sheltered from snow and rain, and even the formations of airplanes had become infrequent in the foggy skies. The planes lay in long rows in fields, sometimes with their wings and noses covered with snow, and it was as though even misery and hardship had withdrawn. But at the Russian front, where the war was under the banner of hate, winter was again the favorite season for battle, because in winter the enemy's suffering is greatest. Armies threw themselves at each other, trying to annihilate; the souls that left their bodies to bounce throughout eternity must have been, in the colorless spirit world, sharp and ice-cold like hail.

Of course, since our homes were beyond the line, we hoped that the German army would be removed as soon as possible. Within the horrors that Germans suffered from the Bolshevik invaders we saw a retaliation for no less horrible crimes. I found no peace when I thought of the Wehrmacht soldiers who, man behind man, were retreating inside the Russian winter, and I hoped that they would succeed in holding back the Russians and, since they had to withdraw, that at least their retreat would not occur in winter.

*

At this time the politicians who succeeded the Fascists met in Bari for their first congress, the "congress of anti-Fascist parties." The episode, marginal in comparison to the big events that were occurring in the world, was of little importance to exhausted Italy at the time.

In the evening, at mess, we talked about it sometimes. We asked ourselves, "What will come out of it?" with an apprehension that would seem strange today, seeing that as officers, for the single fact of keeping ourselves in the armed service, we were in favor of democracy. But our doubts were raised by those men elected by nobody and immediately reunited in a congress similar to a constituent assembly, and by the uncertainty as to whether they intended to respect the freedom of the people or would instead present those unable to express themselves with some grave, irreversible deed.

We followed their work in the shabby papers of the time, in which a violent Communist bias prevailed, directed by the former expositor and champion of Fascist mysticism, Mario Alicata. Back then, Togliatti hadn't been repatriated from Russia, and Communist extremism had no limits; it was a striking experience, and totally new to us.

The other parties' newspapers did not manage to be any more comforting. Although they furiously disputed among themselves, all congressmen, in fact, agreed on the same thing: asking and pretending. Not even one of them spoke of giving.

"They look too much like vultures around a dying man," a few men commented.

"But maybe," others said, "we're shocked by these types of quarrels because we've always lived under a dictatorship. We've never seen anything like it."

"Could be. But who elected them?"

"And who can assure us that they truly represent the people? And then to what extent?" These weren't arbitrary questions, seeing that one of the most pretentious and impatient men in the elections, with expectations from those parties, the ones of "action," revealed himself afterwards to be all but without action.

Leading the congress somehow was the most authoritative of the anti-Fascists of that time, the seventy-plus-year-old philosopher Benedetto Croce, who openly assumed an attitude as supreme "reformer" of Italy. (He considered himself as such—will those who read this believe it?—because of a kind of responsibility directly conferred on him by History. I'm not joking.)

A few old, unqualified politicians participated in the congress by Croce's side, and seemed to underscore the pretense of a constituent assembly whose inability to stand up to the Red subversion had in due course paved the way for fascism. "Because, in fact," several of us remembered, "twenty years ago the majority of Italians, somehow or another, accepted fascism, having seen in it the only defense against the Red subversion. If during the time of the occupation of the factories and of the great postwar disorders the democratic leaders had reacted with the necessary vigor, there would not have been a Fascist dictatorship. How can these inept men now pretend to return to lead the nation? And to scold it too?"

Yes, wishful thinkers, they scolded and asked and pretended, but at times they also burst out in tears: the resolution of the Alicata Communists by their side assumed a particularly sinister form.

Some who had just arrived in Italy were present at the behest of the Allies, and part of the congress had almost no other authority than that. The most haughty of these, the "republican" Count Sforza (an unpleasant old-school figure whose arrival in Italy had been, as reported in the parties' newspapers, prepared by the American press) did nothing but furiously insult the king during all of his sessions, because he didn't want to abdicate. It was clear—even if incredible to us—that Sforza intended to replace him as the head of state.

Fortunately, there were men concerned with the common good and sincere democrats of different leanings (some of whom were, for young men like us, of somewhat obscure significance; we saw, however, the men's sincerity). We wanted to help them. But in what way? Many of us endured by giving strength back to the army, the institutional defender of lawfulness, thanks to which we would one day be able to have free elections and democracy. In any case it was these true democrats' powerlessness in the face of the exploiters' unbridled greed, who turned to asking and shouting and competing with those who for all practical purposes were on their side, that stirred worries in some of us.

In the end, as was its duty, the legitimate government rejected the demands of the congressmen, who had assumed that power would immediately be transferred to them without waiting for a popular vote. It was able to do this, I think, mainly due to the strength that came from us, the army, which although reduced and in bad shape remained faithful. The new politicians' increasing aversion to us stemmed from this, even, unfortunately, among many democrats (how much cowardice can develop in Italy!). In any case, as soldiers, to whom should we have been faithful if not to the legitimate authority?

It must be said that, at least in Puglia, not only the majority of soldiers but also most of the population remained indifferent in the face of such disorder. The civilians I spoke to shrugged their shoulders; if I insisted, they answered that they were more inclined to forgive the king for his past mistakes than to accept "this mass of unknown exploiters." "If nothing else," they said bitterly, "we became used to his majesty."

In the area of Italy free of Germans, a type of de facto division became increasingly evident: the half that gravitated toward Puglia continued to recognize the king and legitimate authority. Thanks also to the Puglian feudal respect for the army, there was always a certain order, in contrast to the paroxysms that appeared in the other half. This other half gravitated toward Naples; there legitimate authority was almost nonexistent, replaced by anti-Fascists who were sustained—according to reports—by some important Allied circles. As for Sicily, it was on its own with all the talk of "separatism."

Those were very bitter days, when it seemed as though we could lose all hope in the fate of Italy.

And they were the days of our youth, which went by, as we reached forward, hoping that it would pass fast, faster . . .

But in a certain sense, life is always like this.

19

ON ONE OF THOSE DAYS, or rather, on a dismal evening, the beginning of a mutiny took place at a reorganization camp situated about ten kilometers from ours. We received the order to take up arms and surround the camp.

Drawing up our men, gathered from battery to battery, in columns, we began marching in the dark, wearing the few helmets that we owned. We shuffled gloomily along an asphalt road, between prickly pears and olive trees damp from the fog. "Everything is falling apart, everything is going to pieces. Italy is becoming like a South American republic or an Arab country: if rebellions are starting even in the army, it's really the end . . ."

I was filled with a rage without words. How would these men, who until yesterday were disbanded, respond? But it didn't matter, there was incentive for everyone: "Enough retreats. Absolutely enough yielding!"

After a couple of hours of marching we received the order to halt. In a column ahead on the road, I noticed Antonio Moroni, pale and full of dignity, and Antonio Castelli, serious under his helmet, with a German submachine gun on his chest. We waited sullenly without exchanging a single word. Then came the order to about-face and return to our quarters.

I never found out how the situation was resolved in the camp that we were meant to surround.

*

On another evening, I happened to experience, very unexpectedly, a sort of apology.

A young officer with a German name had arrived from the lines. Born in Vienna, he had adopted Milan a few years before the war after he had fallen in love with the Milanese environment; for this reason he sometimes took his place next to me, a Milanese.

"Excuse my clothes," he said, sitting down.

"It's OK," I answered, "we're all used to seeing those who arrive from the Balkans."

"There's always someone who's worse off, isn't there?" he said. "Not even those from the Balkans, I think, are in as bad a shape as the survivors I saw come out from the Russian pockets."

"From the Russian pockets? Where did you see those survivors?"

"At Starobelsk. I was part of the Eighth Army's command."

"What a coincidence!" I smiled, shaking my head. "Would you believe me if I told you that I too arrived in Starobelsk after I came out of the Cerkovo pocket? So I probably was one of those poor wretches."

"No, really?" he said. He studied me: "From Cerkovo, as a matter of fact, they were coming precisely from Cerkovo . . ." He agreed, "Well, I'll admit that you were in worse shape than I am right now."

"Much worse," I concurred. "But what a coincidence! You know? It's always the same ones who dance," I concluded, with trite soldierly rhetoric.

All of a sudden his face reminded me of something. "Hey, try to remember," I said to him. "Wasn't it you, by chance, who on the . . . let's see, the eighteenth, no, the seventeenth of January, at Starobelsk, was called on by a Russian girl to try to chase out of a hut[5] three of those poor fellows who had gone in to sleep?"

"Ah!" he exclaimed, after having stared at my eyes. "Those light, crazed eyes were yours!"

Ten months later, the incident came back to us. Those of us who had come out of the pocket had gobbled fresh white bread and subsequent courses set up on tables at the mess of the army's headquarters. Afterwards I had wandered around the streets of the city with two unknown colleagues as poorly dressed as I, in search of any kind of shelter. Finally, we had slipped inside a hut, after having pushed away an old lady who tried to bar the way (she probably feared—rightfully so—that we would fill her house with lice).

We had taken the only two beds and the floor. The old woman's daughter was young and beautiful. She ran to the Italian command where she had some friends; shortly after, we heard a car stop outside the hut. An elegantly dressed second lieutenant, the one who was now sitting by my side, entered. "Soldiers," he commanded, "you know that Italian orders forbid us from entering Russian houses and bothering civilians. You must leave immediately."

5. A Russian log hut.

"Colleague," I answered, barely lifting my head from the pillow, "we don't intend to bother any civilians; we're only trying to sleep. We're not capable of doing anything else. You'll be the one to leave immediately, understood?"

Now in the small mess of the reorganization camp of Guagnano, he recalled our encounter. "'Colleague,' I remember, 'colleague' . . . you had such eyes!"

At present he was in need of everything, so after dinner I welcomed him in my room and gladly had him bring a mattress and some blankets. It was for the pettiness of assuming myself generous, but after all, it was he who gave me a lesson in generosity by following the miserable fate of his elected nation. Nevertheless, I liked finishing that small episode with an apologetic ending.

20

CHRISTMAS CAME.

It was on the eve of the Epiphany in 1944 that the two Antonios, Guatelli and I, became part of the Nembo Division.

An unfamiliar lieutenant with the standing of major, Leandro Giaccone, had come into our camp and had called Antonio Castelli (I wonder who had told him about Castelli). "What are you doing in the army?" he had asked him.

"Huh, what? What are you asking?" Castelli had answered.

"Don't you ever ask yourself?" Giaccone insisted.

"Yes," Castelli admitted, "sometimes I ask myself."

"All right," Giaccone approved. "Well, our authorities have managed to bring to the front the most able division in Sardegna: the Nembo. Since they are paratroopers, and therefore without artillery, I was given the assignment of forming a group of field artillery for that division. Are you prepared to be part of it?"

Castelli's face darkened, he thought about it, and finally agreed. "Yes, all right," he answered, not gladly.

Giaccone agreed in turn. "Good," he continued, "I also need other officers. In this camp, who's got . . . ?" (he used an anatomical term).

Castelli resumed thinking, his face growing dim again, then gave three names: Moroni's, Guatelli's, and mine. ("The prank of a nonbeliever," I wouldn't miss telling him afterwards, "is to make one greatly regret practical jokes.")

Without wasting time Giaccone sent for us one after the other, studied us with his penetrating eyes, and directed his invitation to each. All three of us accepted, and a fifth officer offered himself, the Milanese Captain Clerici, who was like a personification of goodwill. Following our example, in the space of a few hours about fifty more men, both noncommissioned officers and soldiers, offered themselves.

Once Giaccone left, we four friends tried to understand what had just happened. I noticed that a deep emotion, or, more precisely, a secret joy filled the other three, although it was concealed by Castelli's dry look, Moroni's customary irreprehensibility, and Guatelli's equally customary composure. "But do they know what war is? Yes, of course they know it . . ."

"That commander," I observed, "must have actually had his brain in pieces to like three faces such as yours."

"Like yours, you mean," all three of them answered together.

An Italian unit of five thousand men, the First Motorized Group, had been on the line with the Americans for a month, since the beginning of December. At the time many of the Allies in charge didn't want Italians by their side: there had been arguments and resistance. Those soldiers—at the request of the general staff—had been employed immediately for the conquest of Montelungo, an outpost of Monte Cassino. It had been a good decision, thus giving others who were vegetating in the army the right to fight and contribute to Italy's liberation. (A platoon of university students was part of those five thousand; it was the only time I saw university students do something truly positive. Giuseppe Cederle, from Vicenza, second lieutenant of infantry and a university student at the Cattolica di Milano, had dragged them along; he was very similar—according to the description given to me—to my friend Zorzi. Cederle was among the first to fall, and is buried in the sunny Italian military cemetery of Montelungo, at a lone bend in the Via Casilina, among the stones and cicadas. If in the face of God one finds friendship along with all else that is good, those two young men, Cederle and Zorzi, who arrived sharing such similar fates, are surely good friends up there.)

*

A few days after Giaccone's visit, I received the order to reach the town of Surbo with the soldiers of my battery—about twenty—who had joined the fighting unit. We didn't know it yet, but we would constitute the nucleus of the future Artillery Regiment Nembo.

After the evening rations, we climbed into a truck. "Don't forget," said Antonio Moroni, "as soon as the truck is moving, don't begin imagining that you're arriving as liberator of Margherita's city, and that she's throwing you flowers, while soldiers are saying, 'Oh, the lieutenant's girl is so beautiful!' Think that you're grown up by now."

"Try instead to find a room for us too at Surbo, given we'll be there tomorrow or later," Antonio Castelli said. "The army be damned!"

Guatelli and Clerici were laughing.

Since the colonel was Sicilian, and people from that region have a habit of gathering when away from home, the officers in the camp were largely Sicilians. We had reproached them several times for their separatism, and couldn't figure out whether it was within them too. That evening I didn't bother to go say good-bye to them, but they came to me and, crowding around the truck, sought to shake my hand. They were so kind!

Colonel Giaccone was waiting for us in the dark in Surbo, alone like a monument in front of the elementary school building. "Come forward," he said, and led our group along a corridor to the only lighted classroom. He pointed to a field kettle on the floor: "That's all that the group has available today. But it's full of hot coffee."

"At this hour coffee is better than equipment for an entire regiment," my orderly Morandi said; the others gathered without hesitation.

Afterward, at my request, the soldiers divided the floor; everyone put down his gear in his own square, from which he could take out a mess tin to drink coffee.

Giaccone called me aside. "Take a good look around," he said seriously. He had a face that seemed carved with intelligence, but also a weakness for airs. "Today I received the assignment to put together not only one group, but a light two-group regiment. And you are the first officer, I repeat, the first officer," he went on, "who comes—to a regiment—with the duty— to open the way—for the Italians who intend—to pick themselves up again—from the current state of prostitution."

I didn't speak, even if I much liked this adventure. But since the colonel seemed waiting: "Well, right now I feel pretty important," I stated. "I'd say almost as much as the coffee kettle."

Giaccone grimaced.

21

NO PLACE at that time looked more Arabic than Surbo. In general, it consisted of one-floor houses, one against the other to protect against the sun, like sheep pressed against each other during very hot hours to make it difficult for the sun's rays to find their woolen backs. There were wealthier houses, usually lined with vegetable gardens and parched outer walls that prevented one's seeing inside. Against all expectation those interiors turned out to be rich with water and green; a few were painted with aquatic landscapes. Everything was for the heat.

We had to march in the mud, and run in the mud in squads, dragging 75/27 guns.

Men and materials had begun pouring in, and we grew in strength every day, while close by other units of the army were transformed into work units assigned to unload Allied ships. We went back to cultivating our military talents. Having seen the Allied forces close up, we better appreciated our training and realized we could rely on it.

While we were engaged in such activity, we received an inspection from the heir apparent to the crown, Umberto.

To welcome him, the group lined up in a clearing in an olive grove a short distance from our quarters. Slowly inspecting the troops, he stopped to shake the hand of each officer. Surely he was aware that some among us were against monarchy; nevertheless, he politely said a few words to each of us.

He asked me if I had crossed the lines; without a doubt he guessed it by my uniform. I answered that I had and gave a sign to mean that it was for this reason that I wore almost a soldier's uniform. The prince realized the contrast between his elegant twill uniform and mine and seemed to want to apologize; he softly said that, in any case, it was the only suit he had available. I experienced both embarrassment and an impulse of sympathy for this man, above all for his adventurous journey from Rome to Pescara and then to Brindisi, under circumstances in certain aspects similar to mine. And yet, although not against the principle of the monarchy, I didn't wish it for Italy's future (I thought that two courts—civilian and religious—in a single capital would inevitably clash). But the man who was in front of me was now doing his duty, like his father the king, and he performed it despite little applause and numerous insults, at the head of a people skilled in discovering scapegoats for their own cowardice.

After the prince's inspection I found a way to have a tailor in the village make a uniform for me in the Nembo style (he had made a uniform already for Colonel Giaccone), without collar and with an almost sporty cut.

*

The training hastily continued. The soldiers, especially those who were entrusted assignments with responsibility, became transformed into active, eager individuals.

As fate would have it, I wouldn't stay with them.

In fact, after Giaccone had transferred himself to the nearby village of Squinzano to put together the rest of the regiment, another officer with whom I wouldn't have been able to stay assumed command of our group.

I didn't know whether he had been useful to the army or to the nation; certainly he was well-deserving in those days. He was tireless, gifted with initiative, and thus useful to Italy. The voice of that commander stands out in my memory of the inactive period in Surbo: his shouting voice, hard on our heels from morning until night, reverberated on every drill, on all practices, even at night after dinner during our fatigue when he gathered us officers for the "instructions on panels." Since that pressing voice has begun to fade, the Surbo elementary school building must remain dreamlike . . . He had paid in person. When he attempted to cross the lines, the Germans had left him for dead on the ground in his own blood among his dead companions.

But he had had an important assignment in the division where my soldiers and I had been encircled on the Russian front. Shortly before the encirclement the command had abandoned our troops on the line, saving itself while most of us were annihilated.

I didn't know how responsible that officer was for this episode; the incident, however, was between us, and we both realized it. It was therefore impossible to overlook. My friends and dead soldiers visited me with reproachful faces, saying, "You didn't forget about us?" I began to be tormented because in refusing to stay I would be going against someone who, in those days, was useful to Italy, and it was not as though there weren't already enough squabbles in the German-free zone, which abounded in quarrels more than in anything else.

Giaccone had arguments from Squinzano with all the artillery men present in Puglia, to tear away from them men and materials necessary to us; they were arguments with uncertain outcomes, even though the Ministry of War was on our side (it was a meager ministry back then). The colonel engaged in one battle after another with vigor, in the end stirring in us admiration, so difficult to do in Italians. Our group's commander helped him with this: I saw it, and spent months without making up my mind, my soul turned into a mirror of my circumstances.

Nor was it easy to abandon the soldiers who had come with me from the reorganization camp, as well as the two Antonios and Guatelli. A new friend had been added in Surbo, Second Lieutenant Ferruccio Schiavi, whom we called by his Julian nickname Cèt. He had lost his father, an infantry colonel, in Greece, and although an only child, he had left his mother and crossed the lines to keep his officer's oath. He belonged to a limited group who with their generosity compensated for the selfishness of many. Besides his generosity, which was his primary trait, he was innately courteous and brave, to the extent that I irrationally asked myself several times if by chance, given his perfection, he wasn't destined to die, like Zorzi. Cèt, however, would not be killed: a different painful fate was in store for him.

*

One morning I was banished from the group after reacting harshly to one of the commander's words. It was in April. Colonel Giaccone summoned me into his office in Squinzano.

"You know," he said, "that there are now many subordinate officers who want to come fight against the Germans. I have to turn many down even though they are excellent. You know that, right?"

"I know."

"You deserve to be sent to a port with the workers, like your group's commander. Instead I'll transfer you to the second group of the regiment."

"Thank you," I said. "I wouldn't have gone to the port, under foreign corporals, with the uniform of an Italian officer. I would have deserted."

His face became drawn. "You know that your words go against military discipline?"

"I know. But I'm not saying this for lack of discipline. And not even out of pride; at least, I don't think so. As a man it's different, but given that I'm an Italian officer I wouldn't have gone." Giaccone studied me in silence. He had stood out as a strict commander, made for the times; since the regiment had begun to form itself, he had demoted several men for minor transgressions and once demoted thirty noncommissioned officers simultaneously. Not even an intervention from the head of the army's general staff had been able to make him back down. Still, I asked him, "If you were in my shoes, would you go work under foreign corporals?" He must have been asking himself that same question because he concluded, "That's enough. Present yourself to the command of the second group."

I sprang to a salute and left the office. I did not tell him the real reason, beyond the recent squabble, for my disagreement with the commander of the first group; by that point I would keep it to myself.

22

I WENT TO the elementary school building of Squinzano immediately, where the second group was quartered. By chance I ran into its commander at the entrance, Major Pelaformiche, who—as I imagined—had already been informed of my arrival. He was a man of few and disagreeable words; he told me clearly that he didn't like me at all and ordered me "for now" to present myself to the commander of the headquarters unit.

This was the Piedmontese Lieutenant Francescoli. I didn't know him, but I had heard that he was witty and brilliant, the most brilliant officer of the regiment.

When I entered his office (most likely the janitor's room) he thought it appropriate to assume a demeanor of importance. He was almost two meters tall, blond, with glasses. "You're the new officer?" he asked me.

"Let's say, almost new," I answered, "at least very little used in this regiment."

"They've told me that you had problems with the commander of the first group, that you're stubborn."

"Stubborn?"

"Let's understand each other, I don't dislike hardheads."

"I believe it," I said. "You can tell right away that yours isn't soft either."

He became uncertain. "But I'm talking to you in an official manner!" he observed.

"That's true," I concurred. "That's why you're talking nonsense. You've mistaken me for a recruit, I suppose."

Francescoli fell silent, then burst out laughing and gave me a slap on the back. "I think the two of us will become friends," he said. "All right. Like in Surbo, here you'll assume the command of a patrol OC (*Osservazione e Collegamento*),[6] new like you. Actually even newer, since it doesn't really ex-

---

6. Observation and Connection.

ist yet." He gave me some instructions concerning it, then as I was leaving, suggested, "Try to stay clear of the major. He's very irritated that they've assigned you to the second group. He's formal and doesn't want his group to be transformed into a '*refugium peccatorum.*'"

"I know," I said. "When I met him a short while ago at the door, he told me."

I didn't assign too much importance to the matter; it seemed like there were many other things to worry about in those days, and anyway I thought that the problem would resolve itself after the major saw me work with my usual goodwill.

Francescoli saw my carelessness. "Be careful because he's an obstinate fellow."

I nodded. "All right, thank you for the warning."

Afterward Commander Francescoli and I would become friends.

*

Guatelli had preceded me to the second group by a couple of weeks, called there by the need for an experienced adjutant. He was displeased with the assignment. "My destiny," he said, kicking the small stones of the school's courtyard, "is to remain eternally among piles of paper."

In the space of a few days I made another friend: Don Romano, recently assigned to the regiment as chaplain. He was blond and robust, with the white and red face of some of the peasants from the Mantuan plains, from which he came.

My orderly, Morandi, finally joined me in Squinzano from Surbo. "You promised that you'd request me from the first group," he said, presenting himself cheerfully, "and I thought I should back up your request. I made myself undesirable at Surbo: I acquired forty days of punishment in a short while, and they let me go."

Morandi, a Piedmontese mountaineer, was a bear, short and fair, with the eyebrows and hair almost of an albino and exaggerated muscular legs. He had been captured by the British in Sicily and escaped, but was stopped by the *carabinieri* while he was walking up all of Italy toward his home. He had brought an incredible hunger with him to the reorganization camp of Guagnano; for this reason, and since he belonged to Margherita's province, I let myself become partial in his regard. I appointed him cook, the position most sought after during those days of hunger. Later he confessed that he had renounced deserting while with us because of that little bit of consideration.

Now, after giving me a wake-up call, he polished the boots given to me by Guatelli while he spoke unfailingly of mountains (meanwhile, moaning at the cold water and occasionally encouraging myself, I washed my head and chest). "Here, if you look around, you see everything flat," he said. "Little by little our ideas too become flat." After the war he wanted to take me chamois hunting, which "on our mountains are divided into two kinds: the ones from the glaciers and the ones from the woods who are slower and heavier. With the scenes that you make in the morning just because the water is a little cold, I think that it'll be something if we can catch one of the slow and heavy ones."

The gigantic Sergeant Canèr was already part of my embryonic group. He had placed at the top (first, if I remember correctly) of a reserve officers' course that concluded in the south after the armistice. He would have found himself on leave, waiting for appointment as second lieutenant, but he renounced that appointment to be able to fight. Freddi, the patient lance corporal, a noncommissioned officer observer no less valuable than Canèr, was also part of the group.

As was my procedure, from the first day I began to hold a dialogue with my new soldiers. I acquainted myself with the city, the home, and the work of each one; I tried to grasp his identity, his irreplaceability, the reason God had created him like he was, different from all the others.

*

The short convoy of the group (about fifteen men) began moving with me on the outskirts of the village in a single line among the olive trees and wheat, laying down telephone lines, installing and dismantling observatories, conducting radio drills, or training under the shade of a tree.

Water birds appeared in the puddles the rain had left; they were abandoning the swamps on the coast and flying to the north. The good season was coming.

Unexpectedly, when most of the work seemed done, the sense of our uselessness, which had never completely vanished, came back again. There was no news from the paratroopers from Sardegna who were to meet us. Instead came news of disputes—serious ones, it seemed—between the British authorities and ours. The surrounding units were used to retrieve and seize the equipment that we had taken from them; we all realized that the regiment existed because of Colonel Giaccone's tenacity. In this state of affairs our daily sources of irritation and discomfort barely seemed tolerable.

It is true that even in social organisms, as in the human body, each part is connected to everything else and feels its condition. It was impossible, regardless of our goodwill, that we, a small part of the army, wouldn't feel the general state of disintegration. For me, it was a new, unexpected veiling of the "society of saints."

The disagreements between the superior commands disappeared.

Those of us from the second group weren't able to complete our training. At first it was interrupted by regimental athletic events; later on, having received news that the paratroopers were arriving from Sardegna, the politicians remembered us and there was a grotesque succession of official visits. After the arrival of Togliatti from Russia in April, the new politicians had let him convince them to become part of the king's hated government, and now several of them wanted to satisfy their fancies of having a regiment present arms.

We assembled, marched, did their "present arms," silently swallowing this too.

Soldiers complained. "They could have remembered us before," they said. "At least write once in their newspapers that there's still an army."

"In the newspapers? They'll make sure not to write anything. After they'll have us present arms, they'll carry on quietly, because the army doesn't belong to any party."

As officers we abstained from criticizing, but we agreed with the soldiers.

The undersecretary of war, a Communist, came last.

While I waited for him, lined up with the others, I felt so agitated that I had trouble standing and holding my ground.

From my experience in the Russian world I knew with certainty, outside of all polemics, that the Communists had deported and executed millions of defenseless human beings, particularly Ukrainian and Cossack peasants. I knew that there almost wasn't a Ukrainian or Cossack family that hadn't had someone killed or deported. Back then this may not have been known by others, but it was not news to me. I knew that if by chance German soldiers captured a Communist, he was denounced—"*Comissàr . . . comissàr . . .*"—and his execution was asked for. Either the commissioner was necessarily one of those big oafs—an alarming possibility—with a shaved head, raised without a soul, an utmost and perfect result of Stalinism, in which case he was huddled on himself like a captured wild beast, or on the contrary, he was at times a humanitarian type, one of those laymen with a bright face, once even living among us, who must have killed men on the terrifying scale of millions, absolutely certain they were doing good. Even before I was able to study the Communist phenomenon, my conclusion was that we had to fight with all our strength, and die if necessary, to prevent a similar plague upon our people: this was what I was telling myself while, quivering, I waited for the arrival of the undersecretary.

But an insignificant man appeared, dressed in a light suit almost like something one would wear to the beach, in order to seem more democratic. Moreover, his face was ridiculously Neapolitan.

"This one isn't like the Communists you were talking about," Guatelli whispered, giggling at attention at my side.

"No," I agreed.

After the inspection, the undersecretary found nothing better to do than to eat out of a mess kit among the soldiers, and did so ostentatiously, looking around theatrically, just like Fascist leaders used to do. Like back then, the officers had to suggest softly to the soldiers that they not avoid him, but stand near him.

23

ON MAY 24 our small regiment, sixteen guns in all—not much more than the equipment of a standard group—left Puglia.

We immersed ourselves in the ocher-colored world of the Allied armies on the large roads covered with road signs in English. Once in a while we saw ammunition depots in the countryside, some enormous; along the roads, column after column of British and American trucks followed and intersected each other, interminably.

Our short columns, darker and more plain in color, were a good expression of our people, who wandered around sadly, full of needs, among that overflowing wealth.

We crossed the town of Puglia for the last time with its poverty-stricken Arab houses on the periphery and dignified ones in town; we savored again the weak and bitter frustration of the south. At sunset we heard (I wondered if I would ever hear it again) the songs of peasants coming back from the fields on their small multicolored carts, those solitary songs, between a howl and a whine, that evoked the sunsets of the deserted and oblique African sun. I remember the discussions I had with Antonio back while we were discovering Puglia: these towns, we told each other, should simply be removed with scrapers, no longer being of use. We had to build new ones, as well as industries, above all industries . . . But there was the war. Fight the war first, and later build towns and industries, also reshape people's outlook, everything from scratch . . . Right, but where would we have found the means? I shook my head, as I had before. (I was very far from imagining that during the postwar period a few decades of help from the state and of work by the Puglian people would be enough to separate these areas from their century-old delays.)

*

The following day we traveled among the mountains of Irpinia, with golden-yellow brooms flowering on every overhang. "Have you noticed," Sabatini, the very young Tuscan driver, asked me, "how the British behave differently from the Americans?"

In fact the British sat formally, some stiffly, on the seats of their strangely old-fashioned cars, while the Americans, who wore better made and styled uniforms (at times even ironed!) seemed to choose more nonchalant attitudes in their very modern cars.

"I like the Americans better," Sabatini affirmed, "because whenever we came to blows with the British at the port, they ran to give us a hand. It seems like they like us too."

"Isn't it possible that they simply dislike the British?"

Sabatini was doubtful for a moment, then motioned no. "When we fought with the Americans, the British never came to give us a hand," he said.

*

We set up our tents in Beneventano, a short distance from the two small paratrooper regiments that had arrived from Sardegna a few days before.

Almost immediately—we had expected a month of maneuvers—the agile Nembo Division (about half the personnel of an ordinary division) began moving toward the Abruzzi front. So here was a thread, ours, beginning to pull free from the disheartening tangle of national disorder.

Since the paratroopers were almost without motor vehicles, British convoys drove them; very soon the exuberance of the *parà* infected several British drivers, causing disorderly races between trucks. Since we traveled on unpaved roads, we all reached the rear of the front covered in dust. The last hours of the journey, in Molise and Abruzzi, were across devastated soil, half-destroyed villages, minefields: we no longer ran under the sun, but proceeded slowly inside the shade of the sunset, while far ahead of us the guns roared.

The second group pitched camp for the night in a mangy field on the northern edge of Lanciano. After visiting the group's two tents ("So? Rev up, we're finally there") I stretched out in mine, on my bed.

Gradually the voices ceased, and each of us remained alone in the near darkness, with a stupefied sense of waiting.

"Who will be left behind this time?" I wondered, troubled. "Maybe, it

will be me? Or that one, or that other one with his worried face, poor fellow? Because it's certain that this time too one of us will be left behind . . . "
A firefly—there were many in the surrounding countryside—entered my tent silently, zigzagged a little, then left. "Will it prove to be another massacre?" I wondered all of a sudden. "No, make it that it isn't!" I called up to our Lady—the one of my people, the *Madonna del Bosco*[7]—like I used to at the Russian front in times of great danger. Then I crossed myself and fell asleep.

I dreamed I was a child and chased fireflies in the field in front of our house, as I used to do; I ran and ran, and yet always found myself in the same spot, while far away, strangely, the guns roared.

We entered the line the following morning.

7. The Madonna of the Forest.

Part Three

1 IT IS TIME to return to our entrance into Chieti.

Back then, large numbers of townspeople used to stroll every evening along the main street lined with long porticos that crossed the middle of the city.

The evening of that day we too, soldiers of the *Corpo di Liberazione*, strolled with the townspeople. We were all there, strutting in Chieti, just liberated. The paratroopers were more numerous, with their proud badges on their ill-fitting jackets (each one on a blue background with a dagger surmounting a golden wing); the horse-drawn artillerymen followed with their heavy, stubborn step of mountain dwellers. Even in that time of relaxation they tended to walk in close groups, ready to crowd around; their faces, many of them bearded, had in them something childlike and joyful, like country schoolboys on vacation. Finally, there was us, the few field artillerymen of the groups who, we reminded ourselves, belonged to the trained force, flaunting a certain arrogance toward the others who in truth were all more martial than we were.

"Thank you, Lord," I said, walking among the crowd on the street, "for this nice evening, and for the smiling faces of women around us."

I lingered in front of the town's theater to look at a few notices of the Nembo Company Revue, decorated with rough drawings of parachutes and submachine guns, announcing a show.

"Italians, a race of histrionics!" Curzio Favretto, a member of the first group, exclaimed at my shoulders with an English accent. I slowly turned my head with a fake frown: when our eyes met, we burst out laughing like two boys. All things considered, the idea that the paratroopers, having laid down their weapons a short while ago, were now taking up some type of artistic show didn't displease me. "But it isn't necessary to go see them," I said. "If anything we'll read the report in the division's newspaper."

"No theater," Favretto agreed, his face turned serious beneath his crew-cut. "You know what?" He interrupted himself and nodded. "We should instead try to pick up a girl."

"There's a very original idea," I exclaimed. "You want to bet that not even one of these soldiers is thinking that same thing?"

"It doesn't matter," he said. "It still remains a timeless and opportune idea and, in short, the product of a great mind."

"All right, let's leave it at that," I said. "If nothing else, we can try."

This settled, we resumed walking side by side, equal in height and age, drawn and also intrigued at the prospect of having to devise playful lines to pick up girls. (It was strange that devising witty lines for girls intrigued us, since we used them regularly between us . . . The fact is that, being very young, the idea of a woman seemed very big.)

We had covered maybe twenty meters when a very beautiful girl crossed the street after having scrutinized me from the other side. "Excuse me," she said. Then she seemed to change her mind, and politely stretched out her hand. "One moment . . . first I'll introduce myself: my name is Giulia." Her dark face blushed with emotion. "What I wanted to ask you is if by any chance you were the brother of . . . ? It's incredible how much you look like him."

It wasn't an excuse to pick us up (I already wondered if our intentions could have been that obvious on our faces). With true Abruzzese simplicity, Giulia was looking for news of someone who a few months back, before crossing the line, had stayed in her house.

With her fortunate blunder cleared up, the two of us promptly joined her and her friend, Chiara, and began talking hurriedly. Looking around excitedly (and also with slight embarrassment, being respectable girls), they answered us kindly, intent on showing gratitude to their soldiers or, rather, as they said several times, to their liberators.

While I did my best to capture her interest, I took a good look at Giulia, her youthful face, her graceful brown hair, as she walked next to me. I didn't harbor improper intentions, nor did I devise illicit or unbecoming thoughts, even though I was very aware, I must admit, of her attractiveness. Giulia noticed that I was observing her and gave me a questioning look. "Well," I tried to explain, "I was simply noticing that a sparrow appears different when one holds it in the palm of one's hand."

She smiled with natural sweetness, and I devoted myself mostly to her, while Favretto talked with Chiara. And since it was difficult to walk in four in that crowd, we ended up by losing him—with his cooperation—and Chiara.

When Giulia realized it, she became worried. "Why do Americans always have to be in numbers when they are with girls?" I asked her. "You'll see them . . . They own huge military armed forces, but with women they seem . . . how should I put this? In trouble. Even more than us."

"How are the Americans?" she asked, interested.

I tried to see them through her eyes rather than mine, and described them to her. To maintain her interest, I combined clichés and rubbish with maybe some interesting observations; we slowly went back and forth talking like this, blending in with the crowd along the long street through the center of Chieti bordered by porticos. Once in a while, however, Giulia became worried again. At times, she no longer listened to me and, giving in to the clichés of nice girls her age, even ended by saying, "It's not proper to walk around at night with a young stranger," and, "What will people say?"

The soldiers that we met envied me for having such a beautiful girl by my side; this made me even more fearful of losing her.

To keep this from happening, I threw myself with complete devotion into telling her about our daily lives, which would surely interest her if she was sensitive. And, indeed, she was interested; at times, she listened to me entranced. Some of the things I told her were as fresh as foaming milk from the cow. Nevertheless, she wasn't able to let go of her own apprehension. Suddenly, when we found ourselves passing in front of the door of her house for the second or third time, she took her leave. "It's time for me to go in," she said, stretching out her right hand. "Good-bye, then."

It was the only day that we would be staying in the city. "Good-bye," I answered her, without letting go of her hand. "Tomorrow already, the war will start again for us . . . Saying it might not seem like anything, but you don't know how much . . . the brutality of war." I was ashamed to be talking this way, almost pleading, in the end behaving like an adolescent, like the boy I in fact still was, in spite of so many tragic experiences. "I wouldn't beg like this for anything else but femininity," I thought, to justify it.

"Good-bye," Giulia repeated, "may the Lord be with you."

"Good-bye," I said, and let go of her hand.

Afterwards I found myself alone once again in the middle of the crowd. I barely noticed the people who walked by me.

"I was clumsy," I told myself after having begun strolling again. "Clumsy like a kid . . ." Right, but in the end, what did I want to accomplish? Certainly not take her to bed. I had not known a woman physically, and, as my Christian morals prescribed, I was resolved not to know one outside of marriage. So? "Well, I only wanted some . . . company, there, nothing else: the company of a girl during this only night of truce that the war allowed . . ." We're always good at creating excuses with words and arguments. In truth, when I looked deeper, I didn't just desire her company. The girl had stirred in me an extraordinarily strong attraction that still remained. She had awakened in my heart of hearts even my physical impulse toward women, which, after all, I knew well, like every healthy man my age. In order to control it, to cope with it, I had to sometimes devote to it energy and strength as strong as that which I devoted to the war. Slowly, I tried to look at the situation in the most objective manner: "Her company? Let's suppose that she had stayed with me a little longer, and a little longer, and longer . . . I must honestly admit that it wouldn't have been enough. Not even if the two of us had remained alone to stroll here on the street after all the others had left . . . On the contrary, staying with her longer in the end would have increased my yearning. Therefore—whether I like it or not—I must admit that she was right to leave." This is what I told myself, among other similar things, as I walked in solitude among the people. Although it was a well-founded argument, I wasn't able to accept it, so sharply did I miss her dark, slender figure at my side: I missed the girl as though someone had torn out a part of me.

*

In the following weeks I had the opportunity to return twice on official business to the benevolent city of Chieti. Even though when I left Giulia I had believed that I would only see her again with God at the end of time, I found her again both times, thanks to the general strolling that everybody took part in. Both times I was still attracted by her youthfulness. Chiara cried when I told her that Favretto had been wounded (in the Marches, while he was fighting bravely—his serious face had suddenly appeared tired when they took him away). Perhaps, I told myself, Giulia would have cried too if I had been wounded. Nonetheless, I uselessly began to solicit her company again. On the other hand, even if it hadn't been useless, I became increasingly convinced that her company alone would not have been enough, and in the end would have only added to my yearning.

That is how it came to a close with Giulia. Our meeting didn't amount to anything more, and I imagine her today as a sensible housewife, there in the kind Abruzzi, although at times I also think regretfully that maybe, even before being born, a beautiful friendship was lost inside the soundless well of time, which by now it is useless to look into.

2

THE FOLLOWING MORNING, June 12, the Sixteenth Battalion and other groups left the city, once again passing between the two wings of the applauding crowd, and resumed the march forward.

The heat loomed over the long descent that led through many curves to the industrial outskirts; we entered a main road among the fields, leaving behind, at the end of the descent, the few factories that were then part of Chieti, all ravaged by the enemy. We didn't see a single farmer working in those fields because, we learned, less then twenty-four hours before German patrols had still been in that area.

In midafternoon we came to a halt in the village of Cerratina. Here some of the paratroopers were quartered in rooms that civilians happily offered, while others pitched their tents. The parish priest had come to meet our column, followed by a small crowd of peasants, and at the entrance of the dwellings had briefly addressed Major Pellagatta, who had listened to him contritely, with his dark oxlike head staring at the ground in front of his feet. A few hours later the irregular walls of the houses appeared covered with banners praising the Italian soldiers and the Nembo Division. They were placed in a way to cover the British ones that had been put up not long before our arrival, but we were pleased all the same.

Against all expectations our stay in Cerratina lasted almost a week; in fact, the command of the *Corpo di Liberazione* found itself forced to halt, lacking motor vehicles to pursue the Germans. They were now retreating rapidly, leaving behind for us scattered minefields and blowing up even the smallest road bridges. Moreover, they were destroying all industrial machinery without exception, so it was fortunate that the areas around us did not have any such equipment. In some towns, the Germans even blew up household sewing machines.

In order to antagonize them, the division's only motorcycle company continued pressing the Germans, with help from Polish armored forces by the sea. On June 14, inside the large void left by the retreating Germans, a platoon of our motorcyclists, maneuvering obliquely with extraordinary recklessness, reached L'Aquila, preceded by the British.

Meanwhile, there were rumors that the command of the Eighth Army was irritated with General Morigi, who was commanding the Nembo, because in Chieti he had without orders let us precede the Indian Fourth Division, which was closer to the city than we were. We heard that we would fall under the command of the Polish Corps: the British, irritated, didn't want to concern themselves with us any more. A few people, however, believed, correctly or not, that General Morigi had been right because the entrance of the Indians into Chieti would have been preceded by an air raid.

*

Even the streets of Cerratina became familiar, a small and pleasant place with its unassuming house fronts hung with banners in Italian and English.

My platoon reentered the command of the Second Group, whose area we had reached. In order to make room for me in the officers' tent, pitched like the others in an olive grove, Morandi fitted three sheets of canvas (two as walls and one as roof), rendering it even longer under the jagged shade of the olive trees.

Those days were a quiet period during which Second Lieutenant Canèr, the group's topographer, engaged in wrestling matches with the strongest soldiers of other units and almost always won. In the evening he often lingered to talk with me about the retreat on the Russian front; his experiences gave me a way to know it from another perspective. Canèr, friendly with everyone, gave even less weight than me to Pelaformiche's dislike of us.

Lieutenant Commander Francescoli (the one who upon my arrival at the division's headquarters had welcomed me by jokingly reprimanding me) had an entirely different point of view. Francescoli, in fact, didn't let any opportunity for wit pass by; if by chance someone happened to be visiting, his jests came one after the other with such rhythm as to give the impression of finding oneself in a living room, not a tent. When he was alone, however, Francescoli used to sing softly a song full of melancholy, always the same one, about a woman's white, airy dress hung in a room: the wind filled it and moved it, giving the illusion that it was alive along with the woman to whom the dress had belonged; then the dress would fall again, lifeless, because the woman had died.

Francescoli's fiancée had died a few months before in Turin. She had run to the window during an air raid and fallen backwards with a shell fragment piercing her forehead. He had related the tragic event to me, still with an ache; few men among those close to him realized the sadness hidden in him, the most brilliant officer of the regiment. Later, when my thoughts would return to the days of Cerratina and to the soft singing in the tent under the olive trees, I would ask myself if some foreboding of another end, his own, wasn't in his voice.

3

THE PARTISANS had descended from the mountains to the area in front of us left empty by the Germans and the motorcyclists. Unfortunately they were Communists, who at the time didn't believe at all in the solemn declarations of democracy that their leader Togliatti insisted on making. I ran into them on June 20 while I was on reconnaissance with the headquarters motorcycle in Teramo, since the next day the entire regiment needed to reach the city.

Teramo, its streets spotted with rain, completely lacked the enthusiasm present in all other places for the German evacuation; the methodical hatred with which communism divides minds seemed already to be present in the crude, violent writings and Red symbols on the walls. An almost tangible void surrounded the very few military trucks stopped on the sides of the roads.

"This isn't like Chieti, huh?" the headquarters motorcyclist, Zaccarini, said uncertainly; he pointed with his arm.

Only a few partisans went about the streets. Other human figures, however, were speeding along the sidewalks; all seemed surrounded by a sort of shivering glow, shaped by suspicion and fear.

"It could be that by now they've gotten used to seeing soldiers here," Zaccarini suggested, increasingly uncertain.

The family of some townspeople of mine, industrial managers, lived in Teramo; one of the sons—a school friend of my brother Giovanni—had welcomed my brother for a short vacation on the Adriatic a few years earlier. I decided to visit that family during the one-hour break allowed by the marching schedule.

Since I didn't have the address, I had difficulty finding the residence. When, after climbing a flight of inside stairs, I knocked on the door, two unfamiliar ladies came to open it. They looked sickly and became frightened—one nearly screaming—upon seeing a drenched youth in front of them, with a submachine gun across his back.

"I'm not a partisan," I stated right away, "reassure yourselves. I am an officer in the army."

Then they kindly let me come in. "The family . . . ? But they're . . . gone. They left the apartment in our care. Tell us, maybe they . . . caught up with them along the way?"

"Caught up with them along the way? What do you mean? I'm asking about them only because I'm a friend of theirs. Where did they go?"

"Well . . . North."

"North? Why?"

The two women looked at each other. Then one of them said with much hesitation, "You see, they were considered . . . somewhat Fascist. But," she added immediately, "we have nothing to do with it: as for us, we've never been involved in politics. We come from _____, where our house was destroyed by the war."

"So they left . . ." The first thing that passed through my mind was that I wouldn't be able to get news of my town. "But what did they do? Did they lose their heads? Maybe they were impertinent?"

"What are you saying?" the two women exclaimed in one voice. "Impertinent?"

"Indeed," I agreed, "it's unimaginable."

"Maybe," the same woman explained to me, "but how can one be sure of anything in these times? More than their reputation as Fascists, the _____ feared that they might have some personal enemies among the partisans in the mountains. Signor _____ was the director of a company, and years ago he happened to fire a few workers."

"Because he caught them stealing," the other lady added in a quiet voice.

I took my leave after being forced to accept a surrogate coffee, placed in front of me by their still shaking hands; undoubtedly it would take some time for the two women to recover from the fear my appearance had caused.

*

I went outside in the rain. Now, close to sunset, a rather large number of partisans wandered around the streets of Teramo. They were almost all beardless youths, with red scarves around their necks and weapons on top of their civilian clothes. Fascism had educated them in violence, and here were its fruits. Although Teramo was almost certainly unaware of the enormous massacres committed by communism in Russia (I myself at that time did not know their extent; I knew only that their victims were counted in the millions), they still fully realized the halo of terror connected with that title and went around with severe looks. "Irresponsible men!"

"Maybe we shouldn't have waited so long to leave," Zaccarini said once again, shouting to be heard over the roar of the engine, his wet head turned to the side. "They say that the Germans have already evacuated Ascoli."

Darkness overtook us on the way back. The rain pounded us incessantly and molded around our knees the soaked fabric of our colonial trousers.

The road among the hills and mountains of Abruzzi, for years without lights, was utterly deserted. We briefly left it for the countryside near the ruins of a bridge, in order to reach an area with a more fordable stream. The detours—some short, others long—were by now all transformed into marshes and, with difficulty, we had to push the large motorcycle slowly across those wet places by hand; the engine roared and the rear wheel occasionally skidded, opening the mud like a fan. Reaching the banks, we remounted the seats and crossed the low places. On the opposite hills, the mud began to gather again between the fender and wheels, and sometimes blocked the front one, increasing our difficulties. The detours were countless; after a few hours of such exercise we staggered like puppets from exhaustion.

In the town of _____, where a company of engineers had stopped to reopen the road, we were forced to go in search of gas, since our engine had consumed a great deal more than expected.

It was late at night. A night-owl sapper led us up to a lighted place where officers were gathered. They didn't have any gas because their vehicles were all diesel. They offered me a cup of coffee, after which I reluctantly went back outside. Zaccarini was waiting for me under the drizzle, half seated on the motorcycle; I was cold for him too.

A second lieutenant accompanied us in total darkness through the narrow streets of the town and up to a partisans' command. Instead of gas, which they didn't have, they poured in our tank, "with camaraderie," a bottle of "fuel." These were partisans of uncertain political leanings, with attitudes between the motion-picture cowboy and the tough modern Roman youngster, pretty charming after all and, having barely fought, eager to obtain some glory out of the war.

We resumed traveling through the darkness.

After the Fascists, we now had the Communists, at a time when the nation was exhausted: this was the harsh reality. By force of circumstances they were accepted now as allies to the democrats and were gaining full rights of political participation. Would they become an avalanche and sweep us away? During those days of triumphant Stalinism no one believed the democratic declarations of their leader, Togliatti, reported in the newspapers. I wondered if, once the war was over, we soldiers (in the stump of an army that remained) and the democratic partisans (but how many were they? And tough youngsters like these were included . . .) would be able to stand up to them and keep them from taking hold of Italy. And, anyhow, when would that new, certainly terrible war end? How many more years would we have to fight?

The small beam of the tightly shielded motorcycle's headlight made us feel even more alone in the midst of the dark, smoky mountains.

"Who knows if we'll ever get peace," I told myself. Every now and then I also thought about the family that had fled Teramo, abandoning everything. "Where do they think they can escape? To the bottom of the net?" I wasn't able to tear my mind away from similar reasons for concern.

It was almost dawn when we arrived at the last detour, covered in mud, our arms ready to fall off our bodies. Without waiting for the outcome of our reconnaissance, the regiment was beginning to cross the first river in a howl of engines.

4

TWO DAYS LATER I returned to my acquaintances' apartment, intending to search among their papers for some letter with news from my town.

I realized how peculiar, to say the least, such a search was, but in the regiment, halted at the periphery of Teramo, there was nothing for me to do but be idle since every activity was focused on retrieving parts from the many scraps of Italian trucks abandoned by the Germans (we had no other way of obtaining replacement parts). Therefore I told myself that any search would be a better way of spending my time.

The two refugee women no longer lived in the apartment: one of the Communist leaders had thrown them out and taken their place. I was notified, with great caution, by a tenant as I was going up the stairs: "Be careful, lieutenant, he's one of the most dangerous individuals . . ." I rang the bell; the Communist came to the door. He wasn't one of the usual boys; he was a middle-aged man, short and sturdy, with a heavy head and hair that went down the nape of his neck like a short mane.

"What do you want?" he asked me, opening the door a crack.

"First of all, to come in," I answered. He waited a little, then slowly opened the door and let me go by, looking at me in silence.

"Is it possible," I asked him, "to speak with the two ladies who live here?"

He continued to look at me silently from head to toe. "I was the right-hand man of the commander-in-chief up on the mountain," he finally announced. I realized that he had a nervous tic, almost imperceptibly jerking his head down and up; he must have been very tense. "Since the command assigned this house to me, I'm doing an inventory of the furniture."

"Assigned?"

After another pause, with increasing impatience: "Yes, the Fascists burnt mine."

"And the two ladies? Where are they now?"

"I don't know. What do I know about Fascists' plans? On top of it all those two are sick and I have to bring my family in here. What does it have to do with the army?"

"Do you know where I can find them?"

"No."

"Well," I said, "I wanted to ask them to let me search through the papers of this house, whose owners are my fellow townspeople."

"Fellow townspeople?"

He looked at me seriously, with dull suspicion.

Never give bullies the impression that you fear them. I nodded, then let out, "Actually, I'd even call them my friends."

He jumped, almost as though I had said something monstrous; then he moved away from me—like I no longer existed—and resumed slowly dictating, as he saw fit, the names of furniture and objects to a guard from police headquarters who was visibly disturbed by my presence. Nor was he lacking witnesses; there were also two small boys who now seemed paralyzed.

"Inventory, huh?" I couldn't keep from mocking him. "It's apparent here, near the cradle of the law, that you have an innate sense of legality . . ." Then I began methodically opening furniture drawers, one after the other, and searching through papers.

Occasionally the Communist looked at me from the corner of his eye; clearly, he was especially bothered by the pistol I carried on my holster belt. After having stared at it, he took his own out of his pocket several times, a very small one (during those moments I felt extremely tense), made it jump in the palm of his hand, and put it back in his pocket.

"That gun is very small. I wouldn't trust a weapon like that," I said to him at one point, as though I was expressing a technical opinion, to show that I wasn't frightened.

"I've killed several people with this," he answered.

After staying lost in thought for some time, he interrupted his inventory, came next to me and, against all my expectations, devoted himself to helping my search; obviously so that I would get out of his way as soon as possible. He also began telling me—maybe with the hidden intention of intimidating me—some of the deeds accomplished by the Communists. "We didn't do anything to the Germans who surrendered. We took away their weapons and said, 'Beat it, *camaràd.*' But we killed all the Fascists, those dogs."

"Why one method for the Germans and another method for the Fascists?"

"Because the Fascists are Fascists," he answered. He uttered the abhorred word with indescribable hatred. It was truly horrifying. His teachers in hatred must have overloaded him to the point where he no longer cared about the possibility of using his mind. In those moments it seemed to me that I was no longer dealing with a human being.

Almost as though he realized my thought, he tried to be witty. "But listen to this: we didn't kill a Fascist woman, a member of the Women's Army Auxiliary Corps that we caught on one of their trucks. That one we passed around the band as a 'consolation prize.' Uh? Uh?" and he snickered, self-congratulatory, with his barely perceptible head jerk. "Around the band as a consolation prize! Uh?"

Once in a while as we were passing drawers around, old editions of the *Corriere Della Sera*[1] fell into our hands. "Here's the newspaper of the Crespi," he said then, naming the publishers, again with irrepressible hatred, and looked at me several times, as though waiting; for him it was irrefutable that one should hate that name, so that each time he seemed somewhat surprised that I, even if rival in all else, didn't share that hatred.

Finally he gave the newspapers that he had gradually placed under his arm to one of the boys who now followed us, trying to be useful (the other one was gone, maybe to the partisans' command? He had to be careful!); even the guard from the police headquarters followed us, disconcerted, still holding the list he had begun in one hand and a pen in the other. "You'll hang the newspapers in the command's toilet; we'll use them to _____" the Communist said to the boy, concluding vulgarly.

And to me: "Surely the sons in this house received these: they were the Fascists." He paused. "They escaped, sure. But in the north there are more of us who'll make sure to give them the appropriate welcome."

When we entered the living room the portraits of the master of the house and his wife welcomed us unexpectedly: two large, true-to-life paintings on a wall, as was customary to have back then in many Lombard houses. I stopped speechless: the lady's dark dress made me imagine her in the early morning ready to go out to Mass, like so many mothers in my Brianza.

Now those two, perhaps because of mistakes or the foolishness their sons (who undoubtedly had meant to defend them) had committed in the general confusion, were roaming who knows where, without a home: they who

---

1. *The Evening Courier.*

had lived honorable lives. For the first time I felt the physical sensation of finding myself inside a civil war; it was no longer an abstract concept but a fierce reality that I was immersed in all the way up to my neck. "Those two are there, and there's the Communist," I thought suddenly, "and after all, it seems clear that right now I find myself on the Communist's side." I felt the same repugnance that I felt in Russia, when I reflected on how I was on the Nazis' side, fighting against the Bolsheviks. "Then we wished that the Nazis would get rid of the Bolsheviks and that, in turn, the Allies would get rid of the Nazis: many of us hoped for this: all the civilians, one could say. Poles, for instance, said it to us all the time . . . Too decisive, indeed. It would have been too good!" But I had to stay alert to any possible rash movement from the Communist and not let myself get carried away in thought.

My useless search ended with the room. In order not to leave empty-handed, I took a postcard from one of the last drawers that bore the address of a teacher who wasn't yet twenty years old, from the province of Teramo: Lina, whom my brother Giovanni had met a few years earlier during his stay on the Adriatic. It was by chance that I recognized her family name, different from us Lombards, and her first name. Who knows if she would be able to give me news of my brother? The possibility was so tenuous that, in spite of the next days of idleness, I thought best simply to overlook it.

5

HOWEVER, a few days later when, with a few trucks, I happened to drive by the foothill on which Lina's town stood (the road sign informed me), I decided to pay her a visit.

Once the column stopped, I transferred its command to Sergeant Canèr and went up with our truck—the nice 626 Fiat—to the village.

As soon as the car, overloaded with heavy drums, stopped in the square, people ran up from everywhere to greet us joyfully. There were no Communist partisans here, so the Abruzzese environment was unaffected and courteous. Everyone knew the house where Lina lived with an elderly aunt who was also a teacher, and three or four boys kindly escorted me to it.

The old and young teachers were on the threshold, curious like the others about the arrival of the military truck. The aunt had two worn braids around her gray head and a face so full of goodness that she seemed an allegory of patient benevolence. The young one had brown eyes and two large braids wrapped around her head; slender and smiling, she brought to mind the delicate Madonnas of medieval painters.

The two women enthusiastically let me into their house and made me take a seat in a tiny living room filled with knickknacks. They must have used it rarely, yet still, even in that carefully kept clean room, one felt a vague sense of benches and children's eyes and hair, and of freckles, and ink stains from years of shaking pen tips; at least that's how it seemed to me.

"The last letter from your brother Giovanni," Lina said, not to my surprise, "is a greeting card that he sent me for Easter. I'll show it to you now." She went to get it and handed it to me.

"So until Easter he was free and at home," I thought. Recognizing the handwriting, I read the few words. "Up to this date he was out of danger," I said. "He wasn't a partisan or anything like it. I'm glad."

"He certainly would become a partisan," Lina exclaimed, misunderstanding me and unaware of being prophetic. "Partisan of Italy with a tri-color scarf like they wear up north."

"It is such an honor, lieutenant," exclaimed the elderly teacher, who couldn't stop looking at me admiringly, "to have you come into our home! You, a brave officer who fights to remove the foreigner from his country. It is an . . . immense honor."

"Well . . . ," I said, and smiled, embarrassed, not knowing how to answer in the least.

"Tell me," the elderly lady continued in a hopeful tone. "You're a *Bersagliere* officer, aren't you?"

"Yes." I realized I was lying. Then, trying to make up for it: "We're . . . assault troops."

"It couldn't have been otherwise," she exclaimed, putting her hands together. "Oh, the *Bersaglieri* of Italy!" I imagined her, moved and excited, telling her kids year after year how the bold *Bersaglieri* of the *Risorgimento* chased the foreigners from Italy, those *Bersaglieri* of old, with feathers on their hats, who must have had hearts very much like hers. "That's why she insisted on looking at the beret in my hands," I thought. "She couldn't make out the feathers."

Not able to get more news, I stood up after some pleasant conversation and said that I had to take my leave. "Wait, lieutenant," the lady said, and with a mysterious look ran into the nearby room. She came back with an already prepared bundle of flowers, white and red, with some greenery: the Italian tricolor. She placed it in my hand without saying a word, extremely moved.

I offered the elderly teacher a deep bow, feeling as though I was saying good-bye to a dear world now gone. I shook the hand of the young smiling woman; then, proudly seizing the tricolor bundle of flowers, I returned to the truck, followed by a mob of scamps. The driver, Sabatini, started up right away.

*

Now that we too were in Teramo, people began to cheer up and, although not reporting it, they at least talked about the Communists' violence.

Soon incidents broke out between the paratroopers and the partisans. An officer, hearing from the street the terrified screams of a woman—the wife of a Fascist in prison—whom a partisan leader, having extorted money in exchange for her husband's life, was trying to rape, vigorously knocked on the door. To keep him from going inside, the Communist fired several shots from a window; the officer, however, succeeded in getting him out by dropping hand grenades.

In front of a brothel ten or fifteen paratroopers, after having had the upper hand in a brawl with as many partisans, made them get on their knees and, overdoing it as always, forced them to kiss a Fascist identity card. This episode echoed in the provisional national parliament where the head of the Communists, Togliatti, went as far as asking for the dissolution of our division. By that time we were already far from Teramo and Abruzzi, and were fighting in the Marches.

The city between the two rivers had some peace—precarious and temporary, because once planted, the root of hate is difficult to eradicate—only after Polish soldiers, by order of the Allied military government, arrested the principal Communist leaders. As for the character I had met in the house of my acquaintances, I don't know if he was arrested under those circumstances. I know, however, that years later, having committed other crimes and, among other things, killed his blood brother for money, he was denounced by the Communists themselves. Surrounded by squads of *carabinieri* inside a cabin in the woods, he refused to surrender and continued to shoot until he was killed by the concentrated fire of dozens of submachine guns.

6

THE MOTORCYCLIST company that had pursued the Germans alone, like wasps chase a wild beast, since Chieti suddenly asked for reinforcements: the enemy had turned to bite them.

After also evacuating Ascoli Piceno, the Germans had stopped in front of Macerata, taking up position from the Apennines to the sea. Some motorcyclists had run into their line and now lay dead on the ground among their overturned vehicles, or had fallen prisoner after furiously defending themselves with submachine guns positioned on their motorcycles. Back then we feared that the Germans, not recognizing our government, would hang those of us who ended up in their hands: thank God, however, this did not occur. In front of us were the 278th and 71st Grenadiers divisions. The 278th was constituted of men largely from units destroyed on the Russian front and therefore proven soldiers, and the 71st was composed of Austrians: all people who would, on the whole, behave in a civilized manner.

At that time the paratroopers, like all other infantry of the unmotorized *Corpo di Liberazione,* were laboriously moving toward Teramo. One of the two regiments was motorized; the First Artillery accompanied it.

A few days later the Second Artillery also left Teramo and joined the new rear zone.

When our dust-covered column came to a halt and the cars slowly finished closing together, I noticed the Milanese Captain Clerici, a commander, stopped on the edge of the road, observing us with the kind of satisfaction someone on the line always shows at the arrival of reinforcements. When he saw me he came to my truck. "Bad news," he announced, "we've had our first fatalities."

"How many?" I asked, troubled.

"Three. The topographical unit was practically destroyed. Along with Lieutenant Tiberio, two of his technicians were killed: Bencini and Boselli."

"Then only one man from the topographical unit is alive."

The captain nodded. "Corporal Kribar. Do you remember him? He was part of your platoon in Surbo."

"I remember him well."

"All by mortar shell," the captain specified. "There's also an artilleryman wounded rather seriously, Zaccagnini. It seems to me that he was part of your platoon too."

"Yes, that's right. Zaccagnini had come to Surbo from the reorganization camp like me."

"We thought we'd be able to break through the Macerata defense fairly easily; instead we encountered a lot of resistance. Until now it hasn't been possible."

A soldier ran up to summon him to a nearby country house—maybe his command's headquarters. A halftrack had arrived at the line, from which they unloaded a long sack.

My orderly, Morandi, having come down from the truck in spite of the detours, followed to listen. He returned almost immediately to report, "They've brought Cominini back from the line, dead: a gunshot wound through his head . . . *Por Cuminin*," he commented, "*por diau!*" (poor devil!). Cominini, from the headquarters of the First Group, was a mountain dweller just like Morandi and came from the Alpine artillery; if I remember correctly, he belonged to a very poor family from Valtellino.

"Dirty war!" I murmured.

"*Parei 'dco Cuminin rivrà pi nèn a baita* (So then Cominini won't be returning home)," Morandi concluded, sadly shaking his head.

*

Leaving shortly after, we went to take position near the village of San Ginesio, twelve kilometers to the right of the paratroopers' regiment and of the First Group, without any communication with them. The British who advanced to the west of the Italian deployment were maybe fifty kilometers from us, between the Apennines: as I mentioned, during the entire summer campaign we would not see even one of them.

At San Ginesio we found the only motorcyclist squad that constituted a checkpoint and a swarm of Mazzinian partisans. We were welcomed with enthusiasm, as in all the other towns we passed throughout the day, but without noise, because here an acute sensation of danger lingered in the evening air: in fact the Germans, outnumbering us, were deployed a few kilometers away along the Chienti River.

In the morning, after leaving the land surrounding the rocky summit of Gran Sasso and the Communist chill, we once again found ourselves surrounded by Italian enthusiasm. The Marches—a region less passionate than Abruzzi—presents a flatter, more sweeping landscape. The houses were particularly attractive, larger and more solid even though often poor (especially the poorest), because of something classical and old that characterized their design. In these areas, the work of man—incredible for us modern people—had rendered the natural environment more beautiful, so that almost all views were a beautiful sight. The inhabitants were different also and didn't have the patriarchal majesty nor the hidden, inextinguishable fire of the Abruzzese, but were stout and curt in their speech. In some towns we found improvised relief stations where young women, merrily stopping our trucks, distributed sandwiches, beverages, even flowers. The practical spirit of the north was beginning to proclaim itself.

Under the red sunset the soldiers placed the group's eight 100-mm guns among the rows of vines, stretched camouflage nets on top of the trucks, and pitched the tents near the stone walls of San Ginesio.

The next day and the following ones, when duty allowed, I roamed the streets of the village, situated on top of a hill like the medieval ones usually are. It consisted of many buildings from antiquity, in a design that builders over the centuries had not changed much, so that everything appeared to be of the Renaissance era.

The surrounding wall, of brilliant stone, was preserved perfectly, with all its arched gates intact. I liked walking along those walls very much, both inside and outside, and I secretly felt happy that such walls existed in the world, and houses like these, and roofs with red curved tile, and in the middle of the town a little portico built centuries before by hands endowed with beauty that must have been in love with their own work! How I felt this place never heard of before, San Ginesio, to be mine! It was not only part of my land, but part of myself.

The Mazzinian partisans of the formation *Giustizia e Libertà,* dressed and armed like the British, greeted us cordially when we met them on the street; we answered with as much cordiality. But although I had felt relief upon seeing them upon our arrival—after the Communists in Teramo—they now seemed out of place in such surroundings. I experienced the sensation of someone who notices something foreign in a beautiful old building: for instance, some furniture or other objects made out of plastic, which in spite of their usefulness and comfort appear out of place and, in sum, wrong.

How could so many undoubtedly generous youths, I wondered, be Mazzinian today? The humanitarian ideals of the nineteenth century, substituting for Christianity . . . surely filled still in some way by Christianity, but . . . in Russia I had seen where those ideals led, where those humanitarians with their enlightened faces found themselves in the end: they had ended up as executioners of others on the scale of millions, and executioners of themselves . . .

7

ON ONE OF THOSE quiet days I received a letter from the hospital of Sarnano, nearby in the rear zone, from Zaccagnini, the wounded artilleryman from the First Group, asking me to come visit him. I was surprised, because I had lived near him for months without realizing his affection.

I found him stretched out on a cot, his face hollow, like a stump sunken in pillows.

"Thank you for coming, lieutenant," he said, smiling with apparent difficulty. He had the accent from the Pontine in Lazio. "I asked you to come because . . . I wanted to listen to you speak."

"You lazy-bones!" I exclaimed, sitting down next to him. "You succeeded in finding a way to get leave and want to take a look at the faces of those who are still around, don't you? You scoundrel. You'll be home before the vintage; right, you were always thinking about the vintage."

"Maybe . . . I'm in bad shape, but I think I'll be able to keep from dying." He was smiling laboriously, occasionally stopping in a half-smile grimace.

"You scoundrel," I said even more aggressively, because right there I couldn't cure that good soldier instantly with my hands. "Speaking of dying when you have a leave in your pocket!" Trite words. "Look at how much war I've fought," I said in his country manner. "And yet, a smart splinter never came to give me leave, never."

"To listen to you, it almost seems like a party . . ." he replied, pleased.

So at first we spoke of the usual things.

Then I spoke to him about the reasons why we were fighting. He had called me for this: to help him understand that his suffering wasn't senseless. I spoke to him of our country: one almost had trouble naming it after all the slander its name had been through; but our country, I tried to explain, wasn't an abstraction like many believed, nor something limited to solemn discussions, or monuments, or the words in history books that are only rhetorical in regard to our country. As far as we were concerned such rhetoric could also go to the dogs, but not our country, the inheritance left to us by our fathers. And that is therefore, I continued, trying to express his own thoughts, most of all made up of real people: our families and others like us; and then our way of life, which is different from that of other people (he had witnessed this, hadn't he, having been in contact with foreigners?); our country is moreover our land and our home, which we always remember when we are away and continually miss. Our country is even the fields and the vineyards where girls sing during the vintage: "You're going to choose a bride this year, aren't you? You'll be the only one in town to have fought the liberation war, the only one with a victorious face. If we all do our part like you, we'll be able to fix things a little bit at a time. You'll see, finally we'll be able to live like we want to, and raise our sons in peace: not like outsiders, but as Italians and Christians, with the right sentiments."

After a while, realizing that I was tiring him out, I stopped talking and simply stayed near him, a hand on his shoulder and a friendly face, while he thought it over seriously with his eyes fixed on the ceiling, and occasionally nodded, impressing the concepts in his mind. We were surrounded by the silence of the hospital, like a hand with transparent fingers closed upon us.

When finally I stood up to take my leave, Zaccagnini reminded me: "Those dead . . . They brought Lieutenant Tiberio to his home in Pescara. But they buried Bencini and Boselli here, in the cemetery of Sarnano."

"Yes," I answered. "I'll go visit them now."

*

The cemetery, surrounded by trees with bright green foliage, was very beautiful, like almost everything man-made in that area back then.

The fallen of the *Corpo di Liberazione,* paratroopers and artillerymen, lay one next to the other under two long, fresh piles of dirt. I stopped in front of them with my head lowered. How many times, at twenty-three, had I already found myself like this . . .

I knew well the three deceased from the First Group. I knew, therefore, that the mountain dweller Cominini, in some sense a simple soul, had always had death in the back of his mind. It seemed to him like the fitting conclusion of the difficult trial that is life; not a desired end, but for someone who walks in the mountains each arrival always holds something good.

Bencini, with a Tuscan face and pronounced cheek bones, had come to the front for idealistic reasons. Having been very religious, he probably pondered death; in the last weeks, in any case, he had foreseen it, and had therefore entrusted the chaplain with a letter written for his mother, who was waiting on the other side of the lines: a spiritual testament so noble that Don Romano had decided to distribute a copy to each man of the regiment, but he would not make it in time because he too was about to be killed.

The Lombard Boselli, a tall and shy boy with big eyes, never spoke of death, or only in joking terms, because he didn't understand it and was afraid of it. In Puglia, during reconnaissance practice on the roofs of farms encrusted with lichens, I had heard him a couple of times daydreaming out loud about the fastest way to get home if—thanks to a miracle—the fronts that cut through Italy disappeared. He made plans that were both colorful and reasonable, like those of the lichens that spotted the windy flat roofs of Puglia. Now all three were dead and lined up in the ground near the paratroopers, whose attack on the Germans had been suddenly interrupted. At this moment, their spirits, I thought, must be finding themselves in a sort of crucible that was shattering all impediments to the bliss for which man is designed and created: perfect bliss, present only in his union with God. Therefore they were suffering bitterly. Who more suitable to tear them away from this suffering than the Virgin Mary, who in Cana of Galilee proved willing to subvert preordained boundaries to alleviate the distress of the common people?

"Virgin Mother," I invoked her, "the Lord Jesus left us on the cross: he left each of us, one by one. Entering in the great beyond, these soldiers have found you instead of their own mothers who are waiting for them at home unaware. Under these terrible circumstances, give them the help that they would have received from them. Help them all, artillerymen and paratroopers. Better yet, take all these dead soldiers' souls in your arms, tear them away from the soiled residue of blasphemies, of the sins of desire that are so easy in youth, away from all filth and misery: take them to God and lay them down with God. I beseech you, Mother of ours!"

*

That evening when I returned from Sarnano, San Ginesio was in a great state of alarm at the news that a battalion of German Alpine soldiers of the 71st Division had crossed over the Chienti River again and was marching toward us.

First some partisans had brought the news to Major Pelaformiche; then a motorcyclist from the Nembo command from the rear zone; finally another motorcyclist, also from the command, who had warned us to stay ready: probably in the course of the night we would be encircled and attacked.

It was very possible. The Germans, informed by some Fascist spy about the isolation of our group and knowing the almost total lack of preparation of the Italian artillery—too specialized for infantry war—could have decided to annihilate us. In doing so they would have given an example to all of Italy.

Fortunately it was only a false alarm.

Near tears is laughter. The person who in my memory dominates those hours is the Ancestor, who had been with our group since our departure from Teramo.

That day I had seen him come toward me just as we were about to leave, all smiles from the good memories of that brave night at the observatory post Margherita. He had greeted me effusively. Next to us the vehicles and guns were already drawn up in columns. "You know, I've found out about a place where they sell magnificent rabbits," he had said to me, with his eyeglass shining. "What would you say about going with a vehicle to buy a couple?" Since at the time Pelaformiche, on line with the halftracks, was making one of his usual scenes, I had answered thoughtfully, "Rabbits? But the major is crazy about rabbit! We should ask him for a vehicle." The Ancestor had looked at me with some hesitation; nevertheless he must have found my face, and those of the soldiers who had gathered around, so sincere that without delay he had reached the major. While the old man was talking to him, Pelaformiche had become livid with rage; then we witnessed a thunder of words come out of his mouth. The term "old scarecrow" was yelled frequently. The Ancestor had come back to us puzzled; far from scolding me for the prank, he had pulled me aside. "The major is having a nervous breakdown. He's sick, I'm telling you. He needs care! And to think that these were rabbits reared on carrots!" He sighed. Reaching my truck, in a perfectly natural manner he pulled himself up to my seat near Sabatini, the driver, and, while I wondered where on earth I would sit, he began to show signs of boredom because we were taking a long time to leave.

The evening of the alarm at San Ginesio, the Ancestor was very agitated, and sleepy.

At the start he directed all his anger for the Germans on his orderly, a freeloader that some command unit had gotten him to accept in order to rid themselves of him. He said to me, "Put him on the lookout in a visible area. That rascal steals my soap." His anger produced more anger. He tightened his fists and said in a terrible voice, but softly so that his orderly wouldn't hear him: "I'll end up by putting that swindler under *arresti* for continuously making my soap disappear!"

Then he sat at the rough table of the farmhouse where the group's command was on the alert, placed his bald head on his fists, and dozed off. Shortly after he woke up, he raised his face, frightened. "Uh? The Germans?"

"No, captain," Francescoli said, with the light of the lantern on his myopic face. "Go to sleep; there's no danger at all."

"No, no," he said, "I know that they're coming. But I have a hand grenade," he exclaimed proudly. Rousing his drowsy body, he stumbled out of the farmhouse through the squads of armed men with helmets on their heads seated on the ground against the wall. He held the grenade in his hand. "When they arrive," he said, grinding his teeth, "I'm throwing this." The soldiers cheerfully agreed.

He came back inside. "Did you put my orderly on the lookout?"

"Of course, captain."

"Double that scoundrel's watch. My soap! I'll need to find a lock to put on my casket." And he dozed off again.

8

THE PARATROOPERS made a new onslaught against the Macerata defense. This time, the Germans at first retreated slowly from the city, then evacuated it.

We entered behind the paratroopers. It was the afternoon of July 1, and the blazing summer heat loomed over the beautiful, time-worn, brick-colored houses and the silent streets. Since the population had left en masse, only a few people were at the crossings to see us go by, and they clapped their hands without comments. At one of the column's pauses an old man ran up to our truck. He was holding a ham and a large loaf of fresh bread, the best he had to offer; he handed them to us, standing on tiptoes, his eyes filled with emotion. In response to our joyful thanks he slapped the boot of the soldier closest to him, without a word.

Beyond the city the column of the Second Group found itself for some time between Polish armored columns. Since the mines prevented us from using the main roads, we were all forced to advance on secondary roads, which our passage rapidly transformed into dust; a thick cloud of dust hung in the sun like fog.

My heart went out to the Polish people, who alone bore the cross between the two countries of modern barbarity. I knew, moreover, that these soldiers from Anders's army corps—fifty thousand men—were the only ones remaining from the three hundred thousand Polish soldiers taken prisoner by the Bolsheviks during the invasion of Poland; the rest were all dead, many killed with a blow to the back of the neck (in Katyn and elsewhere), the large majority from hunger and hardship during two brutal years in captivity. Adding to my emotions, I realized suddenly that they wore the badge of the Polish cavalry on their British tanker caps.

"The cavalry!" I said excitedly to Canèr, seated next to me in the cab, and to the driver, Sabatini. "You see those badges? They're cavalry soldiers ..." And since neither of them seemed to grasp what I was alluding to:

"Don't you remember the charges of the Polish cavalry, lances at rest, against the German tanks in '39?"

Sabatini remembered. "Ah, yes," he said, "it's true." And after a while: "What madness, though! Why did they do it? By then Poland was won . . ."

Because of it, precisely because of it. It had been a gesture of great pride for their ensuing years of slavery, to hand down to their children, along with memories of the days of freedom.

For many it had seemed as though the beauty of the old days had died forever with this gesture, flattened by the indifferent steel machines. Now, on these other machines, the survivors of the charge carried on, regardless of the uproar of engines and caterpillar treads, and the smell of gas, and dust in the sun, and sun in the dust . . .

We waved to them, leaning over the turrets or perched on the backs of Shermans, while they left our course to return to the coast where their zone was located. They waved back, their rough, smiling faces framed by dust-covered hair and white eyelashes. The Poles always answered with gratitude to our display of kinship.

Some of them were also among the German troops we were pursuing: captives forced to fight against their own country. Up ahead I heard paratroopers talk about seeing Polish soldiers on two opposite deployments cease fire because they had recognized each other, and run up to each other and embrace each other, crying in the middle of the battle. So even these sorts of events, which seemed from another time, took place during the war in Italy.

*

We continued to advance in the following days, passing several groups of hills, one after the other, running from the Apennines to the sea. Now the guns thundered from morning until night, because the Germans, pressed by the paratroopers, were retaliating with their artillery, hitting crossroads, areas where the roads stood out from the hills, and every other suspected area.

The surrounding countryside was green and still very beautiful, rich with crops, with vines propped up by elms, divided in orderly rows.

We came to a halt for a day and night in the land of Forano near an old monastery with a wide open door. The monastery had remained open day and night for the Germans too, with a Franciscan offer of peace to all. Since, however, the Germans hadn't gone in, we too at first didn't enter; we were held back by a confused restraint. Maybe we, who carried weapons, even if out of necessity, didn't want to contaminate the brothers of us all, who had chosen expiation for all. Even if as soldiers we felt, in fact, in some way expiators, there wasn't one of us who didn't acknowledge the superiority of contemplative atonement that wasn't mixed with killing and wounding. Because of this, I think, we didn't enter the low stone corridors of the rustic monastery.

When, however, an artilleryman (it was B., the alcoholic one) was seized with unexplainable pain, we decided to entrust him to the care of the monks, since the medical lieutenant and his ambulance were elsewhere. I brought him inside the monastery myself, with two soldiers who carried him.

The monks welcomed him gratefully in their arms and laid him down in a cell to take care of him.

"We monks," one of them said, "are also responsible for all these sufferings. The church is going through a bad period, like many other times, but we, as few, weren't able to play the part like those good soldiers who though few were able to play the part of many."

The other monks assented to such words.

"When this is over, we'll return to our homes," two artillerymen interjected. "You'll still stay here to do penance. Does that seem little to you? What more could you do?"

"When one takes a pledge," the monks answered, shaking their shaved heads like lambs, "one should care to fulfill it well, especially a pledge like ours. But we are not fulfilling it well. We haven't compensated in front of God for the sins provoked by the war, and even now many of those who are dying have a fate of damnation only because we, for little love of sacrifice, are not gaining their grace."

"You see," a young monk emphasized, "we're even arrogant enough to think such things: arrogant enough to feel useful. We're bad monks."

"Quite a military life for them too, huh?" the two artillerymen commented.

*

The following day after a farther advance, we established the observation post on top of a long, green ridge.

In front of us the land went down to form a wide valley interposed with farms, which on its slope culminated in a town of tall houses close together that reminded one—from a distance—of an uneven, stern fortress. We read its name on the maps: Filottrano.

We didn't know that many of us would die fighting around it, and that the rest of us would remember it forever.

The regiment's guns had opened fire the day we arrived: not only ours, but also those of the First Group, positioned two kilometers to our right. The firing continued in the following days. Meanwhile all the remaining artillery of the *Corpo di Liberazione* left behind their unmotorized infantry below. As soon as they arrived the groups took position among the rows of vines and carried out organized fire.

I wondered if the command expected a strong German resistance to protect Ancona. Or perhaps they had carried on their offensive in the central sector of the front against the British, or in the Tyrrhenian one against the Americans?

The paratroopers' battalions had taken position just below us, in the closest farmhouses and in the first ditches of the wide valley. The Germans, clearly fewer in number, were in front of them, but still on our ridge, in other farmhouses, in other ditches. They resisted, but we thought that they would surrender their positions again when our men moved forward decisively.

The observation post was located in a pit on the edge of a large cornfield. During the slow passing of hours Canèr, Freddi, and I, surrounded by countless dark green stalks, took turns scrutinizing each detail of the valley through binoculars.

A quiet sense of time succeeded the intoxicating sense of movement, hovered imperturbably over our circumstances and all others, and moved forward without a sound. Occasionally, the blasting fire of the Italian batteries exploded behind us, followed by the long whistle of shells and then, below in the valley, the thick smoke of explosions whose echo, sometimes powerful, sometimes weak, reached us.

During my off-duty hours I silently observed insects, ants and others that I couldn't name, that passed by us on the dark earth along their imperceptible paths. Without minding us (they paid attention to men only to dodge them) those tiny creatures quickly bustled about on unknown tasks among the rustic overturned crowns that surround the base of corn.

"What peace!" some engrossed soldiers said at times.

The Germans, however, began concentrating their artillery fire on our ridge. A battery of large-caliber guns, which opened fire at regular intervals, adjusted its shooting onto road intersections not far from the observation post. Mortars were added. At night, in front of the paratroopers' positions, one could see long volleys fly from the automatic weapons of the opposite side, like a snake sparkling in different spots as he sways: it was a sign that tension was increasing.

Since the enemy didn't seem to want to withdraw, our nerves began to tighten too; among other things that kept us on edge was the fact that the Italian deployment was dominated by the German observers in Filottrano. Furthermore, peasants had stayed in all the houses of the valley, hoping for a swift passing of the front. Each time that we opened fire, their presence came back to mind.

9

IT WAS THEREFORE with relief that on the dawn of July 6 we saw paratroopers' infantries push forward. On our right, out of sight, the Poles also put themselves in motion; far away their artillery, much more powerful than ours, fired and fired without pause, with a sort of endless roar. From the observatory, I watched through binoculars as our platoons entered the yards of the closest farms; some farmers ran up to them with their arms wide open.

The Germans retreated without hurry, still fighting, like proud dogs; our men pursued them, defilading cautiously behind hedges, behind every cover. Eventually, we lost sight of them. The air was filled with the thick croaking of submachine guns. Then that too began to weaken. The group's guns raised their sights and finally shifted their fire onto the entries into Filottrano, opening fire as though their mouths were pointing to the sky.

Not far from us, in one of the battery's observation posts, a soldier who was a native of Filottrano was in the corn. From time to time we heard his excited voice, joyful over the imminent liberation of his town, anguished by the shells with which we were striking it. All of us began looking at him; perhaps not used to being the center of attention, he thought that he had to perform for us but didn't really understand which part to play. By noon he had become a wreck. Many tried not to look at him, but he continued to act.

In the afternoon, the Germans were only left with the long ridge where the town rose. The mistaken conviction spread among us that they had evacuated that too, or were about to do so. The gratifying sense of relief that follows successful battles began to spread among us, along with an awareness of our exhaustion.

*

The false rumor that the Germans had evacuated Filottrano must have spread among civilians too.

In fact, once in a while, countrywomen holding children's hands came from the rear zone to reach their men who had stayed in the valley. When they drew level with the deployment, the sentries ordered them to stop and sent them back.

A small group of women and girls, black against the bright sky, negotiated with a sentry from our ridge, who was telling them that yes, they were right, and that their wish to know their husbands' fate was more than fair but, given the orders, they could not go by. Soldiers, the sentry said, obey orders every day that do not make sense; once in a while they too should obey. The grumbling countrywomen finally decided to turn back, but as they reached the place where their small road merged with the white of the large road, a whistling shell came down on them from above.

The few soldiers who were outside the pits threw themselves on the ground, and one of them who happened to be at the intersection shouted for the women to do the same, but the women didn't understand and stayed standing. We saw a violent cloud of smoke explode in their midst and cover them. Figures stirred in the smoke like specters, and some of them came out of it running. Rushing to them, we made out gray bodies writhing on the ground; some children screamed with whatever voice they had, huddled on themselves.

We lifted and transported the wounded to the closest farm, where the group's command had established itself. Francescoli urgently sent a motorcyclist to call the lieutenant doctor.

An old woman in her seventies, her arm broken, was spraying red drops on the ground like an aspergillum as she was carried by soldiers to the floor of the kitchen where Guatelli's regimental office was located. Two or three of us tied her arm tightly above her wound. The toothless mouth of the old woman, who was entirely lifeless, was half open and her whitish pupils were motionless; only her miserable chest moved for breath.

At the same time, in the yard Guatelli was treating a young girl of about fourteen, wounded on her head. "Please, give me a hand," he called to me as soon as he saw that I was available. "Yes, come," added Francescoli, "I have a problem touching blood. First the girl." When I went near him, he muttered, "At no other age is one more afraid of death and so unprepared for it."

I helped Guatelli cut the hair around the wound, which we covered with sterile gauze, then bandaged her head. "My stomach," the girl, held up sitting on a stool, continued screaming. "My stomach hurts." We discovered that a cylinder of wet, yellow fat was coming out of a centimeter-long hole in her stomach.

"What can we do for a wound like this?" Guatelli, who carried out the treatment calmly and methodically, asked me.

"We have no choice but to wait for the doctor," I answered him. "Meanwhile, you take care of her. I'm going back to the old woman in your office."

The old woman, having stayed alone after our brief treatment, had unexpectedly recovered and, pointing the stump of her broken arm toward the ground, had seized a table leg available with her hand and was trying to stand on her feet. The lifeless part of her broken arm swung like a foreign object in another large puddle of blood.

Guatelli's clerk had also rushed over. We laid the woman back down on the floor almost by force and, kneeling around her, we performed another tighter binding on top of the last one.

Since her clothes were soaked in blood, we thought that she must have had other wounds as well and began searching, but didn't find any: all that blood, which now covered our hands, came from her arm.

The poor woman now moaned and once in a while tried to weakly cover her stomach and chest with her cut-up clothes. We helped her, after which she once again became lifeless. I felt as though she was about to die, so I said, "Pray to the Lord, Grandma, because you are about to face his judgment. Can you hear me? Pray to the Lord."

"Pray to the Lord . . . Pray to the Lord . . ." the troubled scribe repeated, while she gasped in agony.

In the yard, the soldiers had also treated a boy of maybe eight who, held sitting up against the dust-covered tire of a truck, now wouldn't stop screaming. Even an artilleryman—the one who had thrown himself to the ground near the group of women—had been wounded superficially on his back. His squad companions had treated him; now he was lying face down in the grass near the farm, his forehead on top of his folded arms, and once in a while he let out a sigh.

A woman, the mother of the two wounded children, had been killed. The soldiers had removed her from the road and settled her in the clean shade of a straw stack.

I went to see her: she appeared to be a mild countrywoman of about thirty-five or forty years old. On her chest, her gray dress was stained red, but not much. Strangely, her face assumed the expression of a smile.

"Just think," the Ancestor said, coming behind me and sounding like someone who repeats something that's already been said. "When I heard the whistle I was urinating behind a hedge . . ."

"Be quiet!" I commanded.

Silently, with the Ancestor at my side, I invoked with torment that God also welcome the soul of this gentle creature that we men had found a way to kill.

"Stinking war!" the soldiers of the command's unit said, coming to take a look at the dead woman, as in procession. "Lousy war!" We said these words softly, and didn't curse, so as not to offend her—she who was delicately smiling even after she had been killed. Thus, the soldiers expressed their sorrow.

Afterwards I lowered the eyelids of the deceased with the tips of my fingers, and I kept them lowered until her eyes remained shut; then we laid out a tent-cloth on the dead mother.

The doctor finally arrived and, in a great hurry, took with him the wounded and the deceased on the motor ambulance toward the hospital of Macerata. As he moved away in the distance along the white road, the ambulance raised a thick plume of dust, reminiscent of the smoke of a running train, such a small vehicle containing so many lives and destinies.

With the early darkness, I began my observation shift. I sat on the edge of the observation pit, among the thick cornstalks that the breeze occasionally stirred. I had washed my hands, stained with blood up to my wrists, with an acrid-smelling disinfecting soap, and this smell blended now with that of blood and wouldn't leave me. While the insects in their fields, heedless of us, recited their nightly prayers, I uselessly held my hands behind my back.

10

ANTICIPATING MOVEMENT forward as soon as we attained success, the following night I engaged the platoon in extending the telephone line from the current zone to the zone of the future deployment of artillery.

The night of our wait was dark on the earth; in the sky, however, was a pale moonlight.

A few German airplanes passed above us low and slowly, in search of targets to shatter. We silently observed their easily recognizable silhouettes against the unraveled silver clouds.

One of them, reaching Filottrano, dropped a cloud of phosphorus plates that lit up in a huge cluster of yellow flames: the entire slope seemed bathed in blazes, like a sudden apocalyptic spectacle. Gradually, they all went out.

When we passed by the deployment of the First Group, I saw an officer walking alone, back and forth near the guns. I realized that it was—well, well—Antonio Moroni: he was pensively smoking a cigarette.

"Hey, hi Antonio."

"Oh, look who it is! Hi."

He came over to our cart road.

"What's going on?" I asked him. "You're once again in battery?"

"For a while, luckily."

"And your colonel, the 'little *Napoleone*'?"

"He left the fighting troops."

"Even though he had nothing to do?"

"Even though he had nothing to do. It seems that the war was exhausting for him all the same."

Antonio smiled at me kindly in the dark. "Tell me instead: do you have to go all the way to the line?"

"Yes."

"If you come across our patrolman Curzio Favretto, tell him that his brother has arrived from Sardegna. He's been waiting for him for over a month."

"All right."

"Tell him that he's here at our command."

"I'll try to track him down and give him the news."

Behind Antonio, one could spot the eight guns of seventy-five of the First Group—dark and lined-up outlines—each with its camouflage net stretched on top like a wing.

"Well, bye, then."

"Bye."

Our truck passed over cart roads and larger roads, leaving behind the telephone wire that the gigantic Sergeant Canèr, or Scirea, or others gradually hung on the trunks of trees, on bushes, on the poles of the telegraph, or on the short pickets of field fences. We entered wooded gorges under the hard, outstretched branches of oaks. Once in a while, the truck came to a halt, then started again, teetering as it proceeded. It once again stopped in a difficult area near a farm where a dog that had barked at us from afar now whimpered on the threshing floor; doors and windows were shut.

Everyone slept between lookouts, in houses, in tents, undoubtedly even in the pits of the line. It seemed like the men wanted to catch as much sleep as possible, which our tired bodies welcomed, before the battle.

We spent a good deal of the night stretching those six or seven kilometers of line. In the dark, it was difficult to locate the minor courses traced on the topographical map, difficult to find the streams' most fordable spots; as far as the bridges were concerned, even the smallest ones had been turned into blocks of debris enveloped by running water.

The line was ready only a few hours before dawn.

Our front now formed a semicircle below Filottrano; we were located at its right arm, on a ridge that emerged obliquely from the town's highest crest. The Polish line, constituting the Fifth Kressowa and Third Carpathian Divisions and some other divisions and armored brigades, began at a fair distance more to the right, stretching all the way to the Adriatic.

"Come on," I said to Morandi, while the others, shivering in the morning cold, stretched out to sleep in the grass around the truck. "Let's try to track down Lieutenant Favretto before combat begins."

Morandi came behind me with his submachine gun slung over his shoulder, wobbling in the dark with his bearlike walk, his hands in his pockets, his beret pressed on his forehead, and the tiny collar of his uniform raised.

Once in a while, we could make out the silhouette of some paratrooper in the open cornfield wrapped up in a blanket; everyone was still sleeping.

"By now," Morandi muttered, "they've learned how to load the mules. See? They've taken the blankets with them."

After a brief search, we found Favretto's patrol at a halt a little farther ahead on the same ridge as ours, in a farm three-quarters exposed to the enemy.

A drowsy sentinel told me that Favretto was sleeping with the others inside the stable. When I pushed the door open, I collided with a stifling smell of heat and stench: there were also animals in there. I found Favretto with the faint light of a taper candle; he was lying down in the hay wrapped in deep sleep, his face tired. I woke him up, energetically shaking one of his shoulders. "Hey, sleep patrol."

"Oh, hi," he murmured. "I'm dead tired."

"But I'm not. Tell you what, your brother is at your group's command. He arrived yesterday from Sardegna."

"Oh," he said, "Sardegna . . ."

"Did you understand? Your brother."

I left him, and we returned to the truck.

*

Some movement began on the line even before dawn. With daylight, Polish artillery laid siege to Filottrano from the right side, along with ours. The German guns answered immediately, opposing violence with violence; there were fewer of theirs than ours, but they didn't seem few.

As I waited for orders, I looked for an observation spot in the area of Favretto's farm; Morandi, Canèr, and Freddi were following me. We ran into Favretto.

"What in God's name were you telling me last night about my brother? Where were you coming from?"

"Right from Chieti. You know? I met that girl, what was her name? Ah, Chiara. In short, she wanted me to tell you that she can no longer live without you."

The artillery fire continued without a break; the Polish shells passed in fast volleys above our heads.

"Did my brother arrive from Sardegna?"

"Yes. He's at your group's command."

"He's an idiot. He wants to be part of the war. He's thinking about his duty to his country, you know?"

"What can you do about it?" I offered sympathetically.

"Whoever dies for his country," Morandi pronounced instead, proverbially, "dies by being killed."

Almost as a confirmation, an irregularly short Polish volley brushed over our heads and exploded only thirty steps from us in the middle of the corn. Some screams came out of the field: two paratroopers had been hit, one of them, we learned shortly after, very seriously.

Taking our leave from Favretto and waiting for orders, Canèr, Freddi, and I settled ourselves on the ground under a hedge, in good position to observe what we could of the battle.

All of the steep slope in front of and around Filottrano was being systematically raked by Italian and Polish fire; the air was a constant rumble of explosions. Occasionally a few shells leaped outside of the pandemonium of smoke clouds with a whirling tail of fine smoke that looked like a game of fireworks and, drawing a parabola, fell back down. Slowly the shooting began to focus on the town's points of access. The Germans continued to react with heavy fire. They hit the valley and our ridge a little everywhere.

Then the paratroopers sprang into attack: the submachine guns began to howl agonizingly. The Germans responded, their machine guns sounding shorter and quicker: our Breda machine guns, with their neurotic shelling and different howl, blended with their overwhelming and compact Spandaus or MG4s, while hand grenades punctuated all the uproar. At times, we heard screaming: "Nembo . . . Nembo . . ." a sign that somewhere paratroopers were attacking with bayonets.

We thought that the enemy soldiers weren't numerous, and in fact—as we would learn weeks later—they were few, only two battalions. They were firmly positioned, however, like a fortress, inside and around the town, with the order to resist and protect Ancona at any cost. Meanwhile, camps, trees, everything slowly became flooded with sunlight; it was painful to look at the beauty of the branches hanging in front of our eyes and trembling in the air full of explosions.

Around noon, I was sent for by Colonel Commander Giaccone, who had followed the battle from another area on our ridge. He ordered us to lay down a few short telephone lines and to dig a pit for his observation area near the observation pit of the division's command. Two other generals of the *Corpo di Liberazione* were there, along with Paratrooper General Morigi—commander of the Nembo—a Polish liaison lieutenant colonel, and some superior officers of General Staff.

Thus, I was able to follow closely the direction of a battle and observe how badly it looked in the end, as actual events coordinated only meagerly with predetermined strategy. I remembered Tolstoy: "If I didn't see with my very own eyes how the Germans fight the war," I thought, "I too would reach his mistaken conclusion: that everything in war, and maybe not only in war, is due to chance. Not after having seen the Germans though . . ." But it wasn't the time for reflection.

The paratroopers pressed on toward Filottrano. The artillery, especially ours, did its best now to open the road for them, hitting the entrances to the town and the first houses. Occasionally we could see roofing tiles and pieces of beams or frames fly up in the air.

In the early afternoon, a few of our units entered the town and fought fiercely between the houses that the artillery continued to hit. They had several dead, and killed several; they also took many prisoners.

By the time the leading units retreated—at times, I learned, even in a disorderly manner—victory seemed close.

As soon as such news reached General Morigi he began screaming and jumping like a crazy man. Romagnese, with eyes dark as nails, crew-cut hair, slim and solid, without hips (physically he couldn't have been any more Romagnese than he was), he yelled in the telephone to attack again, he didn't want to listen to reason; they used to say that he was a real paratroopers' commander, full of courage, not a strategist suited to lead battles. Those who were there with the highest ranks tried to pacify him, showing a calm that seemed almost excessive; the commanders from the units that had stayed behind along the roads of the Marches were less affected by the events.

But why were the paratroopers retreating after having finally reached their objectives?

There were rumors that the Germans had counterattacked with tanks (actually they had armored self-propelled cannons) and that our men, who had had to leave behind their anti-tank guns, would not have been able to contain them. However it was, the town was lost; one battalion, however, the Fifteenth, refused to retreat and shut itself off in a large apartment house, where it remained surrounded.

Polish Sherman tanks were called, and arrived only in late afternoon: one or two, very exposed to the enemy, were blown up by long German 75 anti-tank guns that fired with a sort of howl well known to me.

Now the superior officers of the command assumed self-important demeanors, as though they were each conducting everything, and no longer approved of the news that came from the action. Arguments developed between them; I heard some of them toss resounding orders over the telephone, their only goal obviously to blame others. In a way, since things were no longer going well, none of those commanders believed that until now they actually had had anything to do with the battle, seeing that they hadn't managed it alone: our individualism is that exaggerated. On the other hand, they hadn't had much to do with anything.

Among the wild orders, I was greatly amused by one given to Antonio Castelli, ready with two 75 guns on the anti-tank line: he was ordered to "exit and attack the Tiger tanks." Imagining Castelli's confusion at that boastful order, Canèr and I secretly giggled.

Once again the exhausted paratroopers closed in below the town. Would they attack again?

They didn't attack.

Night fell, and with it so did some calm. I heard General Morigi on the telephone refuse the offer, which was being made from very distant rear zones, for bomber formations to level the town to the ground. Becoming angry, he brought to their attention that our civilians were in the cellars.

I heard the general commanding artillery affirm that the Italian artillery had fired five thousands shots that day.

It had been, up to that point, the hardest day in the history of our division.

11

WITH THE COMING OF darkness, the Second Group lined up behind our ridge, and we reentered it.

The next day, July 9, Sunday, I woke up when the sun had already risen. There was not one shot; a great calm reigned, and no one seemed to pay attention to the suspended battle.

Don Romano, the regiment's chaplain, came over to celebrate mass. The entire group attended, with units organized in a field of stubble on the same ridge defiladed from the valley of the battle and the view of Filottrano. The sun was bright and the sky a beautiful blue; everything was in vivid colors.

The robust chaplain performed the signs of sacrifice in front of the field's altar, even more massive due to its creased gold paraments, which made it shake every time that he brushed against it; then, as usual, his orderly's ready hand stopped it. On the altar were a few stiff linens and two candles with permanently horizontal flames from the wind. As always, those of us present felt peace in the incommensurable size of what was being performed in that stubble field between earth and sky, and in the simplicity of the place, and in those four pieces of linen and that poor chalice. It was as though these material things were suited to contain the immaterial Presence. We too felt like we were vessels of God, in spite of our troubles, the viscid sins of the flesh, the blasphemies and idiocies that sometimes came out of our mouths. For the One who had given us the right, we could have moved the levers that lead beyond the almost unimaginable abyss of all things and of power: millions of light years, and the sum of the forces of the universe. Everything that morning, inside and outside of us, was like all field masses.

However, it was our chaplain's last mass. By the end of the day he would be murdered. He could not have known it, and no one realized to what extent he was similar to Christ who was sacrificed on the altar in his hands;

he was similar to the unconscious lamb about to be sacrificed, meek and draped in gold.

*

As soon as the assembly was dispersed, word spread that the *Tricolore* waved on Filottrano.[2]

In groups, we went where the general command had been located the previous day; in the pits only a few sleepy telephone operators now remained, wrapped up in their coats. In order to get there, we had to cross through the widespread smell of decomposing flesh.

The *Tricolore* waved indeed from the town's highest point, a reservoir of reinforced cement for drinking water. The Germans had evacuated during the night, uncertain that they would be able to sustain another attack.

While we talked about it, we heard some distant guns, followed by whistles, then explosions: German shells were arriving again. Isolated at first, they became more frequent within a short time, and the town was again under siege. Once again clouds of smoke rose from the roofs or, when the shells struck closer inside, they slowly came out from all the cracks between the roofing tiles. The air was once again filled with explosions.

*

During midmorning my platoon received the order from the regiment's command to immediately go with the truck to Tornazzano, a suburb east of Filottrano; there we would be given instructions from the colonel commander for setting up an observation post. A glance at the map, and away we went on the roaring Fiat 626 along a cart road bordered by hedges and oaks that went almost all the way up our ridge.

Occasionally, we passed the strong smell of decomposing flesh. There two, no, three of our trucks were overturned by the side of the cart road, one next to the other, their wheels up in the air: those wheel sets seemed more solid and powerful than one had expected. Carcasses of large white cows near a farm, probably dragged out of stalls, were swollen as though they would blow up, their legs pointed up in the air.

We took the wrong road, then found the right one again. When we turned onto the main road, which led to Filottrano from the east, we could see it was scattered with small square holes, very recent, less than a hand deep and not much wider. A mine had been extracted from each hole; the

2. The Italian tricolor flag.

164

mines, all of the wooden anti-tank type, now lay piled here and there in a precise manner on the side of the road. The magnetic mine detectors must have located them only with difficulty, by the small metal nails that bound them. It was possible that a few hadn't been located, since the white powder of the road was undoubtedly scattered with splinters. Therefore, we proceeded with increasing caution.

We reached the first group of houses, all lined up on the northern side of the road, very decimated. Polish paratroopers and soldiers from the Kressowa Division (their arm badges showed a mermaid with a brandished sword) were spread out among the ruins. There in front of us, at a short distance by now, German shells continued exploding with tall clouds of smoke around and above Filottrano.

The fifteen men of the patrol were silent. They insisted on looking at the mine holes from the slow-moving truck. Occasionally, I felt their eyes pointed at the back of my neck through the rear window of the cabin. The driver, Sabatini, almost a boy, held his neck stiffly and followed my instructions carefully: "Turn a little to the left . . . There. Now to the right. Slowly . . . Move to the middle. That's it." He gave me several furtive looks.

"Don't worry," I said to him cockily. "I've fought enough war to know what to do."

"I know," he answered. "We all trust you." Then: "Did other trucks come by before ours?"

"I think so." But perhaps the few trail marks in the dust were from a jeep.

A jeep was now coming from the opposite direction, and it intersected us. It was driven by a noncommissioned officer of the regiment's command. On the back seat was a tiny old woman, hunchbacked, all smeared in blood. "I never thought that a person could look so much like a wounded bird," Sabatini said, expressing my thoughts exactly. She panted and held her small face turned up; she tried to look around.

Polish squads were positioned in another group of houses, with a few Bren submachine guns at the shattered windows on the north side, toward the enemy. The bizarre British equipment, all meticulous pockets and straps, hindered these soldiers and made them look like heavy horses resigned to harnesses.

On this stretch of road many mines had been left near their holes: the mine removal must have been done in a hurry. At the entrance of Tornazzano, I decided to stop the truck in an appropriate spot, in the shelter of a house, and to proceed on foot.

We went into the suburb in single file. We didn't find any orders waiting for us; the small place, completely destroyed, was nearly deserted. I left two men there in case the orders arrived late, and we moved forward with good speed.

*

Someone called out to us from an odd weapon pit: "Hey, platoon. Hey!"

We looked more closely and recognized two 75 cannons, undoubtedly Castelli's "assault guns"; they were placed in some kind of devastated hen-house.

"I have an order to give to you," the sergeant major who had called us announced as he came out. His name was Dioli; he was a farmer, even bigger and tougher than Canèr. The artillery's bandoleer cut across his chest from his left shoulder to his right hip, almost in a horizontal fashion; it looked like one of his little brother's garments that he had put on by mistake. He reached us on the road and, after having given me the salute, spelled out: "The colonel has told me to give to you the order to enter Filottrano with the truck. You will find instructions there."

"Good."

"He said," he repeated, "that you must enter Filottrano with the truck."

"I understand, thank you."

"Good fellow," Castelli exclaimed, at this turn coming out from the henhouse. His uniform, including his shirt with that unbearable collar in the latest trend, was in good order as always; his helmet covered his receding hairline. "Your truck must give the regiment the honor of being the first car to enter the town. The disputed town," he emphasized.

"Right. But tell me something: how many Tigers did you catch?"

"What Tigers? Ah . . . How do you know about that order?"

"I heard it being given."

"For heaven's sake!" His face darkened as usual. "Think if one of those inexperienced guys had been there instead of me . . ."

"Do you know that we enjoyed hearing that order?"

"Ah, yes? Well, now I'm going to enjoy myself. Since you don't have Susanna the goose to help save you from the mines."

"What goose? Right. By the way, I don't see her. Where is she?" (Susanna the goose was the assault division's good-luck charm: she was said to be gifted with spell-casting virtues and, in addition, an extraordinary intelligence, not only for a goose.)

"She's safe in a hideout," Sergeant Major Dioli responded very seriously, instead of Castelli.

"If a goose dies," Morandi intervened, "it isn't like a soldier that the government can replace right away by simply sending a postcard. Geese are expensive." He rubbed his thumb and index finger together.

We all smiled. "How much talk," I thought meanwhile, "for a battle that's already over! But no, it's because sometimes a little humor can help." I stretched my hand out to Castelli. "Bye, nonbeliever with a helmet," I said in farewell.

"Bye, priestly man," he answered, "I'm going back to the hen-house, seeing that the hideout is for the goose."

*

We returned to the truck, climbed back up, and continued to advance cautiously. Then, angrily. The road, still heading east-west, traveled a crest that after Tornazzano had become similar to a viaduct or a rampart. To our left was the basin where the battle had unfolded; to our right, toward the north, the terrain descended and later gradually ascended again in the distance, thus forming another wide and bluish basin, this one completely in the enemy's hands. He undoubtedly observed us from his side, the houses having become fewer, but unless he resorted to anti-tank guns, it would have been difficult for him to hit us while we were moving. Indeed, some mortar shells fell nearby without our concern: the mines worried us enough.

We saw these abandoned everywhere. I judged that they had been removed from their holes in an increasing rush; maybe the minesweepers had been pressured by enemy fire. We were almost in Filottrano when I decided that we couldn't sensibly proceed farther on a road in such conditions. I resolved to stop the truck, then I made it go down slowly to the left, in the yard of a colonial house defiladed from the rampart.

"Look over here," Canèr called me.

A German Spandau was positioned in a weapon pit dug on the edge of the threshing-floor, where the machine-gunner sat motionless. Only his head leaned a little bit forward, covered with his heavy helmet.

Infrequent paratroopers traveled cautiously up and down the quiet road of the rampart. Shell volleys insisted now on hitting more spots, including behind us.

I began searching, with only Freddi and Morandi, for Colonel Giaccone. After circling around a small square adorned with flower beds at the en-

167

trance of the town, which enemy fire attacked furiously, we entered among the houses. Filottrano was deserted and in ruins.

We passed through several empty streets, one after the other, while German fire now showed signs of becoming unsteady once again; occasionally, we stopped and called out loud for the colonel. No one answered. Finally, we went back.

"Did you notice?" Freddi noted, stopping and indicating the white powder that covered the road. "Here there aren't any tire tracks. So no car has come all the way here."

"Indeed." I thought it over. "So the few tracks stop at the small square that we weren't able to cross, at the town's entrance . . . Maybe we'll find the colonel there."

We didn't find him in the square, but we found his car, hit and abandoned, near a gigantic, half-burnt Polish Sherman and a paratroopers' jeep shattered by a mine.

"Here are the first cars that entered the town, the disputed town," I said to my two companions, pointing at them. "See the nice results! But we've got to admit that the colonel didn't limit himself to getting others—in this case us—into trouble: he got into it himself first." But where was he now? And was he alive? Unharmed?

12

HE WAS ALIVE and unharmed. A captain of the regiment's command (a Sardinian—a taciturn race) who by order of the colonel was looking for us in that deserted place told us, "A mortar shell made a direct hit on the Millecento.[3] Everyone wounded, except him."

"He's right to consider himself a lucky man," I observed. "But it's nice to run into you: finally a human being. This looked like the earth after the flood."

"Come to the colonel. He's waiting for you."

The colonel, standing underneath a small canopy near the square, didn't seem shaken by what had happened to him. On the contrary, he had a shadow of irony in his eye, like in Puglia when he had had to fight against all those absurd bureaucratic obstacles in order to form the regiment. It was as though he was now mocking, in the same manner, the mortar shells and the obstacles arisen from fate.

He approved with sharp gravity (was he also laughing at this?) my modification of his order to enter the town with the truck. Then he gave me instructions to set up an observation post in a house on the northern margins of Filottrano. He made the same captain, who was at that moment his dispatch—the others had been lost—take us to the selected house.

Enemy fire had ceased almost completely. We walked at a good pace along the deserted streets, among the tall houses. When we arrived at the reinforced cement water reservoir, where the flag waved, a few civilians appeared at the door of its cellar: they were the first that we met.

"Hurray for our liberators! You've saved us from death," a woman exclaimed, unable to shout within the silence. The other peasants nodded.

---

3. A Millecento was a small car built by the Italian car maker Fiat.

"We would have liked to save you with less damage," said the taciturn captain, letting out a few words and stopping in an instant. The civilians nodded at this too. "What more could you have done, our poor sons?" women's voices murmured. "You've been very good."

"Let's hope that we're able to force them farther away soon," Lance Corporal Freddi said kindly, while we began walking again, "so that you can finally have some peace."

Farther away: Freddi said it well. But farther away were other women and children and civilians. There was no respite if one thought of having to fight and fight again, to transfer the war always farther away. The Germans were right to do all they could to keep it outside of their borders . . .

The captain indicated the house selected for the observation post. I put Freddi and Morandi to work: "Begin by making an opening in this wall."

"There aren't enough walls with holes in this town," Morandi explained to Freddi. "You understand? We have to make a hole in another one."

*

I returned to the truck and divided the platoon into two squads of six men each. One of them, preceded by Sergeant Canèr with an enormous roll of cable on his shoulders, began immediately laying down the telephone line backwards across the countryside toward the group's telephone exchange. The other squad followed me in single file toward the observation post under construction.

The German artillery and mortars had begun their fire once again. The firing soon became more intense than it had been that morning. The small square of flower beds and torn cars came under attack from continuous volleys and was impassable once again: we outflanked it a second time, walking again on the southern slope, in the middle of vegetable gardens, defiladed from sight but not from enemy fire. The terrain appeared to be scattered with blackish holes made by shells. Here and there were corpses among the vegetables and crushed corn, both ours and Germans. The stench was strong. We recovered some submachine guns by removing them from the dead.

Animals now free from their yards moved through the tufts of giant dust-covered reeds on the edges of vegetable gardens, or went from one fence to another through broken segments. Dead ones also lay on the ground, especially rabbits, swollen, disgusting.

The enemy volleys didn't cease. A few fell even on our slope: we bent over quickly or knelt down; crouched and deafened by the rumble, we watched the clouds of smoke open violently, each time unexpectedly.

Still proceeding along the slope, we passed next to rabbit cages where the animals, dazed by fear and hunger, looked at us with strangely glossy eyes. After several steps we went back to free them, so that they could escape wherever they could. An unnatural, rhythmic gasp drew me to a stall where a wounded cow lay on the hay since who knows when, contorted and fearfully alone in her agony; I raised my submachine gun and gave her reprieve with one shot to the head.

We once again entered among the houses. All the German fire also moved above the town, as though it was pursuing us.

We went ahead along paved streets, among the tall, beautiful buildings with the protruding cornices of Central Italy; with each explosion, the glass remaining on countless windows shook with a dull sound. Occasionally a window rumbled down the wall of a building. Now and then, shells exploded on the roofs of the houses near us; then a deluge of roofing tiles and debris would rain down from the cornices, shattering and bouncing on the street, while we pressed ourselves into a corner between the wall and the pavement.

We were beginning to feel fatigued. We stopped for a few minutes in a cellar with strong vaults that was packed with civilians. Standing among folded mattresses and piles of household objects, they offered us food, wine; they raced to talk to us.

A poor man, dazed and perspiring, turned to me, and forcing a smile, said, "By now, it's about to end." Then his eyes suddenly filled with tears: "I lost two sons this week, two sons." He raised a hand in front of my face, two fingers outstretched.

After passing piles of ruins that obstructed the road, we arrived at the house of the observation post. To enter it we had to climb over one last pile two or three meters high; it was half of a caved-in house, and the smell of decomposing flesh was coming from there too. Freddi and Morandi had made an opening in the wall and had found themselves in a walled-in room where, maybe to save it from German requisitions (or from ours?) a car in excellent condition had been hidden. From the northern side of the house, the large, bluish basin of land in enemy hands stretched into the distance; it was here that we would put the observation aperture, but only after it grew dark. While waiting, I started a temporary observation post nearby in an adjoining house.

The men had split up the work: while some saw to widening the already open breach with pickaxes, others had gone outside to stretch the piece of telephone line across town and up to the truck.

I wasn't able to see any traces of the enemy's presence through the binoculars; even their guns, which continued to fire, must have been located in areas well defiladed, because I couldn't see a single smoke cloud. I decided to suspend the observation for a while (after all, until the telephone line began functioning, we wouldn't be able to direct return fire) in order to make contact with the command of the Fourteenth Battalion, the only paratroopers' command present in Filottrano. There, I was informed that only a few companies were lined up in front of the town: most of the division had been withdrawn to its starting position, outside of enemy shelling range.

Returning to the observation post, I found that while the others continued to keep busy, Morandi was sleeping stretched out on the floor, his white and red mountaineer face redder than usual, and his hair, so light it seemed white, glued to his head.

I shook him. He mumbled about German grenades that he would have liked to eat; he was dead drunk. "It was the civilians' wine," Lance Corporal Freddi explained to me, with a pickax in his hands, turning his face— sweaty and dirty with dust—in my direction.

Later, this episode would remain impressed in Morandi's mind more than any other he had lived through during the war. He would talk about it several times, with satisfaction: "I said 'I want to eat 149–grenades,' huh? I must have been so drunk!"

A wall unexpectedly collapsed near the temporary observation post; we had to evacuate and substitute another one. Even the line, once connected with the one stretched out by Canèr all the way to the group's telephone exchange, was interrupted by splinters several times, which forced us to go outside to make repairs.

*

When at night, after a long interruption, the telephone line began working again, we received bad news. The major, as always doing something he wasn't supposed to, had personally set out to bring us our rations. Along the rampart, however, his halftrack had been hit by a shell: three men, among them Second Lieutenant Provera, had been wounded. Now the major, turning back hastily, notified us through the operator that we wouldn't receive rations.

Although we had some dry provisions available and were exhausted, we decided not to give up on warm rations. Especially, I must also admit, we wanted to show the major that bringing us provisions wasn't such a difficult enterprise. (I still hadn't forgotten his insults at Villa Consalvi: that's why I couldn't keep myself from making fun of him . . . I was at university age, sure, but now, in the senseless skirmish that he had started, the fault was no longer one-sided . . .) Sergeant Canèr—he too at university age—left, staggering with exhaustion, to go get the rations: out of necessity, he used the truck, regardless of the terrible danger from mines.

The observation post designated by the colonel was ready. It became necessary to go out again several times to repair the telephone line, which had once again been cut by enemy fire.

Finally, we arranged our pallets in a room on the ground floor, the one most protected, where I had carried Morandi during the day, along with the most valuable observation tools. I placed a sentry outside the door.

In the dark, seated on our pallets, tired and idle, we ate the rations brought back by Canèr.

13

THE ENEMY VOLLEYS, which had succeeded one another in an irregular way throughout the day, became denser with the night; their explosions and the collapse of roof tiles and stones seemed even louder in the dark. The mournful howl of an abandoned dog chained in a nearby yard began following the loudest explosions. The stench of decomposition now came up to our window from the landslide of debris.

The last men returned from working along the telephone line. After eating, we all lay down to sleep on the pallets.

Shortly after, the telephone rang. The major had had time to think it over and ordered me to "immediately" lay down the new telephone line from the observatory to the hospital of Filottrano. "Immediately, do you understand? Until now, you've worked for the regiment; now it's time that you worked for the group."

Dazed as I was, regardless of that "immediately" and his agitated voice, I asked him for a couple of hours of rest. "Before dawn the line will be ready just the same."

He answered me with a series of insults, extended vehemently to my soldiers too, "bastards" like me; he repeated the order, then broke off communication.

I felt everyone's eyes turn toward me in the dark. I wasn't able to find any irony, to turn the insults into a joke. "Did you hear?" I said, and I cursed with anger.

"Yes, we heard," Sabatini, the driver, answered.

"He called us a bunch of bastards," Canèr specified softly.

"That's right," I said, and cursed again. "Those three of you less tired get ready to come out with me."

The room filled with curses and blasphemies. The shelling outside didn't seem like much compared to the rage that was building inside us.

"Don't be angry, lieutenant." I heard the patient voice of Lance Corporal Freddi, who was already sitting on his pallet, putting on his shoes. "The major's nerves aren't sound, so he isn't responsible for what he says."

"Sound nerves?" the Tuscan Sabatini exclaimed. "He's a ____ actually a ____." Many others insulted him, and cursed again; it seemed like it was good for us. One of them said, "We're animals. We, who could have gone to a port with the 'workers,' or deserted, and instead we came here to risk our lives under a ____ like him. Once already they've brought this army to hell."

"Must we do everything?" bitterly exclaimed one of the men who remained lying down. "What are the others in the unit's command doing?"

"I think we're better off than them, with the major in their face day and night," Freddi let out, always with his patient voice.

But the other man, maybe angry for not having gotten up, started insulting the major again alone. "Well, that's enough," I said wearily. The place fell back silent.

We headed toward the exit with a few rolls of telephone line and instruments slung over our shoulders. Morandi was now on sentry duty; he was in the dark space of the door, his helmet on his head, his shoulders larger in his coat, looking like an owl in his garret. "You sobered up, huh, you animal?" I greeted him. "Move aside."

He smiled, pleased. "Almost sober, lieutenant" (he was a mountaineer, as we know, and, whenever he was called to drink, he felt in some way united with mountain people). Some explosions loudly covered his voice. I noticed that swarms of German tracer bullets were being fired from the countryside not far from the town and, after passing above our house, became lost with furious speed in the sky.

We waited a little while for the Abruzzese recruit Pasquali, who had been sent to the shelters to look for a civilian to show us the shortest way to the hospital. Then, fragments of glass and debris crunched under the soles of our boots. Meter by meter the telephone wire unwound along the deserted roads and among the ruins. One of the three soldiers staggered. The civilian went to take his roll of wire and guided us, stooped under it.

The work was completed in a couple of hours, and we returned to our observation post.

*

Before we fell asleep, the phone rang again. "Line Tester," the uncertain voice of the operator announced.

"Piece of ____," briefly responded the soldier on duty, in charge of the telephone, the red-headed Scirea, from my mother's town.

"I have news for the lieutenant."

"News for you," Scirea then said, gropingly passing me the receiver.

This was the news: a half hour earlier, in the small square, a truck from the regiment's command had blown up on a mine. "Both the chaplain and Lieutenant Bruschi of radio were wounded very gravely: they have both lost a leg at the groin. The others who were in the truck were unharmed." I immediately thought about our truck, which had previously crossed the square, with Canèr and the driver Sabatini, along the only road that could be traveled, passing maybe within a few centimeters of the mine. And without any need for it!

The German fire increased, still directed on the houses, and began to pound like it had during the battle. We should be grateful, I told myself, if Don Romano only lost his leg.

The following day, he and the other wounded man still spoke—for a short time—in a normal manner, from their respective hospital beds. "Priest," Bruschi, a Romagnese, said, "you led me miserably." And then, to defend himself: "Luckily I brought you. Don't you understand? We'll take each other's arms, and together we'll still have two legs. I've saved you half the trouble of walking."

They both died before nightfall.

Dead, poor chaplain of Christ, with his mother waiting for him in the countryside of Mantova, beating the endless hours on rosary beads. He was done fighting in that obstinate way of his, one hand in the hand of God, against others and against his own youth. The Mantuan women would no longer torment him at the confessional because he was handsome and strong: he would no longer complain of it with us, his friends; things that a priest doesn't discuss easily, not even at the front.

*

The German fire seemed to focus on our quarters. The volleys opened with a crash that permeated everything; walls, wood, windows shook continuously. Each living thing felt the need to sink into the earth. Suddenly, our house jumped as though a powerful hand had seized and shaken it with force; the sound of breathing continued to be heard among us.

The house's foundations shook a second time.

"What could it have been?" someone muttered.

"The attic exploded," another answered, grumbling. Most kept quiet or continued to sleep.

Morandi came from outside, gropingly searching for my pallet. "Lieutenant."

"What is it?"

"You told me to come wake you if the firing point of the German tracer bullets were to move closer. It seems like now it's closer."

I went out with him. I felt my aching body as something distinctly separated from me and my will; it took longer for it to obey than usual, and I followed, as though from a distance, its individual movements. The German tracer bullets seemed to be firing from the field just below the town, and rose almost perpendicularly in the sky, like very fast stars. Maybe some enemy patrol had come forward in reconnaissance? The howl, clearly recognizable, of our Breda 30 machine guns seemed to have become nervous.

"Has the truck been hit?"

"No. Only some debris on the tarpaulin."

"Where did the two explosions that made the house shake come from?"

"I don't know."

Since the firing around us continued furiously, I made all the men wake up. In the darkness, continuously torn by the glare of explosions, I pushed them inside a nearby vaulted cellar (which at least in theory would be better able to withstand the eventual landslide of walls). Before I entered myself, I paid a visit to the command of the paratroopers' Fourteenth Battalion, to see if there was any news from the companies on the line. No news. I returned quickly. The smell of decomposing flesh from the landslide was more defined in the cool of the night; it hit me in the face like a sheet hung in the wind.

The explosions continued all around us, and the dog now howled non-stop, as though he had gone mad, and tried continuously to tear loose from his chain. "Let's end it with this dog," a bewildered soldier said, standing like everyone else in the damp cellar. "Let's shoot him."

"Let him be," another answered, equally bewildered. "Maybe he hasn't eaten in days, poor animal, him too."

The driver Sabatini added with his Tuscan accent, "Maybe it's not hunger, but the smell of the dead that makes him like this. Maybe his owner is rotting under that landslide . . . It's as though the dead don't exist for us, but dogs can sense it." The incessant howling rose in the night, mixing with the enraged clinking of the chain; in those sounds, it seemed like nature was re-belling against the actions of men, attempting to free itself from us.

The German fire finally moved above the center of town. We went back to lying on our pallets and fell asleep.

*

At the first signs of light, the sentinel on duty woke me up. I visited im-mediately the premises of the observation post: it was a collection of ruins, undoubtedly resulting from the two blows that violently shook the house. We began working and quickly prepared a new observation post—the fourth.

Shortly after, a platoon of the regiment's command, announced by tele-phone, came to take it over. It was under the tall Second Lieutenant Lainati, a Milanese (and he was mindful of it in each moment) who, arriving at the head of his short column, greeted me with, "Hi, *milanés ariùs* (Milanese country-folk)."

"Hi, *meneghìn centpéé* (centipede, or complicated man)," I complied.

"So, all the work we did has been for someone else . . ." grumbled the artilleryman, Bertolini.

I agreed, knitting my brows: "Indeed."

But Lainati and his men would have to evacuate the next day, because of the stench coming from the landslide.

14

WE HEADED IN single file toward the hospital, the tired men loaded with equipment, while in my mind I sifted the new burning insults received from the major.

It was almost dawn, and there was some calm. The youngest of the platoon, the Abruzzese recruit Pasquali, kidded around while walking bent under his load; all he needed to make him happy was for the sun to rise. Since no one backed him up, he occasionally alternated his banter with some bits of song:

> 'My mamma used to tell me
> don't look at blondes,
> because they're all vagabonds,
> vagabonds with love.'

Behind Pasquali trekked Artilleryman B., as always the last in line, as always his beret slanted, "Our assigned drunk," as Canèr defined him.

Canèr, in a bad mood, moaned at my shoulder, "Soon, we'll see the major's face again . . . Last night, he made a frightful scene with my brother, only because he had asked to replace me along the telephone line."

"We're well aware what these superior officers, these God Almighties, are worth," I exclaimed, generalizing angrily. "We all see in what kind of situation they've put us in . . . But enough!" I shook my head and resentfully interrupted my sentence.

Pasquali began another piece of song:

> 'My mamma used to tell me
> don't look at brunettes,
> because they're all traitors,
> traitors of love .'

179

"Brunettes are traitors, and majors are traitors," the orderly Morandi delivered, who followed Canèr in line.

All of us snorted with laughter.

The cliff of the hospital was also dominated by the enemy-occupied countryside to the north, now spotted with long shadows from the barely risen sun.

There he was, the major, near a straw stack, looking grim, seated behind a goniometer, with one of his usual sharp pencils pointed at the map on his knees. Several soldiers of the command unit were there also. Second Lieutenant Canèr, the sergeant's brother, greeted us with a vexed head nod: the previous night, I would learn later, he too had received the brunt of the major's scolding.

Reaching them, we came to a halt. On the inside ground floor of the nearby hospital, whose façade was riddled with shrapnel, we caught a glimpse of a line of wounded people on the floor and nuns bustling around them, like doves full of love beneath their white wimples.

"Once you leave the platoon's men and unnecessary equipment," the major's order immediately reached me by means of a clerk, "three radiotelegraphists will join you, reach Villa Centofinestre and the Sixteenth Battalion that's about to begin the advance. Carry it out, immediately."

*

Almost without speaking, I cut my line of men in half and, followed by six or seven and by the three radiotelegraphists (who were already waiting there with an RF2 portable station), started up toward the Villa Centofinestre, located beyond Tornazzano on top of the ridge where we had followed the battle two days earlier.

Now in the small square of mangled cars was also the regiment's command truck in which, during the course of the night, the chaplain and Bruschi had been mortally wounded; the truck seemed to be kneeling on the crater opened by the explosion.

Leaving the town behind, we traveled again the whole road of the rampart, still proceeding in single file. The square holes and mosaic of disposed mines were beginning to fill up with a thick cloud of dust. After Tornazzano, we entered a park among well-tended hedges until we arrived at the large villa with a peacefully colored front. The façade seemed to suggest, "In the time when I was built, the passage of man on earth wasn't an out-of-breath race, like yours today."

The Sixteenth Battalion was by no means on location; fortunately, there were some soldiers from the First Group, from whom we learned that the battalion was to the south of the town, in the valley where the battle had been fought.

We crossed the fields, still in single file, wandering beneath the rising sun in our search. Like the villa's park, the fields also appeared devastated by shells; in several spots hedges were uprooted, and trees had fallen or had wounded trunks or hanging branches with limp leaves.

Once in a while, we also recognized bloodstains encrusted in the earth, from which swarms of flies rose buzzing, only to immediately plunge back with a strange violence. In the grass were some abandoned objects, sometimes bloody rags.

After having walked for a couple of hours, we advanced ever more slowly. The men frequently exchanged the two heavy radio boxes. However, several proceeded with such slowness that we had to stop to wait for them. This was, I told myself, what my light-hearted response to insults and offenses was leading to: in essence, my senseless skirmish with the dangerous Sicilian major . . . I hadn't been the one to start it, but since I was part of it, couldn't I devise a way to get out of it? I didn't see a way.

We reached the battalion just as it was about to begin its march. Although Paratrooper Major Pellagatta had immediately informed me that our unreliable radio would be the only means of communication with the command's superiors, the platoon followed the battalion, gradually losing ground; those who carried the radio boxes on their shoulders were walking at a snail's pace, so that I turned around continuously to look for their drawn faces under their helmets. Soon we would no longer have been able to continue . . .

But, quite unexpectedly, for a reason that we couldn't grasp, the battalion halted for one, two, actually three hours. It was our salvation, to throw ourselves down on a worn-out field, some with our foreheads against the ground. To rest. To eat. Next to us, the paratroopers too were stocking up on rest.

When around one o'clock we felt the heat of the sun's rays straight up in the sky, we resumed the march. In a thin, single file the battalion climbed the rampart road that we had traveled several times and, entering a path among the corn, dropped into the green valley occupied by the enemy.

*

We proceeded in silence.

Some of the whistling volleys passed above us; the projectiles broke with dull detonations beyond the rampart, toward Centofinestre.

We knew that the Fourteenth Battalion was advancing to our right, parallel to us, but it kept itself about a kilometer away and we couldn't see it. We knew nothing else, and the sense of the unknown kept us hanging on.

The scouting platoon oversaw the head and the right of our long, winding column by keeping itself a little ahead on that side. Once in a while, we saw some helmets or a submachine gun barrel in that direction sparkle in the green.

Here we were, then, once again engaged in tracking down the enemies in order to destroy them; in the same manner, they committed themselves, one by one, to destroy us, or at least to harm us as much as possible . . . Where were those who protected us positioned right now? I wondered, just like my companions. And mostly I wondered whether there would be fighting before nighttime.

Yes, there was fighting. It was the Fourteenth Battalion's turn: some paratroopers were killed, but by far the greatest casualties were on the enemy's side. One of their formations was wiped out. As a matter of fact, the battle went very well: it took place according to the paratroopers' dispositions, that is, close up, so that some men were almost cut in half from the volleys of the Italian submachine guns.

If we had known this at the beginning of the march, we should have been pleased since, reasonably, things couldn't have gone better than they did . . . Pleased? Alas, no, not at all, just as we weren't at the conclusion of events. We didn't want the war; indeed, we killed against our will, only because we were compelled to. Did the others, the Germans, want the war? No, not even the Germans wanted it: had I not seen them on the night of the armistice throw their berets up in the air because they had thought it to be over? They had been enthusiastic and happy, in spite of their cold disposition, no less so than Italian soldiers. Maybe their generals wanted the war? In my opinion, not even their generals wanted it (in fact, we would learn with certainty years later that most of the German officers of their General Staff had even conspired to keep the war from beginning).

But we men didn't want many other things: for instance, to jump from the top floors of our houses, or to open big mountain dikes with mines. And obviously, we didn't do, nor would we ever do, these senseless things. Why did we fight in a war then? I mean, what was it that compelled men who wouldn't jump from top-floor windows or blow up dikes down this senseless road, that made them fight in war one against the other?

"Certainly it is not a supernatural intervention, nor a miracle," I told myself as I walked. "One can't really think that God performs absurd miracles . . . What was it that compelled us? Not God, nor things (how could animals or plants or minerals compel us to such a choice?). If it isn't someone or something outside of us, we are the only ones remaining: it is we, therefore, who are compelled. Or better yet, it is something that we bring into existence freely, without constraints, which at some point forces us to act in this way, even if our will is against it. What?"

We are only completely free in our moral order, that is, truly free (I had experienced this once and for all in Puglia, when my only freedom had been to disapprove of what I was forced to do against my will).[4] Therefore, I thought, it is something that we produce and that gradually builds in the moral order, which at a certain point moves like an avalanche and, regardless of our efforts to the contrary, drags us along. The war, then, comes from a break in the balance of moral order. It is the product of human immorality, nothing more nor less.

"But men will always commit misdeeds," I didn't fail to point out. "Then, will they always slaughter one another and the dreadful modern wars repeat themselves again and again?"

"Look," said a paratrooper second lieutenant who was walking in front of me, interrupting my thoughts; he pointed to some recent weapon pits. "We arrived in the middle of them without noticing."

"It seems like some Spandaus were here," I said. "I have the feeling that they just moved them out."

"One can camouflage himself well in this type of terrain," the second lieutenant said, indicating with his hand the crest darkened by the sun.

We walked for several hours in the luxuriant countryside, worked with care, where birds sang softly. Occasionally we came to a halt, always in silence. Only the patrol's radiotelegraphists, who immediately positioned the RF2, uttered some disconnected sentences, reporting to the division's command the area reached.

A violent thunder of submachine guns unexpectedly exploded about a kilometer to our right, almost immediately mixed with the mowing-down

4. See Part Two, chapter 18.

rumble of German Spandaus. "The Fourteenth fell into it," Major Pellaggatta said, and it was the only comment. We continued to walk: at times, the fire of the opposing automatic arms ceased, then started again, ceased again. More time went by like this.

By now the sun was setting, and the scorching air slowly began to cool off. The radio order of a halt for the night came as we went back up a big grassy crest scattered with Italian 149 grenade holes. There were, I remember, some unexploded ashen grenades that stood out on the blood-stained grass.

The major made the battalion retreat and had it take a position concealed from the enemy's sight, along a country road bordered by trees and hedges that we had just climbed over.

The following day at first light he set it out marching again and lined it up on a series of wooded rises that dominated the Musone River. The Germans were lined up on the rises of the opposing slope and below along the riverbank.

15

IN THE FOLLOWING DAYS, the entire *Corpo di Liberazione* closed in below our line.

The German long-range guns insisted on hitting Filottrano and its surroundings. During one of those firings the only survivor of the First Group's topographical unit, Corporal Major Kribar, was mortally wounded in the park of Centofinestre: a splinter no larger than a corn kernel entered his intestine through his back. The surgery was too late. So not even one man remained alive from Lieutenant Tiberio's topographical squad, made up of Bencini, Boselli and Kribar, that many in Surbo had made fun of for shirking.

The Sixteenth Battalion's command settled on Monte Polesco in a patrician villa surrounded by woods. We unrolled our pallets on the floor of a room with a geometrical pattern assigned to the platoon and stacked our small gear. Against the wall, under a fine window, we lined up our submachine guns with their riddled muffs.

A mournful silence reigned among the civilians in this comfortable place, because as the Germans were leaving they had called the old Count Spada, the owner, to the door and—maybe presuming him to be in the king's favor—had killed him without a word. (According to some, a muddled partisan episode was to blame for that death; the partisans had assaulted a German motorcycle near the villa. However, we didn't encounter any trace of partisans.)

As it was, we found a way to torment ourselves even in this place: Major Pelaformiche ordered me under *arresti* while I conducted fire from a very exposed area, with Sergeant Canèr and Lance Corporal Freddi, on a German battery pointed out to us by a civilian.

This is how it went: unrolling a telephone wire, the three of us had left our lines and ended up on the extreme edge of the wooded hill, in an area where, as if on a balcony, we ruled over the enemy's sector through big holes in the vegetation. After arriving here, we had stretched out on the ground, careful not to make any noise, since the Germans could have been very close. And, in fact, one of them came out in the open there below us, a few dozen meters away, across the small Musone River. No longer a young man, he had his coat unbuttoned and a hand in his pocket. He stopped to chat near a small rustic structure with someone who was hidden from us; we heard the words perfectly, as well as the hateful German accent. My blood began to boil.

Canèr and Freddi eyed me: maybe they too were reminded of the old murdered count. Now, it would have been impossible not to kill this idiot, completely within range, with our first submachine gun shot: it would have been like slaughtering a defenseless animal.

But he wasn't an animal: over there in Germany, there surely must have been some clumsy Lotte or Frida or Erika, wearing a badly cut jacket, whose life depended on his. For an instant, it seemed as though I saw her, with her potatolike face. Maybe at first she would have behaved like the Spartan wife of the fallen, like all other German women. Later, however, an entire life of loneliness would come, children (probably dumb—being his children—but still children) orphaned, or unborn . . .

I didn't lower my eyes from the target. "Take a good look at him," I murmured to my two companions. "You can see close-up what a total nitwit looks like."

They both smiled tiredly; they were terribly tense and ready for action. Those words calmed them down. "Anyway," Lance Corporal Freddi whispered, "at this point, they can't win the war anymore." So, for pity on the unknown Lotte or Frida or Erika with the potatolike face, that man was spared.

With the telephone underneath my chest, I had transmitted very softly the firing specifications: the objective was in a strip of woods a few kilometers from us. But right after the second explosion, Pelaformiche intervened on the line: he had silently listened to my every word and wanted to know based on what criterion I had given the first range variation. He judged it too wide. He wasn't satisfied with my concise and softly spoken explanation; he wanted me to be clearer. He became angry. I became angry. He placed me under *arresti* "for bad technical supervision of fire" and removed me.

Immediately, with my first muttered words, the German nitwit had leaped for cover behind the rustic structure. Canèr and Freddi were tense again, and flattened on the ground, seizing their submachine guns. Canèr cursed softly with rage. I decided not to leave the operation I had begun unfinished, and persisted in recalling the group's command, but Pelaformiche wasn't to be found; the situation could come to a head from one moment to the next.

Fortunately, the southern sergeant major with the prognathic face, commander of the platoon that had been at the Margherita observatory, arrived on his own initiative with five or six paratroopers; he had seen us come out of the lines and had been worried about us. The paratroopers stretched out fanwise on the ground to our side. The red-headed artilleryman Scirea, who seemed to feel in some way obligated to look after my well-being because he was from my mother's town, joined us all by himself. Without saying a word (he always spoke little, as we know), he took his place between me and Freddi. "Who authorized you to come here?" I asked him severely, even if very softly; he said nothing, this time duly.

"There sure are some generous people!" I had to admit.

Shortly after, we were all forced to evacuate in a great hurry, throwing ourselves on the ground every few steps because a German gun, having located us, chased us between the trees with its shells. After each explosion we leaped to our feet, as soon as the whistle of splinters had passed above us.

By this time, it was obvious that the only thing that remained was for me to be thrown out of the Second Group. I had no illusions about it . . .

Paratrooper Major Pellagatta, who had ordered the action, was very irritated because it had been interrupted, and gave a statement to the division's command. But at the time, the division's command, as could be expected, had other things to pay attention to.

*

The *Corpo di Liberazione* remained lined up on those rises for six days; on the seventh, it attacked again, and the battle which took its name from the Musone River unfolded.

But there was nothing left for the platoon to do during that interval of days. At first Major Pelaformiche ordered us, in his usual rude manner, to transfer ourselves to another battalion, then he took away our radio and then, despite the astonished protest of the battalion commander, even telephone connections with the guns.

Incredulous at finding ourselves suddenly idle, we considered our situation . . . Usually we sat at the foot of some large trees that gave off a rural fragrance and rose in front of a rough barn, in the middle of the country-side where the patrol was now positioned. Far in the distance, behind us, one could make out old-fashioned Filottrano.

With the passing days, many of the protests and complaints at the major's outrage were expressed in the usual clichés and mutterings, eternally the same, typical of military life. Until—it didn't seem right to be wasting our time in this manner—one morning I got everyone's attention. "Listen. In reaction to our troubles, we continue having the same conversations: about our homes, our towns, the good times in town, which are maybe only imaginary. Instead of wasting our time like this, why don't we try, instead, to look into how we've gotten into today's situation—I don't mean only the few of us of the platoon, but the whole world—where we're up to our necks in trouble? Or maybe you'd prefer always repeating the same things, which is the same thing as saying nothing at all?"

After a short, surprised pause: "Today's problems?" the orderly Morandi said. "We know those come from the war. Everyone knows this. So what else is there to say?"

Freddi added, "Exactly, today's problems come from the war. And there have always been wars; actually, they get worse with time. That's the reality of it, unfortunately."

"Well, it hasn't always been like this," I observed. "I mean, it's not inevitable that with the passing of time wars become worse."

More uncertainty. Canèr intervened: "What do you mean? From century to century, from the time they used stones and sticks to today, war has always become more deadly. I don't know what you're alluding to."

"I'm alluding to those centuries, unfortunately not many, when Christianity influenced—always up to a certain point, but more than today—people's behavior: that's what I'm alluding to."

Canèr looked at me without understanding.

I had to explain: "Think maybe of the twelfth and thirteenth centuries."

"The Middle Ages, the age of chivalry . . ." he said uncertainly.

All other conversations had stopped, and everyone looked at us attentively, because the terrible problem of war interested them deeply and affected their families, from whom they were separated by war.

"If I understand correctly, you are saying that . . . for hundreds of years, war was less repulsive," Lance Corporal Freddi specified. "Is that what you're saying?"

"I'll give you an example." I directed myself to the others also. "You've heard of the battle of Legnano at school, haven't you?" (It was a well-known name: above all, two regiments of the Legnano Division were part of the *CIL*.) "You know that it was a very important battle: the most important in Italy from that century, the Twelfth Century: to the point that it's still talked about today, eight hundred years later. Well, do you want to know how many lives were taken in the battle of Legnano? Only a few hundred."

The soldiers looked at one another incredulously.

"So did other battles and wars of that period as long as they occurred among Christian people. They had few deaths, and not by accident, but because they did all they could to make it that way." I gave a second example: the siege of Brescia. "Germans against Brescians: both people who don't kid around." The soldiers agreed, nodding their heads. "Both sides, that is the Germans who besieged and the Brescians who were besieged, had reached such fury that surely the conclusion would have been the terrible massacre of the defeated ones. Because of this, I mean, precisely because there would have been a large massacre, the Pope intervened, ordering the Germans to withdraw the siege and the Brescians to let them go without trouble. And everyone, furious or not, understood that that order was right and obeyed."

The entire patrol listened attentively. The recruit Pasquali suddenly shook his head. "The soldiers of that time . . . were—as the sergeant said— also ancient knights, right?"

"Exactly."

"Sure, between them that's fine. But what would they have done if, from the outside, people who were . . . truly determined had attacked them?"

"For you the ancient knights, with plumes on their heads, seem half-stuffed. I understand, with movies and everything else . . . But you're wrong. In those centuries, wars were chivalrous even outside Christian Europe. Although among non-Christians some battles—for example those of Genghis Khan's Mongols, fought a few decades after Legnano and Brescia—caused an incredible number of deaths. The battle between the two sons of Genghis Khan—all made out of knights—appears to have had as many as two hundred thousand deaths in a single day, a number never reached even in modern wars."

At times, as we talked like this, the whistle of a German shell trailed above us in the quiet air, like a bow that cuts through the quiet sea plain. Without stopping, we turned our heads to watch the cloud of smoke open above or around Filottrano.

"Of course," I made sure to tell them, "even in the Christian nations of that time, men weren't perfect, that's taken for granted. Even then they committed nasty tricks of every kind and killed: if not in war, they killed in quarrels among private citizens, for example, or, I don't know, even in carrying out the law, or in other ways. The battle between good and evil existed even back then; it would be foolish to forget it, as it would be foolish to remember any era as perfect. But the fact remains that men in the fairly Christianized society of back then killed infinitely less than today. Today's massacres, in war and in peace (sure, even in peace: think of the slaughters carried out by the Nazis, and those of Communists in Russia) would have been inconceivable in the world back then. I mean, people couldn't have even imagined it."

In their simplicity, the soldiers became emotional:

"It must be true . . ."

"Yes, it's really like that . . ."

"Who would have thought?"

"Then war could really become less repulsive . . ."

"Why doesn't anyone ever speak of it, lieutenant?"

"They do speak of it," I informed them, "but it's usually anti-Christian intellectuals who speak of it badly."

"Why?" several of them asked, once again surprised.

"Precisely because it was an era that strove to be Christian. And the biggest discriminating choice of man remains the same: with God, or against him."

One question followed another. That day and the following ones, the soldiers asked me many questions and attentively listened to my answers, which were often inadequate, seeing that they were still the answers of a young man. The men were especially excited, I remember, when I recited by memory, passage after passage, the account of *Ottone of Frisinga* (that important inverted Tacitus) on the extraordinary dignity of the people in the free Italian communes of the thirteenth century. I caught a glimpse of hope in several of them: indeed, we would finally find the right way to get out of trouble . . . How many times in those years did I see simple soldiers go through similar moods!

16

IT BECAME CLOUDY and began to rain. The scattered blood was washed away from the grass.

The night before the Musone attack, the only regiment of infantry from the *Corpo di Liberazione* marched among the hills' gorges. The infantrymen passed in single file in the drizzle, full-bodied, with creased uniforms. They were unchanged. The armistice had caused some mutations to other branches: the slackening of discipline had permitted an emphasis on distinctive characteristics in some, while others had a new appearance, wearing colonial garments intended for the Aegean Garrison, the only ones recovered from Puglia's depots. The armistice had left no trace on the infantry, whether they were in colonial uniform like these men or in gray-green: for the large majority, it was still our army like it had always been.

Displeased, I observed them walking and stopping with little order. Frankly, they didn't inspire trust. "I'm not going to let myself be killed," one of their officers in front of me actually said. "The general can let himself be killed. At the moment of attack, I'm getting into a hole."

Eventually, even the last men with their model 1891 long rifles sadly turned over on their backs disappeared among the trees. Waiting to attack, they would encamp in the woods under the rain, lacking means as always, their uniforms and bodies already wet.

After a night of intense work stretching out the telephone lines (the major, finding himself forced to make use of the platoon, in the beginning used it repeatedly for similar needs), we saw the pale day rise with explosions. The chorus of artillery was deafening. To our right, between us and the sea, the Polish artillery fired with many large-caliber guns. The hills beyond the Musone became covered with smoke inside every recess, above every summit, around all farms.

Polish airplanes, in small squadrons, prepared their attack from above with resolute care: they struck, machine-gunning, scattering small smoking storms here and there, making somersaults in the sky.

The Germans responded to the fire with force, but although I tried, not even this time was I able to feel sympathy for those valiant soldiers who, by now alone against the world, continued to fight impressively.

At noon, under the assault of the *Arditi* and of the infantry dashing on the other side of the river, the Germans retreated, leaving the ground covered with dead men. Of all the battles that I saw, the battle of Musone was the one the Germans paid for most dearly. In addition to the dead, three thousand prisoners fell into Polish hands and ours: in their sector, the Poles reached the long seashore above Ancona with their tanks, isolating some of the enemy's formations that covered the city.

Once again, the major found a way to torment me, so that after having been at his disposal for a few hours to no end, I turned my back to my useless observation window and threw myself on a rough peasant bed. With the passing of the afternoon hours, the artillery fire lengthened and became less frequent. The thick uproar of rifles and submachine guns weakened in the distance. The great summer heat was over everything: the men who were killing each other, and those who stretched out lazily at the artillery front when the firing stopped, and also over my petty resentment, my irritation at being in the midst of such considerable events without playing a part in them.

At night, only the large Polish calibers fired, raising large explosions down below toward the east between the crests of the hills. They methodically hit the defenses of the Germans who were encircled in Ancona.

*

The following day we crossed the old lines under an intermittent rain. In the woods that completely covered our slope, we noticed small piles of hay soaked with rain everywhere, where at night the infantrymen had slept, like beggars of old. Occasionally, the road was obstructed by men and vehicles.

We had to stop for five or six minutes at the river's ford: some soldiers from the command of the *Corpo,* wearing armlet badges, were making the motor vehicles go through one at a time.

From the patrol's truck, Artilleryman Fiorani addressed whoever was closest to him: "This time the infantry didn't kid around, did they?" he said.

"What infantry? It was the *Arditi* who did everything," the traffic coordinator answered him.

"Sure, the *Arditi* too. But there's only one battalion of them," Fiorani observed: "the battle was big . . ."

"The *Arditi* did everything," he insisted. If you want to know, yesterday I was near General Utili who commands the *CIL:* I was there as an orders dispatcher, a few steps away from him. Well . . .'"

"Get out of here, you must have been in some tavern," Fiorani interrupted.

The traffic coordinator shook his head. "I'm trying to say that the infantry is always the same . . . I don't know how it was back in the First World War; maybe back then it was different, who knows, many say it was. But yesterday a battalion called for reinforcements before attacking. 'What reinforcements?' the general asked, 'You haven't even started.' 'Yes, but it seems like the Germans want to attack us . . .'" He addressed the others too: "You understand? The Lord must have created the infantry on the seventh day, when he was tired."

"The *Arditi* are too few. They couldn't have done everything on their own," the artilleryman Bertolini intervened, backing up Fiorani.

"Few but good. They did everything on their own. In fact, they proved to be better than your paratroopers. This time, the Germans weren't even able to retreat: they almost all stayed on the ground."

Pause. "Well, it's a good thing that someone else woke up," exclaimed a disappointed Fiorani (a stocky guy, with short legs and a long torso, from Emilia just like Bertolini and Freddi). "Every battle was up to us Nembo from the moment we entered the line."

"This time you Nembo, as a matter of fact precisely you artillerymen, seemed to be on the Germans' side. Do you know that your First Group killed six or seven *Arditi?*"

"What? What crap are you talking about?"

"I'm telling you what I know, because I saw the colonel of the *Arditi* with my very eyes. He arrived like a crazy man foaming at the mouth: 'Who is going to bring back soldiers like those nowadays?' he yelled. 'Where am I going to find such soldiers again?' Well, General Utili stayed silent."

At this point, as we could have expected, the artillerymen began arguing with the traffic coordinator, reminding him that "for starters," he was a shirker. In fact, Morandi defined him, with some pertinence, as a "shirker traffic coordinator." I had to intervene to get them to stop.

"The general wouldn't have let Colonel Boschetti make such a fuss, if things weren't really as he said," he grumbled, and moved away, tidying up the band around his arm.

"Could what that command wretch said be true, lieutenant?"

"I don't know."

Later on, we would learn that, unfortunately, the events went exactly as he had described.

We noticed on the shore between the rocks a shoe full of something. An artilleryman descended from a truck in the column in front of ours and went to inspect it. "The foot is still in it," he announced. He took it and placed it outside of the road: it wasn't an ankle boot from the *Arditi*, but an infantry shoe.

"That traffic coordinator could have removed it, instead of talking rubbish," Pasquali, the Abruzzese recruit, said, "so that the truck wouldn't crush the rest of mama's boy."

As we crossed the river, we grazed a small cart without sides that stood out in the middle of the water. In spite of a blanket laid out on top, two dead infantrymen, already swollen, stood out on the chute. The mines hadn't spared them, even after they had died. One had to hope that the foot we had found on the shore belonged to one of them.

We found our dead and the Germans' beyond the lake between the trees. Then, still more dead Germans, isolated or in small groups, continuously. Some had their arms raised to defend their heads from splinters; there were many.

Their half-burnt anti-tank guns lay next to tractors camouflaged in yellow and brown; around, on the blackened earth, were sharp anti-tank shells.

17

BEFORE NIGHT, the group's eight guns were once again in position a few kilometers past the river, near a farm.

A battery was charged with setting up the group's observation post, clearly affronting the platoon. But this doesn't mean that they left us alone. On the contrary: that day, like the previous one, we received and executed with exhausting swiftness orders and counter-orders so difficult that the fruits of the preceding week's stagnation were lost.

As for me, I began to feel not the usual tiredness, but the one typical of the front that settles and gathers in the bones like a slow poison, ungrateful even to remembrance. That night, after we swallowed our rations, we lay down heavily to sleep.

Around two o'clock, a sentinel groped his way to my tent: "Lieutenant Francescoli wants you."

A big silence filled the night. The moonlight barely distinguished the structures of the farm from the straw stacks and our trucks covered by camouflage nets. Only a few stars, intent on following their icy paths, came out in the sky. There was an immense solitude beneath them; the stars were so far from us—a handful of sleeping men—and from the dead scattered in the countryside, each wrapped in his own silence.

The only tent that let out some light was that of Francescoli, the commander of the unit. "One moment," he said as I entered. "I'll finish this off, and I'll be with you." An unusual noncommissioned officer who was taking orders in front of him looked at me, afraid that I would cut in front of him.

"I'll wait on the threshing-floor," I said.

I went to sit on a stump protruding from the grass, under the intangible face of the sky. As I did this, I strangely seemed to feel my angel seated by my side on the stump, as a human would be. It wasn't the first time during those weeks that I felt the presence of my guardian angel (I had felt it also many times, and as intensely, on the Russian front). Urged on by such experiences, at times here in the Marches I even tried to imagine it. How is an angel made? I had tried to put together, in a single figure, the different angelic attributes collected here and there in sacred texts. I told myself that if I could infuse it with enough artistic strength (better yet, if I was able to guess astutely enough the angelic universe), the angel's image would suddenly construct itself before me . . . The synthesis, however, had never worked, for as far as I had leaped, I had always fallen backwards. The angelic figure had never let itself take on concrete form.

Francescoli called me.

"Are you tired?" he asked me when I entered his tent.

He was sitting on a cot. "We all are, aren't we?" I answered.

"Right. The line laid out by the Fourth Battery doesn't seem to want to work."

"Ah, really? Well, it doesn't displease me," I said, somewhat as a joke and somewhat seriously. "It means that, after all, even group's platoons are good for something, don't you think?" (I fear that, in front of such pettiness, my invisible angel went limp, dispirited . . .)

"All right. The major wants you to lay out a new line immediately." He brought the lantern closer to the map on his blanket, projecting the yellow light on the signs—always magical to me—that designated roads, hills, soundless woods, and towns.

"We are here, in this spot," he said. "You have to follow this route." The tip of his pencil zigzagged on the map. "Do you see where the observation post is? On this spur. Before daylight—bear in mind, before daylight—your line must work."

I studied the route carefully, then I folded the map and slipped it inside my bush jacket. "Now I'm going to amuse myself waking up the soldiers," I said. "They'll think that it's an order, for which a counter-order is already on its way, like those other ones today."

"Who knows if that isn't the case . . ." Francescoli let out. We burst out laughing.

At this point, an angry voice rose outside: the major's tent was nearby, and evidently he wasn't sleeping and was listening to us. "Wake up, second lieutenant, stop chatting and move." The voice became agitated: "If the line isn't ready at seven o'clock, I'll do . . . terrible things."

"Terrible things!" I murmured, puzzled, leaving the cube-shaped tent. The tent where Sergeant Canèr and two others were sleeping was next to the patrol truck. "Hey, wake up," I said, inserting my head between the lengths of cloth; a stench of warm air surrounded my face.

"Who is it?" Canèr grumbled.

"The lieutenant. Wake up half the patrol. We have to lay out a line; we'll use the truck."

"A . . . what?"

"Something nice. Come on, wake up half the patrol."

"Something nice . . ." Canèr murmured quietly.

Maybe he was about to fall back asleep. "Wake up, or I'll do terrible things," I exclaimed with a menacing voice. Canèr sat up, shaking the fragile tent. "The lieutenant has gone mad," he moaned.

*

Within a few minutes we left the threshing-floor on the lurching Fiat 626; at the roar of our engine the men inside the tents turned over in their tepid blankets, glad that they hadn't been the ones to have their sweet sleep interrupted. Two sentinels wrapped in their coats were on the edge of the encampment: undoubtedly, they too wished for our engine to leave, in order to continue their thoughts undisturbed; to think of their women, real or fictitious, imagining perhaps their sketched-out shadows next to their own on the ground. What else should a sentinel think about on moonlit nights?

Our tarred wire slowly unwound along country roads. The men gradually hung it from the trunks or branches of trees and the poles of the electrical grid, or set it down on the hedges. The engine lulled, and voices rose only every now and then to give some warning.

Occasionally, the light of the sailing moon revealed an enemy's corpse lying near the road, and sometimes on the road, in which case he came into the very tight semi-circle of our headlights, then stayed behind.

We reached the observation post. The line worked immediately. We slowly returned again.

Morandi, who preceded the truck on foot, suddenly called me: "Come, one of these dead was in the Russian campaign. He has the ribbon. He seems to be an officer."

I joined him; in the beam of the headlights, I leaned over the German who had faced circumstances so similar to mine and, by now, had landed irrevocably on the shore from which there is no return. He was a lieutenant. He lay in the middle of the dirt road; one could see on his chest a "ribbon of the ice," identical to the one I too had worn until the armistice, and another decoration.

He wasn't apathetic like German corpses usually are. Death had stiffened an expression of indescribable terror on his face—his mouth was wide open (as though he had tried to keep death at a distance with a scream). His arms were desperately raised to protect his head. And he was a valiant man: Germans don't give out decorations randomly. Therefore, they too could find the humanity in themselves, if they had suffered enough.

It was the first time that I had seen one of them scream with such force, and I was shocked by it.

"This man is from the race that we think of—or thought of—as demigods, from the race which, simply because it believed it was rational, deprived millions of human beings of their lives. But now he's like all the others who died in war: like those two infantrymen there on the cart, half submerged in the current, for example, and like the Russian peasant soldiers, whose timid faces after they are killed look as though they are asking why."

"Poor fellow!" I said, as we started again on our road.

"Poor fellow him too," Morandi said. "Who knows what he went through!"

The chapter has ended.

Farewell now, Filottrano; and farewell to you too, heart of our youth. With the passing of time who knows how many things would take place down there, and certainly, during the years of political discussions, the opinion of our actions would change several times (the usual nonsense for and against the army . . .). Later on, naturally, the people would forget us entirely.

Down there, only our dead kept our youthful hearts.

18

THE DAY AFTER the angelic night, and for several days after that, we continued to advance.

From Filottrano forward, each new advance required fighting, which the paratroopers and the other infantries of the *Corpo di Liberazione* alternated among themselves. Units theoretically considered at rest had to press to the head on foot without the meager motor vehicles at the disposal of the *Corpo*—the vehicles were transferred to the troops engaged with the enemy—while acrobatically carrying all the equipment behind them. (Up until then the Allies had passed 60 motor vehicles along to us. We would receive another 102 in August: therefore, a number barely sufficient to level out wear and tear.)

The advance of our units, dependent on the changing white road system of the Marches of the time, was similar to a long tide or a dense and laborious swell. The men's faces were hardened by the exertion, while the mules had acquired that sense of participation in human fatigue, a communion of tenacity that forms only when great efforts are shared.

In general all the artillery groups, at least those that were motorized, participated in the actions of the head troops. I won't relate each one of our events, because—due to fatigue—from a certain day forward I ceased taking notes, and some events have become somewhat jumbled in my memory. But then if I don't remember them individually, it is because they weren't much different from each other or from what had come before.

I will mention, however, the night that the platoon received the order to join the column of the San Marco Regiment, which, leaving behind the Italian front, advanced north into territory still infested by enemy units. That day the two *Alpini* battalions and the two *Bersaglieri* of the *Corpo* had broken the German defense in Iesi and liberated the city. The guns of the Second Group had come to line up immediately in its proximity, along the south banks of the Esino River. The platoon, equipped with radios, was sent on a halftrack to join the sailors who had advanced.

Due to the lack of bridges (here too they were all demolished), we crossed the blue Esino outside of the city, in a place where the current widened to form a calm mirror. In the middle of it were some motor vehicles of the *Corpo,* stopped because the water had reached their engines; our halftrack went through unharmed, raising two small waves.

In Iesi there was activity and uproar. At a crossroad, we saw ferocious civilians who punched and kicked some Fascists and pushed them toward the prison. Without stopping, we entered a dust-covered, heavily trampled main road beyond the city, along which the San Marco had advanced.

The sun was setting on that day's events too: on all those we knew about and those we didn't, occurring near and far in the wide stretch of a world that would have been so grateful, on that summer evening, if men hadn't transformed it into an arena of killing and violence.

No Italian motor vehicle had traveled the road before ours; therefore, we had to focus our attention on its white dust, under which some anti-tank mines could be lying.

At dusk, we still proceeded, alone on the solitary road of the damp countryside. Hesperus, the first star to appear, shone already in its spot within the deep blue expanse; a few more stars lit up.

"How could the sailors have gone so far ahead?" the artillerymen asked dubiously, "and not one peasant to give us any information!"

Finally, Sergeant Canèr's voice lifted everyone's eyes from the ash-colored road: "Look over there, in that valley: mules."

"They're tied in a circle for the night . . ."

Once we were within shouting distance, I called: "San Marco train?"

"No, artillery. Fifth Horseback Group."

It was the group of my friend Cèt, Second Lieutenant Schiavi, with whom I had struck up a friendship in Surbo.

"It's one of the groups who backed up the *Alpini* in the fight for Iesi," I told the soldiers. "I didn't know that it had advanced with the San Marco." I raised my voice again and asked: "Where is your command?"

"Farther ahead. Farther ahead on the road."

"The Fifth is the group of Lieutenant Ferruccio Schiavi," Morandi thought best to remind me, sitting higher than anyone else on the pile of gear, his submachine gun between his hands.

"Yes. Let's hope to meet him," I said.

A few minutes later we reached a column of mules loaded with broken-down howitzers, slowly walking on the road. One of the drivers sang a melancholic Bergamese song that quite suited the evening hour: the men and even the mules seemed to harmonize with their slow step.

"Tenth Battery? Is it maybe the Tenth Battery?"

"Yes, it's the Tenth."

Here came Cèt out of the line; I leaped down from the halftrack, and we ran up to each other and shook hands. "I have to establish communication with the San Marco Regiment. Do you by any chance know where I can find its command?" I asked him.

"It's about a kilometer away. The troop is much farther ahead, at least six or seven kilometers from here."

"See you later."

"See you later."

*

The San Marco's command was in an area called Acquasanta and con-sisted of three colonial houses and a small church in the fields astride the road. There was an aristocratic navy officer, with a rank corresponding to a colonel. I explained my charge: "The order is to establish a radio link be-tween the San Marco and the Nembo Second Artillery Group, and to main-tain it until the San Marco finds itself inside the range of the guns. Specif-ically, here at Acquasanta, we are barely within maximum range: the troops are outside."

The colonel, who found himself faced with an odd combination of sat-isfaction and uncertainty (satisfaction because his sailors had entered Belvedere Ostrense, on top of a small hill far in the distance; uncertainty because a short while ago fighting had begun around them) said, aristo-cratically stressing the formal address: "I pray you to communicate, lieu-tenant, that the San Marco Regiment has occupied Belvedere. And the en-emy's reaction has become heavy just now. After such communication, your duty having been fulfilled, you can, if you see fit, return to your group."

"Thank you," I said. "I'd like to bring to your attention that I'll stay on the spot until dawn, near the horseback artillery."

In the dark, as we traveled back on the same road, we ran into three or four overloaded mules. Some drivers, lead by Cèt, pulled them with tired steps: "I too am on patrol with the San Marco. But where are you going?"

I returned with him to his navy colonel. He was now more worried because the German artillery fire and mortars were still increasing and by now filled the darkening peaks of the distant hills with blasts around the regiment. He was standing in front of the biggest of the three houses of Acquasanta, on a sloping field, like on the deck of a ship; he looked at the firing attentively, the collar of his elegant blue navy coat raised, his hands sunk in his pockets.

He didn't request our intervention. We told him that we would keep ourselves at his disposal in the most isolated of the three colonial houses.

At our arrival, some rabbits stole away from the threshing-floor. The house seemed uninhabited. However, when I began knocking vigorously on the door with the ironclad butt of my submachine gun, two old countrywomen hurried to open it.

Cèt's men, who hadn't slept in days, lay in the stable on hay near their mules; mine were in the adjacent kitchen. At my request, the two women showed us to the best room in the house: under the faint light of a candle that one of them held, the place almost seemed elegant.

Suddenly, I realized that Cèt was laughing in his usual youthful, discrete manner (I still hadn't forgotten it): he seemed to enjoy this small episode very much. As I looked at him questioningly, he imitated my gesticulation, which seemed authoritative to him. "That explains your success with peasants," he said, and burst out laughing again. The old women walked away, leaving us in the dark. We leaned our two submachine guns carefully against the wall within reach, then lay down.

"Listen," I told him. "Before we—dazed as we are with exhaustion—fall asleep, do you mind briefly giving me an account of how it went in May on the Mainarde, when we were still in Puglia?"

"I don't mind," he said, still laughing, and he began telling me with a calm voice, without wasting words, how his group and the Piedmont Alpini Battalion (one of the two that were now part of the *CIL*) had fought in an alpine configuration on those steep southern mountains. Cèt revealed the essentials without ever loading it with dead weight; furthermore, he seemed to delight in each thing, as though he was always seeing it for the first time: God had granted him such great gifts. That is precisely why I had asked him to give me an account.

"You know that there were also some French troops in that sector," he said finally.

"Unfortunately! Yes, I know," I answered.

"We were close to them. Well, even the French didn't learn much from the war: in the end, it wasn't pleasant dealing with them. Let's understand each other: the officers were French, and the troops were Moroccan. I happened to go in some house they had just vacated; you know the houses of mountaineers, don't you? Where each object is like a mold of the life of whoever lives there? Well, everything had been shattered, the furniture mostly burnt, and there wasn't even a meter of floor or a table remaining without human dung."

"That's it? You don't know the rest of it?" I asked him.

"What rest of it? What do you mean?"

"You really don't know? Do you remember Lieutenant _____ from our regiment's command: you know, the one with the boyish face?"

"Yes, sure."

"His house was between Naples and Rome, at _____, right on the Moroccans' way. The Moroccans not only raped his mother and his fiancée but also his father, then killed them."

"What did you say?"

"I said, raped and killed, murdered all three of them. Many others in that town, and not only there. _____ has now left the regiment and gone back to what used to be his home."

"I wasn't aware of such things! If the French . . ." Cèt stuttered, "allowed it, it's a sign that . . . Their honor . . . That . . . Poor France!" He sat up on the bed, greatly anxious. "And here we are talking!" he exclaimed.

"Why don't you say: 'And here we are still fighting'?"

He lay back down.

"Why," he answered after a long pause, "it would be like saying: 'And here we are still living.' We are obligated to live."

"That's it."

We didn't feel like conversing any more. Cèt, to whom the information had been completely new, couldn't get his mind around it, and turned around nervously on his bed.

"The Pope," I said compassionately, "managed to get the Moroccans removed from Italy. Did you know? But the Nembo wasn't happy about it; the paratroopers were hoping to run into them. The plan was . . ." I realized that I too was beginning to get excited. "Well, enough, let's be done with it," I concluded.

After a while, Cèt asked me: "How did it go for you?"

I told him in a few words. We both found ourselves dissatisfied. Now we could hear occasionally the volleys of automatic arms outside: since they didn't seem very distant, we set out to listen several times.

"It's unbearable," Cèt said, after another pause.

"What?"

"I'm thinking of the Moroccans."

"Enough, forget about it," I said. "We're the first ones to blame, stabbing France who was already on the ground; and in any case, however you put it, there's nothing we can do about it now. Even talking about it is worse: we felt it too when the news reached us. Let's think instead that the war will eventually have to end, and after going through so many nasty events, we'll finally return home. You'll return to your seashore."

"My sea . . ." Cèt murmured shortly after, half asleep: "The sea of Istria. Who knows if I'll ever be able to see it again . . . My mother is on the island of Cherso."

We were overtaken by sleep.

A dream stayed with me, of Riccione and its many gardens: I traveled the streets, one after the other, whose background is the deep blue stroke of the sea; in that dream they were troublesomely deserted, and I couldn't understand why. I reached the gate of the villa between the pines: nothing had changed, the small Madonna in the terra-cotta low relief still smiled from the wall; in front of it the iron light hung, lit up. "For you," I said to her with gratitude, "the house in the shade is untouched."

The gate was closed, like when I had come to pay Margherita a visit with a song in my heart. But the privet's flowered hedge, which, starting at the hinges, encircled the garden—happiness for the bees and my eyes—was now without flowers.

I leaned my forearms on the gate: I noticed that the gravel of the small paths was littered with dead pine needles, like in the winter, and it saddened me.

Suddenly, I noticed sounds of fighting, shell whistles. So I collected myself. "Margherita," I shouted toward the windows, "come down! The war is coming and everyone has fled. Open up. Come."

Nothing.

I tried to climb the gate, which only came up to my chest, but I couldn't, and I clung to it and strained like a reptile. "Open up," I shouted. I stuttered, breathless: "The Germans are arriving in retreat. They'll drag you out of your house and kill you with their machine guns like they did with Russian girls . . . The Moroccans will come. Open up! Open up! Stinking war . . . Dirty war!"

A shell whistle passed so close by that I woke up.

Lifting myself up on my arm, I heard Cèt's breathing as he slept in the darkness of the peasant's room.

"Ah," I murmured, placing my head on the pillow once again, "thank goodness!" It was a dream, nothing more than a dream . . . The concreteness of the pillow proved to be comforting.

A real whistle came, very close like the one in the dream. Then another one.

A German gun, maybe self-propelled, was firing on Acquasanta, not from the north, from the front, but from the west, from one of the open flanks. The shells brushed past our small house and became buried.

"Cèt." I shook him.

"Yes?"

"Wake up. Listen."

One, two whistles.

"They're passing very close," he said.

"Thank goodness," I observed. "We're awake and armed, and we can defend ourselves well."

"What?" Cèt said.

"Do you hear how they bury themselves without exploding? They must be anti-tank shells."

"I think so too."

We could also hear, from time to time, bursts of submachine guns not very far away. At the same time, we kept hearing the rumble of combat from the side of Belvedere.

"Let's go to the commander of the San Marco," Cèt decided. "He might need artillery."

The commander, however, intended on waiting for the enemy's intentions to become clearer. He didn't ask for the intervention of artillery, so we returned to our small house, next to which, this time, I organized an embryonic guard duty. I positioned one of my artillerymen a few meters away: "Place yourself there, between those two stacks, don't move. Some Germans could be around. If you see any, fire at them. It'll be your way to give off the alarm."

*

We retreated at dawn, taking leave of Cèt and his men. Cèt counted on retreating later.

But he didn't. That day the Germans attacked the San Marco Regiment in force, apparently determined to destroy it. The sailors pressed around

Belvedere and fought violently on three fronts the entire day: the Germans weren't able to break the line.

Cèt was the only patrol who found himself in town. He had positioned the observatory on the bell tower, where the blow of an 88 suddenly ripped off a bell. A few months later, he would narrate the episode himself: "The German shells were coming in compact volleys, a dozen at a time . . . Good soldiers those San Marco sailors: not experienced, but with guts; all in all, one can trust them. The commander, who maybe wasn't aware of how a land battle is led, simply placed himself in the middle of the square, so that he wouldn't be any less exposed than others. 'Long live our commander!' the wounded shouted when they passed near him, carried in the arms of others. I'm telling you: watching it from the bell tower, it seemed like a battle from the *Risorgimento*. Even many peasants fought alongside the sailors: in short, it was a first-rate racket. OK, those in my command exaggerated, they recommended me for a medal."

19

THE ATTEMPT ON the life of Germany's dictator by his own generals led us to believe that the war was ending. Hitler was not killed, but the German soldiers, those lined up on the hills in front of us and the many we fought one by one on other fronts, would they still let themselves get killed when the futility of it was so evident? They continued to let themselves get killed.

It was horrifying to think of so much valor, and such extraordinary loyalty, being wasted in that obstinate manner; a waste, I feared, that would maybe impoverish us all . . .

The Thirteenth Paratrooper Battalion, along with the command unit of the Second Group, halted in a dominating position in Montecarotto—ten kilometers west of Belvedere Ostrense—in the deserted hospital. The enemy, growing fierce under our pressure, battered us with guns that opened large rents in the front and roof of that building. Some of their bright 105 shells, maybe sabotaged by the Italian laborers who had built them, passed through many walls without exploding and finally rebounded madly back and forth inside some rooms, reducing the white varnished beds and the nun's black ones to a strange tangled mass never before seen. The command unit's artillerymen in ready position were gathered in a large room on the first floor. Seated on the floor, they inhaled the smoke of bad English cigarettes in endless drags, like thirsty men drink; above them trails of smoke stagnated in the air.

The fragile ivory-white room was chosen by Francescoli only because it was adjacent to the head of the passageway where the window of the observatory was located. I won't easily forget that room, because it served to remind me, with remarkable clarity, of the provisional nature of human beings. In fact, Francescoli saved all those men from death when he dropped my suggestion—because he was tired, or maybe, I must admit, because he was negligent—to transfer them to a room on the ground floor that seemed better protected. A shell penetrated and exploded precisely in that better-protected room, and probably wouldn't have left even one survivor.

The paratroopers sent away the entire town's population after it appeared certain that spies hid in their midst. How many sick, unmovable people, how many miseries can be in a small town! The parish priest, the only authority left, ran among the people to establish calm, like a shepherd among scared sheep. He was to those peasants what my Lombard priests are to laborers, spending their lives in their midst, pining away at the same difficulties.

Corporal Lisi, a Puglian newly assigned to the patrol, came out of the hospital with Morandi to repair the telephone line and was left deaf and dumb for two hours because a shell exploded almost on top of him. Morandi continued to drag him along the line, sobbing like a child because he thought he was deaf and mute forever.

These were usual circumstances of war, by now tedious to listen to.

However, a new event, at least in my personal regard, took place during those days.

I was assisting the major, in charge of fire (we had placed some self-propelled guns among the olive trees about two kilometers away) when the Germans located us and began to fire on us. The force of the shells that exploded on the side around the observation window burst open the blinds of the shutters, leaving us exposed from head to foot. At that point, we couldn't stay in that location; but neither the major, who had accused me of being afraid at the Margherita stronghold, nor I, with good reason, resolved ourselves to leave. We were under terrible pressure, in the middle of very violent explosions and smoke, as though trapped by our past words. In my heart I asked for God to save me, rather, to save us, and I asked forgiveness because I was testing him. At the same time, I felt a kind of sympathy for the man next to me, who even with all his faults was doing all he could to control his own nerves.

When a shell exploded with indescribable force on the side barely a few meters beneath us, the major quickly bent back, as would be natural, while I was able to stand upright: at that instant, a fragment came out of the explosion, rose swiftly, and fell against my throat. It did not injure me because it was only plaster, but undoubtedly the major must have thought it was a splinter and that my throat had been cut. From that point on, he stopped all animosity toward me; I wondered if it was because of that alarming splinter.

With the arrival of August, the war became increasingly less bearable for those of us most tried: for me, for Castelli, for other soldiers, for Second Lieutenant Canèr—survivor of the Russian front—even for Paratrooper Major Pellagatta, in spite of the strength of his oxlike head, which at times reduced him to an exhausted buffalo capable of operating only fitfully.

We continued fighting because we were called soldiers, but we increasingly found ourselves fighting with our hearts to prevail over our nerves' rebellion. We saw the signs in each other, but we didn't say a word.

20

THE PATROL STAYED for a week with the *Alpini* of the Monte Granero Battalion above the steep town of Barbara.

We recognized the *Alpini* from a distance, with their feathered hats and the unusual compactness of their units, and from close up by their beards, as well as the behavior of those of them who loitered here and there under the sun with their slovenly, proud gait.

We greeted them with some excitement, because although we knew that some Italian ordinary divisions were perhaps the least efficient troops to fight the war, we also knew that the *Alpini* represented the best ones of them all (a mirror again of the whole of human nature, merits and faults). I remembered the still recent retreat from Russia, those frigid encirclements from which the Germans had opened the way for us Italians of ordinary divisions. But not for the *Alpini,* in whose pocket the exact opposite had taken place: in fact, our mountaineers had been the ones who day after day opened the way for the troops encircled with them, including the Germans. The Tridentina Division opened passageways for Italian ordinary troops, the meager remains of a German army corps, and perhaps ten thousand Hungarians—all finally reaching safety, without the help of airplanes, without the help of tanks or other vehicles, thanks only to the incomparable valor of those simple-hearted men.

I was thinking about these events when we met the *Alpini* at Barbara.

Afterwards, we positioned the observation post on a hillock, in one of their trenches shaded by an oak tree and camouflaged by a few riddled branches in the turned earth. I named that noble observation post Caterina, using my sister's name.

Far away among the hills appeared "windy" Urbino, where Raphael had emerged as a painter: my binoculars allowed me to clearly distinguish the two large red towers of the Ducal palace that are part of art history tests. I wondered, observing them worriedly, if by chance our stupid artillery wouldn't become the one to destroy them.

In the meantime, the intoxicating sense of movement was replaced by a sense of stagnancy and of the slow passing of time, which imperturbably rolled over our circumstances and those of all others and moved on without a sound. We spent hours by the *Alpini*'s side, exploring the static enemy zone with binoculars.

Observatory Caterina: butterflies.

They came often, drifting, settling on the edges of the overturned earth of our trenches, perhaps to suck out moisture. One afternoon an especially beautiful one arrived: it was velvety-black, streaked with fire, with white spots. My attention was drawn by the loveliness of its colors, which, I realized, weren't arranged randomly: indeed, even a great painter would have been able to compose them with so much art only in a moment of special grace.

I studied the butterfly closely: certainly she wasn't like this by choice; she didn't even know that she was a butterfly, wasn't aware of it. She wasn't even aware of her own existence; she existed, period, and standing on the edge of the earth of the trenches she moved her wings rhythmically, like someone who is breathing in sleep, unconsciously happy to be part of the great miracle of summer. However, when shortly after another one of the same species appeared, the butterfly rose in flight and began circling around, intentionally showing, one would think, the other one her own colors, flaunting them, hiding them, flaunting them again more gracefully, like a skilled actress.

An insect, an embodiment of something which infinitely transcends it, was also like us. It was a mirror, small like the sparkle of a grain of sand in the sun, of the joy and the colors that are in the mind of God. A butterfly alone, I realized suddenly, would be enough to show the existence of God.

I delighted in that unexpected feast of colors. The incomparable joy that must be in God . . . Indeed, I understood, this is why we men and angels were created, as well as who knows how many billions of intelligent beings gifted with sensitivity: so that we could share in such immeasurable joy!

Beforehand, however, there is the trial (which gives us merit, for which we are not only passive), and for us terrestrials there is also death. Indeed . . . Soon the two butterflies would die. With a shadow of distress, I imagined the slough of all the dead butterflies, poor crumpled and ripped things that ants, doomed also, would drag away toward the end of summer. How nice for us that butterflies exist. And how fair that they are not aware of existing, so that they are then unaware of dying . . .

During the days we spent by the *Alpini*'s side, I was able to observe once again their customs and lifestyle. They were men of the kind of simplicity I had actually forgotten still existed on earth. Among them, yes meant yes, no meant no, and false pretenses and double meanings were unknown. They spoke of the epic feat they had accomplished rarely, and only when they needed to draw from it some sensible teaching. But in a time when Italy was down on its luck and all foolish people exalted the winners and everything about them—gold and pinchbeck—these soldiers maintained a confidence in themselves that was made of stone without any arrogance.

I wasn't the only one to observe them: I realized that Canèr occasionally studied them in silence too.

I remember one of his remarks one day when, finding him with such an expression, I had nodded with a smile: "If only all Italians were like this . . . Instead of always being 'cunning,' and spending so much of their strength making a fool out of the next person. The national pastime, which in turn makes all of us into fools sooner or later." He had shaken his head: "An entire nation of cunning fools! Have you ever thought of it, lieutenant?"

*

In mid-August, while we were in the valley of the Cesano River, we learned that the *Corpo di Liberazione* was about to be transferred into the rear zone at rest. At the time, the English had reached and crossed Florence, and the Americans were in Pisa.

On August 17, Polish units from the Fifth Kressowa Division, recognizable by their mermaid badges, arrived to relieve us. Since as always the paratroopers didn't have enough motor vehicles for the transfer, the Poles unloaded several of theirs and with brotherly spirit put them at the paratroopers' disposal. We knew that in those days the Poles were distressed because of a new brutal tragedy under way in Warsaw. When at the end of July the Soviets had arrived at the suburbs east of the city, the Polish partisan army, which the Soviets had urged to rise several times, had risen. Then the Soviets had stopped, and now they waited for the insurgents—proudly anti-German, but not Communist—to be annihilated by the Germans to the very last man. (For the second time, and in an even bloodier manner than the first, Communists and Nazis, although mortal enemies, found themselves in agreement to crush the Poles, a people determined not to lose their own freedom.) Men had been fighting desperately in the city for several weeks. At first, the American and British air forces had dropped munitions for the insurgents, but those flights had ceased because the Soviet command had prohibited airplanes from stopping within its own lines. Now the Polish pilots continued alone, trying to carry out the drops without making stops. Very often they were not successful: it was said that the British command had strictly forbidden them to take off, but that the Poles refused to obey the order.

So the Polish pilots continued to take off: once in flight, no one knew if they went forward with stone faces, or if they silently cried, or if they yelled out their despair inside the roar of their four-engined aircraft. Their airplanes must have looked like birds that desperately fly around a nest surrounded by much stronger predators: at the end, they can no longer hold up and crash to the ground, and their irrepressible pain ends abruptly along with them, without memory of it. Within a few weeks, all of the heavy Polish air force would fall that way; in the end, we would learn that it no longer existed. The insurgents, after fighting for sixty-two days, were exterminated; the rest of the population was deported, and 85 percent of Warsaw was leveled to the ground.

Men carried out many deeds during the course of the war that any beast would be ashamed of. Others were even bloodier, but none, I believe, was more disgraceful than this one.

*

On the day of our departure from the front, I received by way of the Vatican a postal message from home, the first; a few others would reach me in the following months through the Vatican or the Red Cross. They were all of few words, as was prescribed: my parents asked for some news from me and wrote that they were doing well. If it wasn't true, how would they have had the heart to tell me on these slips of paper?

So ended our first cycle of war.

21

THE ROCKING OF the trucks that carried us into our time of rest was comforting.

Who knows if our destiny held a better house than this disorderly and unattractive one we were passing? And, above all, would it be in a town or a city? Better to be in a city, naturally. A small one, not to throw in our faces too many of the miseries that develop following a war, but big enough to offer us a variety of surroundings, and girls: yes, most of all girls with whom we could exchange a few words.

A few words—I thought disappointedly of Giulia—were permitted even to those who were religious like me, and to those intent on staying faithful to a distant woman, as well as to logicians who know that giving in to the flesh once or more isn't a solution but the opposite. Talking wasn't forbidden for us either.

Meanwhile, city or town, we were still going toward an unfamiliar place, and therefore were surrounded by the gentle appeal of the unknown.

The appeal of an unfamiliar place? Yet another? As though we hadn't encountered enough unfamiliar places in those months, when it seemed that not much could be found beyond the line of each hill. However, there were things on the other side: clearly a piece of the world where one wore out one's soul by stretching it out on top, in order to gain a sense of it and to assimilate it.

Perhaps it was better to go to a place of no importance where there was nothing to do but sleep . . .

Yes, but after sleeping and eating to satiety, and being inactive, our bodies, which were used to exertion, would have found themselves suddenly full of energy and empty of restraint. The usual circumstances of military rest prevailed: the trouble in controlling our inner animal, which becomes increasingly resistant within a still tired spirit. The body, in fact, is like a mule that recovers with only food and rest after battles, but the spirit is more delicate.

Actually, examining this more closely, until then it wasn't so much the prospect of new surroundings that attracted us as much as—underneath that innocent desire to meet girls—a blind pull of matter toward matter. It was not even women we wanted, but women's bodies. Yes, that's how it was. And to think about it, even on account of testing oneself, it became almost an obsession.

We had much to fight off: at that age, every appeal that turned up under our eyes, even minimal, was enough to reawaken it.

"If life was limited to only the days of military rest, Freud's proclamation, which reduces everything to sex, would seem correct," I ended up telling myself. "But the experience of days of hunger, of real hunger, teaches you, in the same way, that everything can be reduced to the need to ingest: one thinks only of food, dreams only of food; and one finds in the effort to dominate oneself the same phenomenon that dominates sex. What about those who have experienced thirst in Africa, real thirst? They testify that all reality can be reduced to the need to drink. It's a pity that Freud did not experience hunger or thirst . . . Maybe, who knows, he would have come up with some opposing inspiration that would have spared the world from his disastrous doctrine."

Freud! He wasn't the only disastrous one . . . Those were the years of juvenile thought; as the trucks continued to drive along the white roads of the Marches, I turned my thinking to the enormous problems that the insertion of Jewish Messianism on the modern world had produced. It was a fact that Jews—finally out of ghettos, as they should have been—even if they had lost their faith in large numbers, they hadn't lost their Messianic expectation. On the contrary, at times their foremost intellectuals only needed any acquisition of knowledge to immediately build a theory—always definitely anti-Christian—on the redemption of man. More than Freud, Marx . . . Similar theories maybe wouldn't have done much damage in an environment firmly Christian; but this situation, wedded with the less christianized environment of today, was producing frightening fruits.

Of course it was cruel to think of Jews, that slaughtered nation, in terms other than compassion. But, while keeping compassion for the victims, one couldn't stop oneself from thinking about what was happening: in fact, one had a duty to think about it. For instance, how could so many intellectual German Jews, creators and divulgers of Marxism (not the uninformed people, the innocents who always pay for the guilty, clearly not the children and unhappy women, in no way different from my mother and from Margherita, and, what's more, consanguineous to the Virgin Mary), how could they be surprised that other Germans, incited by them in every way to deify a given social class, had finally decided to deify a race instead, their own? And instead of "repressing" other classes, like in Russia, that they had chosen to crush non-German races, starting with the Jewish one?

I wasn't able to think at length because the soldiers' sudden thunderous cheers for the body of a pretty girl passing by pulled me away from my thoughts and brought me back to the struggle of sex. Once again . . .

I tried to go back to my initial expectations. But it was wearisome to think in that manner. It made one gloomy. However, I wasn't convinced yet that our rest time would be as much of a disappointment as everything else in that life. Wasn't it enough that we had clenched our teeth at so many disappointments? The heart was such an untamable beast!

So prevention was aroused in me, and prevention ate at the pleasures of expectation. Not at everything, though; a certain amount of gentleness remained. The heart of man is truly untamable.

I unearthed these dissimilar thoughts during the journey toward the rest area, and my companions probably considered very different ones; in the middle of this, night overtook us. Our dust-covered column was stopped by Francescoli, tall in the road on his long legs, who, having preceded us that morning, waved with his flashlight for us to halt.

*

The group's column disassembled following his instructions, and the trucks from the different units slowly entered some minor routes, toward groups of homes or farms buried in the darkness.

The unit's command reached an old rural hamlet, from where we could see with some difficulty in the dark the disorderly roofs overloaded with roofing tiles. Several displeased soldiers asked Francescoli, "Lieutenant, we have to spend our rest time in this place?" Some officers also asked him quietly, "Do we really have to stay here?"

"Tomorrow we'll move somewhere bigger," Francescoli answered everyone impartially. "There are other farms around here."

It began to drizzle on the disappointed soldiers, who set up their tents or laid out their cloth against a wall or around straw stacks. My orderly, Morandi, insulting the division's command out loud and specifying carefully that in his outrage he clumped them all together from General Commander Morigi to the last guard, set up my mosquito net between two piles of wood and put a sheet over it. "Don't trouble yourself," I said to him, "all these preparations aren't necessary for me to sleep."

"Ah, not necessary, not necessary! Do you remember the straw stacks of the 'red house'?" he answered, recalling one of the previous nights. "The mosquitoes were eating us and the *Bersaglieri*. But not the pigs of the command," he continued. "They never felt the mosquitoes, and now they're in a city for sure."

Shortly after, we began hearing the first breaths of those asleep. Two sentinels, walking back and forth on the wet stone threshing-floor, stayed to keep watch on our humiliation.

*

The next morning we kept busy organizing the area, where we believed we would stay for two weeks. Instead, we would be transferred farther south, and later our rest time would be transformed into a time of restructuring our units and renewing our equipment, which would keep us far from the front for months. But unaware of all this that morning, we divided squad by squad over the surrounding farms, as Francescoli had arranged.

When we officers went to inspect the houses before taking the men, each of us projecting his lone shadow on the dirt roads, several soldiers began hoping once again to find a good place to rest, as though, in certain aspects, they hadn't experienced the disappointment of the previous night.

I found the owner of a farmstead—a former official of state railroads—who was overseeing the last labors of the harvest. I asked him politely for two rooms for the soldiers.

Two large white oxen were pulling huge loads of sheaves toward the threshing-floor. Their peaceful bellow rose while they solemnly placed one powerful forked hoof in front of the other; their yoked shadows and that of the carts were clearly drawn on the ground beneath the new sun, as ancient as our civilization. One's heart became lighter in front of this scene, which finally wasn't one of destruction. "What peace! What magnificent peace!" I thought.

"Don't you have your tents?" the owner answered, almost startling me.

"Yes, of course. But during our few days of rest it's better to sleep under a roof. It's more comfortable, especially if it rains like last night, don't you think?"

"Comfortable or uncomfortable! I'm not letting myself be intimidated. I'm from Ancona; I'm an ex-official of state railroads, I am!"

"Hurry up, show me your house," I said. "Let's not waste time."

He was a stocky and robust old man with a stiff neck. The peasants who were lifting big stacks on the threshing-floor interrupted their work. They looked at us; it wasn't clear whose side they were on. Without waiting any longer, I went inside the large, clean house and began to inspect it. The owner and the old bailiff followed me silently; when the tour ended, I indicated the rooms that we would occupy, although without enthusiasm because I didn't feel like arguing.

The owner then burst out shouting; he flew into a rage, and imprudently he glorified the Fascists, singing their praises: "I would have given the rooms to them for sure, not to you soldiers from the other side, and partisans, all of you . . ." he made a significant gesture, for thieves. So it wasn't enough that Pelaformiche was insulting; this one had to add to it. His rage blinded him. I felt a great desire to kick him. But he had white hair and hoary eyebrows . . .

I turned around and, while he continued to shout, I went quietly to get the truck with the soldiers. I went ahead of the vehicle on foot. When we were at the threshing-floor, I signaled to two soldiers with submachine guns in hand, and they—after having stared at me, surprised—brought their weapons to their shoulders, and after receiving my confirmation signal, suddenly opened fire on the flocks of geese and chickens that scratched about. Since a shooting in a peaceful environment, especially if it blends with the screams of frightened women, makes quite an impression, our rooms were at our disposal right away. I ordered the owner to leave, and he left immediately on a bicycle, frightened, pedaling awkwardly.

Afterwards the silence returned to an environment of all soldiers and peasants, and I too tried to penetrate it.

*

In the following days, the artillerymen of the patrol turned up several times on the stacks together with the peasants, working with them: they sweated with their shirts open and threads of hay in their hair. "We too are peasants, lieutenant," they said, while peasant girls looked at them from the corners of their eyes and timidly lowered their dark-skinned faces if their eyes met.

As for me, I liked to lean over a long enclosure of prickly hedges, inside which beehives were aligned among long stalks of untilled grass. The innumerable bees ("Lombard," I daydreamed: "beloved by Virgil, beloved by Ambrose") came and went in the air, each with its destination, like tiny airplanes on a quiet airport. As I contemplated them, absorbed, sometimes I happened to mumble Latin verses from Georgic poetry.

It also became customary for the soldiers to sing all together with the peasants until late into the night, sitting in a circle in the evening in the only large kitchen. "Stay with us," the peasants now said. "Don't leave while the war lasts. Maybe you're not comfortable here?"

"We're comfortable," the soldiers answered, "but we're soldiers."

In fact, not even a week later the Nembo Division received the order to transfer itself to an area farther south. The Second Group reached San Ginesio.

22

THE DIVISION'S COMMAND, however, discovered the beauty of that small city and, with the phenomenal speed of commands when they act to increase their own comfort, they moved there the same day of our arrival, adding themselves to the Second Group.

Upon returning at night to my room, in which I hadn't yet slept, I found it closed, occupied by an unfamiliar division captain; my small gear had been dragged into the hallway.

"The captain said that the division's command has precedence," his orderly explained to me, "and that captains have precedence over second lieutenants."

"Ah, that's what he said?"

"Yes, sir." The soldier didn't look me in the face, ashamed of the role he had to play. The civilian owners of the house had come to the doors of the other rooms, fearful of an incident. "Don't worry," I assured them, "I'm in the army, and therefore bound by discipline, even under the most foul circumstances."

"What's your captain's name?" I asked the soldier.

"Sir, Captain G., of duties."

"You can certainly omit the 'sir': remember that," I said to him.

Afterwards I went straight to the seat of the division. But the two majors on duty, dizzy with wine, their bellies full, did not give me my dues but instead offered me some comforting words and somewhat confusing suggestions on how I could find another room. "Be patient," one of them said to me. "Tomorrow not only you but your whole group will have to move out of San Ginesio. Can't you see that we're tight here even by ourselves?" The other one, less drunk, tried to correct him. "That's not what it's about. It's that the town occupies a central position in the division's zone. Central, you understand? You understand?"

"A central position!" the first one repeated with his hands stretched out, dismayed by such an idea.

Back at the house, I quietly loaded my pallet and other odds and ends on my shoulders; in the meantime, the civilians had squeezed together, leaving another free room for me, but by that time I was too irritated to accept it. I carried my household goods on my shoulders up to Francescoli's house in the dark along the beautiful paved streets of San Ginesio. They pointed out his room to me. He was sleeping; he woke up suddenly when I threw everything on the floor. "What? What's happening?" he asked.

"The Germans have crossed the Chienti once again and are marching toward San Ginesio," I said.

"What?"

"I wish that they really were coming!" I murmured. "We'd see then how quickly these pigs at the command would sneak out."

The next day, right on time, the Second Group received the order to move to a small town in the middle of woods about ten kilometers away.

It was there that news reached us, after about a week, that the units constituting the *Corpo di Liberazione* would soon descend south (where the Allies' depots were located) in order to become two staff divisions, with British arms and equipment. Simultaneously, another four Italian divisions would be prepared: the part of our army that still vegetated; indeed, we learned with surprise that two such divisions—Cremona and Friuli—were already in the preparation phase.

It remained for us to stay away from our homes while the war seemed about to end, and to exchange our uniforms for foreign ones, even if fitted with our badges.

*

Back then, those with the "shopping" truck who went to Macerata twice a week to pick up provisions reported that there was now an uninterrupted transit of British armored vehicles on the main roads, headed for the front that we had left. The Allies were transferring some of their units there from the Tyrrhenian sector; in fact, they surprised the Germans, and near the Adriatic broke through the "Gothic Line," the large defensive line under construction in the Apennines between the two seas, barring the south of Italy. The British emerged in the Po Valley around Rimini, but were stopped there.

Meanwhile, in the small town in the woods, days of almost absolute idleness followed one another. The exhausted Francescoli had suddenly become ill, to the point that the concerned lieutenant doctor had taken him to the hospital of Macerata.

By that point many of us, although still tired and with worn-out nerves, would have preferred to end the triviality of that continuously altered rest time, which had become long, too long.

At times I would gather the soldiers on a field on the edge of town for some instruction. Since there were no benefits to training them with equipment that we would no longer use, I wondered if I wouldn't have been better off spending those hours attending instead to their civilian preparation.

I didn't have books at my disposal, but I knew by heart several episodes from Dante; I went over them by myself and saw that I still knew them thoroughly. One day I asked the soldiers if they would like to comment on them together.

They consented without much astonishment (they all still remembered our history conversations after the battle of Filottrano); some of them, like Lance Corporal Freddi, actually accepted with enthusiasm. So we spent a pleasant hour in the company of Dante: at first, I recited the verses one after the other, letting each soldier—even those more unprepared and uneducated—grasp the meaning of the individual words. Then I recited complete passages; finally, the entire episode, and repeated it several times. It was a new experience for me: after a few initial perplexities, and a few attempts at some sneers, I saw them gradually stick to the text that I was presenting: they tried to grasp, each as well as he could, and with his own point of view, the beauty that I pointed out; in the end, no one, or almost no one, proved to be impervious to the suggestiveness of great poetry.

I was therefore surprised upon seeing a couple of men suddenly giving me strange signals. I understood when Colonel Giaccone's vehicle halted behind me (it was the walled-in civilian car that we had recovered at Filottrano; since his Millecento had been destroyed, the colonel had requisitioned it). I turned and stiffened in salute. Giaccone asked me if our major was in town at the moment; I answered in the affirmative. He asked me what instructions I was giving.

"Literature," I was forced to answer.

"What literature?" Surely he thought that I was explaining a few pages from the artillery manual.

"Italian literature."

"What?"

"We're discussing Dante."

"Ah!"

"The Canto of Ulysses: twenty-six of the Inferno."

"A training a bit . . . eccentric," Giaccone observed.

"I admit it."

The ironic smile that we knew well began to form around his eyes. At first I didn't understand if it was a sign that he was mocking me or that he approved; finally, with a nod of the head, he let me understand that he approved.

"Come on, let's try not to disturb Literature," he said to his driver. "Let's move."

*

A fairly attractive girl, the landlord's daughter, lived an existence unknown to me in the apartment where I was lodged. Without having any intention of it, I began to court her with a few words a day. She seemed receptive; I didn't realize at first how receptive she was.

One evening when no one else was home and the girl was alone at her window, I went over to her side. A large forest covered the surroundings of the small town, bristling on a low hill.

"Have you noticed," I said to her, "how at sunset the sun paints the old wall of the house beneath ours red? If you stretch out your hands, they'll fill with its color."

After having looked in my eyes, she dipped her hands in that tawny copper, then slowly brought them up to offer it to me, as though it was some mysterious treasure. She was like those antique figures finely drawn in copper, her own priestess. Unlike those antique figures, however, the red color of her hands came from the real blood underneath her transparent skin. As her hands entered the shade, she continued holding them out to me, palely.

I felt my blood then like a river, and I felt violently shaken by its force. She looked at me with anxious expectation, her chin raised, without fighting what was within her; in me the angel was fighting the demon, and all the earth in my flesh and, on the opposite side, all the spirit in my soul.

It was the angel that compelled my elbows on the window-sill. I glanced at the fury of the woods reddened by the sunset without seeing it: her closeness invaded me; she was made of what I was looking for, all the flesh against which I had always fought and the femininity that I missed united to shape her.

Finally the angel won, and I won, and I told her softly: "As human be-ings, we must . . . be patient."

She looked at me for some time quietly, then said humbly: "I wanted to give you some peace, because I felt compassion for you, poor boy." As she said this, she left, and I wasn't able to accept what I had done. I saw again her expectation. "Our God is cruel," I cursed.

My eyes stopped far in the distance on the roofs of a monastery that emerged between the tree tops. A former chaplain who I had gone to visit a few days earlier—Father Mario, still under serious trauma from the things he had witnessed at the Russian front—spent his time there on his knees in a slough cell, in front of a cross. He once again found within Christ's gri-mace, hung on wood for all, his infantrymen's grimace as they lay on their backs dying in the snow, when he, with his face toward their faces, kneeled to impart their last absolution.

"Would that be the God, who died for you, who is cruel toward men?" the angel asked me scoffingly.

"Now you decide to speak," I thought.

"The problem is," the angel said, "that your destiny is one of giants."

"Sometimes too much so," I thought.

"Poor boy," the angel said.

23

A FEW DAYS LATER, September 3, Second Lieutenant Canèr and I were banished from the Second Group.

At mess Major Pelaformiche had told us nonchalantly, "You two, this afternoon you'll come with me to the regiment's command," and without any explanation had resumed talking about something else.

The regiment's command was in the village of Caldarola; our truck entered it in the usual thick cloud of dust, under the hot sun, while cicadas sang incessantly. The command was set up in a house that looked over the main square. We went up a flight of stairs with the major, thin and hard like an Arab, in front and the two of us unwittingly behind, shielded by metal banisters. Reaching a landing, the major left us waiting outside and entered the colonel's office.

Once in a while a sentry went by with a tidy uniform, and with an unwitting hint of condescension saluted us by clicking his heels; it was the usual atmosphere of commands.

Canèr, leaning his mighty back against the wall, decided to talk a little to ease the wait. The two of us had a wealth of memories. This time, though, he was barely able to start. "This place reminds me of the gasoline depot of my division, the Sforzesca, in the rear zone of the Don," he said. He took a drag of his cigarette. "These people in the command put on so many airs . . . My regiment, like the others, had to retreat without fuel: even for us it was a major inconvenience. By accident, I went by the divisional gasoline depot, and would you believe it? There were Romanian soldiers smashing gas drums with axes. The Romanians were up to their ankles in gasoline mixed with snow. They were right to destroy them all: otherwise, with all that gasoline that the command hadn't distributed to us, it would have been easier for the Russians to pursue us."

He exhaled a couple of mouthfuls of smoke toward the ceiling. The

smoke had a nice summery color to it, bluish. The attenuated song of cicadas came through the wide-open window, insistent and useless like our
memories, like mine here. "Well, it's nice to feel summer's still around,"
Canèr said, smiling.

"Lieutenant, come in," the major called me suddenly; leaving the door
ajar, he disappeared.

Colonel Giaccone was seated at a large table.

I came to attention in front of him; he left me at attention. "You were
banished from the First Group," he said slowly. "Now you're also banished
from the Second Group." He observed me in silence, almost with weariness. "I don't intend for the regiment to lose you," he continued, with his
intelligent eyes studying me. "Therefore, I'm not sending you to a depot in
Puglia. The regiment still has a unit that you haven't been part of: one only,
the machine-gunner anti-aircraft battery. I'm assigning you to it. See to it
not to get banished from that one."

I stood silent in shock. With our rest time the stimulation of the major's
nerves had lessened, and he had been treating me like the others, except for
a few intolerant remarks from time to time. This announcement was, in
any case, an act loaded with consequences.

"Do you have anything to ask?" the colonel asked.

"Can I ask what I'm being reprimanded for?" I realized that I was speaking with an altered voice. "You have to control yourself," I tried to order
myself.

"Your group's commander declares that he is 'unable to make you obey.'"

"Ah."

"Remember," the colonel said, "that diabolic sin isn't lust, or anything
else, but pride."

"Quite right on the mark," I had to agree to myself.

"I want you to know one thing: I'm not throwing you out because—
aside from your lectures on Dante—I see myself in you when I was young.
Afterwards, however, I had to bend to life: you will bend too . . ."

"Bend?"

"You'll understand better with time."

I was still at attention. "Does my unit's commander know that I'm being banished?" I asked. "It's Lieutenant Francescoli, at the moment at the
hospital of Macerata."

"He knows," the colonel answered as though skipping the subject; then
he discharged me. "That's enough. You can go."

I went out on the landing. "Banished from the Second Group," I informed Canèr. "Go in, he's waiting for you."

I stayed to wait for him, with my back leaning against the wall.

He came out livid. "You too at anti-aircraft artillery?" I asked.

He looked at me. "No, to the depot in Puglia."

We went down to the sunny square side by side.

"Now that the war is far away, the major can make do without us," Canèr said quietly.

It was these walls' turn, these old houses of the Marches, to be the backdrop of our shame. It didn't matter whether it was these or others, and I didn't care about shame: that was foolishness. It was the loss of the platoon, of each of my soldiers, that weighed on me. That was for certain. And having to leave Guatelli, Francescoli, and the two Canèrs.

"Listen," I decided suddenly. "You might think this is strange, but I'm going back to the colonel. Anyway, we're fearless people. I'll see if I'm able to get you to come to the anti-aircraft battery too."

"Forget it," Canèr said harshly.

"No, I'm going. I want to take advantage of some . . . goodwill that he showed me a little while ago."

The colonel, however, received me with a grim face, and with a few severe words made me regret my footsteps.

This didn't stop me: since I had started this, I decided to continue my attempt until the very end. "Canèr went through the Russian retreat; even though few people know about it today, it was one of the most tragic episodes of any war. After the armistice he went with the partisans: you know that he came south sent by them, to bring a message to the army's command. That's not all: here in the Second Group, he has been one of the officers who has applied himself the most. That's still not all," I added with calm determination. "In April, his city, Treviso, was almost entirely destroyed by an air raid, so he is very worried about his family's fate." I paused. The colonel looked at me with a dark face. "Canèr has given much. I'm not saying," I concluded, "that after the war we'll have to regard him in a special way because he was cold in Russia. But, at least while the war lasts and he continues to do his duty, don't throw him in the garbage like this. On the contrary, it seems like we should show men like him a minimum amount of gratitude." I stated this, even though to the soldiers I always said, "Don't expect gratitude from anyone, ever."

"Have you finished your pleading?" the colonel asked me.

"Yes, sir."

"Keep in mind that gratitude for those who deserved it has been one of the causes of Italy's ruin. However, I never change my decisions. You can go."

It wasn't long before Colonel Giaccone was also sent away from the regiment. I imagine that his words on gratitude would have come back to him—he who had spent his life in the army and had put together the regiment with his own tough hands. But he had signed the surrender of Rome to the Germans; in fact, he, a simple lieutenant colonel, even if of General Staff, had dealt with the enemy personally, even with Field Marshal Kesserling, because all the generals who were always on the streets of the capital had suddenly disappeared when faced with danger and responsibility. He, however, had remained at his post, and since it was indispensable that someone negotiate, he had negotiated. (Being an authentic leader, he had also exceeded the confusing mandate bestowed upon him by his hiding superiors, obtaining for Rome, on his own initiative, the status of "open city.") In any case, he had signed the surrender of Rome; therefore, they would now put him on trial.

When we arrived at the truck that would take us back to the group, the major—who knows how pleased he must have been for the nice blow he had inflicted on the two of us—pretended to be in a great hurry, and turned the bony back of his neck. We weren't aware that he was trying to join the territorial command of his city, and that within a few weeks he would be gone from the fighting units.

*

The next day, I made Sergeant Canèr assemble the patrol for the last time.

He assembled it on the field on the edge of the small town; however, only seven or eight artillerymen gathered, because the other seven or eight were scattered at different jobs. Knowing that they wouldn't be able to take part in the assembly, they had bid me farewell. Later, perhaps, they might have regretted not having been present, but it made no difference, nothing mattered all that much.

I positioned myself on the devastated grass in front of those convened. There they were, arranged in a single line: the patient Lance Corporal Observer Freddi, the orderly Morandi, the red-headed artilleryman Scirea from my mother's town, who without ever saying a word looked to take on an additional load in moments of great weariness, and Corporal Lisi, the last one to arrive, who at Montecarrotto had remained deaf and dumb for two hours; surely he didn't even remember it any more. There was also the driver Sabatini, with his crew-cut and his sagacious Tuscan accent, and the Abruzzese recruit (no longer a recruit by now) Pasquali. Each one with faces given them by God; faces that had become so familiar to me. They behaved, in their attitude, as though they were of a large unit, and for me, indeed, they had been.

I spoke, therefore, to that handful of men. "Much of it doesn't really matter," I said. "What really matters, for me at least, is that I have to leave you. It seems like the same old ceremonial words, but there's a difference: I truly feel what I'm saying, and not only because of the power of the moment. Well, today I'm leaving. You know that tomorrow the sergeant will leave too, and some of you will undoubtedly be transferred; the community that we put together, and that the war reinforced, is breaking up. The best advice that I can give you is, instead of scowling, find another one. Along with our families on the other side of the lines, this patrol family has mattered more than one would think, at least for me. The world today is really in bad shape, and together we created a small barrier around us. In any case, whatever you might encounter, I urge you to continue to do your duty. Then, once the war is over—I'll tell you for the last time—don't expect gratitude from anyone. You shouldn't scowl at that idea either: we must look to God, not to men. It would be a joke if we were to go through this much and die, for what? Perhaps for the gratitude of four idiots, who above all can't be bothered to show any gratitude."

Since a knot was beginning to form in my throat, I concluded with something amusing. "When one of you had a tantrum, remember that I would say: 'Be good: if you're good, I'll take you to see the colonel when he dies.' I think that's the only serious pledge that I didn't keep, but it's not my fault, it's the colonel's."

This said, with tears swelling in my eyes I shook the hands of that ridiculous handful of men, one by one. Finally, I walked toward the truck, followed by Canèr and the driver Sabatini, while the others dispersed.

*

The truck (the platoon's beautiful 626 Fiat, on which I climbed for the last time) took me to another small town a few kilometers away, where my new battery was quartered.

The following day the two Canèr brothers left for Puglia; in fact, even the sergeant had asked for transfer; he who, after the armistice, had renounced an officer's rank in order to be able to fight immediately. When I bid farewell to the patrol gathered on the field, Lance Corporal Freddi wasn't able to keep from crying. He had almost never laughed, and that time he cried.

Afterward, I no longer succeeded in communicating, either by voice or by letter, with the Canèrs. They didn't write to anyone at the regiment. It was only by accident that we learned that the lieutenant had been assigned to a depot where they sent the refuse from harbor workers' units: insubordinates, recidivists, and thieves. Later, we learned that he was under punishment in a fortress because, unable to control himself when a soldier had insulted him, he had with his incredible strength killed the man with one slap.

That is how the military career of the Canèrs—two of the most generous young men I have ever met—came to an end.

24

MY NEW ANTI-AIRCRAFT battery was by no means new. The soldiers, tired of war, looked upon changes of officers with hostility; they too annoyed me. Fortunately, the commander I found was fed up because he had spent a large part of the war in Libya and didn't want to lecture anyone: he was someone who got tired when letting out a few grunts related to duty. However, there was another commander, higher in rank and just arrived, who was glad to reprimand me. Thrusting his hands in his holster belt, looking at me from below because of his lack of height yet trying to give the impression that he was looking at me from above, he declared that he wasn't afraid of undisciplined junior officers; on the contrary, he had so much command ability that he almost preferred them. After all, he said, observing his fingernails, no man is worth more than a certain amount, because he could have been born simply from a handling error by his parents. This matter, of course, didn't concern the two of us, even though, in an admirable gesture of forbearance, he said he wasn't entirely sure about himself. I looked him in the face, to see if by chance he intended on insulting me in some way; but no, he was someone who, assuming a command after having been without one for many months, satisfied his needs by hearing himself talk to inferiors.

While he continued, I turned my thoughts to an entirely new set of ideas. "This fool," I thought, "could one day be part of the 'angelic butterfly,' which I too hope to be part of in eternity. And along with him Pelaformiche could also be part of it, and . . . who else? Let's see, those quivering bourgeois cheese vendors, for instance, who, charity aside, are such repugnant human beings. Surely, we can't know how that future corps will be today, but it's evident and indispensable that there will be fire for each of us . . . to tear away stupidity, cowardice, corpulence, and the smell of cheese (a lot of fire will be needed for that one), and . . . and also the presumptuousness with which I judge and define, which surely can't be pleasant for those who have to live close to me. Imagine what misfortune, being immersed in these things for all eternity! Without mentioning then our incompatibility with God, on whose life ours will be grafted like a shoot on a vine . . . Yes," I concurred to myself, "fire, as unpleasant as it might be, is necessary."

Meanwhile, because I had giggled at the idea of the smell of cheese, the future commander did his best to disguise the foolish things that he was talking about into logic and no longer stopped talking. Unwillingly, I ended up thinking back to when I had presented myself to Francescoli after I had been banished the first time, and the interruption of his comical reprimand that had marked the beginning of our friendship, and I grew sad.

Within forty-eight hours, my unyielding orderly, Morandi, joined me at the anti-aircraft battery, following his concept of military duty, which among Italians was based more on loyalty to people than to institutions.

Such loyalty cheered me up a little.

Nonetheless, some truly painful days followed for me. "These are rotten days," I told myself, whenever I told myself anything, "but meanwhile they go by. Take comfort in that, and don't give a damn about anything else: the war will have to end."

Sometimes I took shelter in the memory of Margherita, especially when I was in the presence of something that conveyed beauty. For instance, on top of a rustic bridge that my new soldiers were slothfully repairing, I thought of her, the girl I barely knew, if the wind waved the branches of a nearby row of white poplars, turning all the leaves silver, or, farther out, bent a stretch of marsh reeds in long green waves. Our encounters had been so brief, and yet she had engraved my spirit so deeply. In those moments, it seemed as though in a world desolately rotten, the beauty of things sadly recalled Margherita's beauty, and I almost wept from it.

Sometimes I also thought about my father. Who knows how he struggled to keep something for all of us to live on while I, because of my convictions ("Is there anything more volatile than a conviction?"), placed the front between my family and me . . .

Many days passed this way, or it seems like many now when I think back, because they weighed so much.

*

During one of these days, Captain Bevilacqua, regiment adjutant, came to pick me up with his car in order to take me to visit Francescoli, who was dying in Macerata. Two or three other friends of the sick man were with him. Back then, the civilian hospital of Macerata took in so many soldiers that it felt like a military hospital.

When we emerged from a flight of stairs into the hallway that led to Francescoli's room, we saw Second Lieutenant Provera come forward, alone in the yellowish light of the hallway, in his bathrobe, his head lowered, his face emaciated. He was still there because of the wound he had suffered in Filottrano the night when he had set out with the major to bring my platoon its rations, that inauspicious night when the chaplain and Lieutenant Bruschi had been mortally wounded. We knew that for several days Provera too had remained between life and death.

"Provera!" I called out to him.

He looked around and, knitting his brow, scrutinized our group, which was the only one in the halfway, then came toward us with open arms, dragging himself along in a hurry: "Corti!"

"Those rations haven't arrived yet," I said, hugging him. "I'm getting the feeling that you're taking this delay a bit too far."

"Tell me about it," he said softly. "Do you know that I was on the brink of death?"

"As a matter of fact, we knew it."

"Now, though, I'm fine. Actually, do you know? I'm getting engaged."

"What?"

"Yes, with a Red Cross nurse who took care of me. She's Piedmontese too, like me."

"Ah, this explains all the delays," I exclaimed, too forcefully.

The others too, disturbed by Provera's gaunt appearance, smiled more than necessary.

"Come, come," he said, still softly. "I'm fine now; it's Francescoli who's not doing well. He's not likely to make it. If he hadn't been so worn out . . . Come see him."

Francescoli, the only one bedridden, was lying in the middle of a small white room; he was so tall that his cot barely contained him, but by now he was no longer heavy.

"Hey, Franco," we exclaimed noisily while we approached him, alarmed by his ashen thinness.

He greeted us by weakly waving a hand, unable to raise it even from the sheet. He also murmured a few words, but his voice was so soft that we couldn't understand him.

"Hey, Franco," we said then, our voices suddenly softer. "How's it going? It doesn't look like you're sick after all . . ." The usual foolishness, while we knew there wasn't a cure: Francescoli too was about to leave.

He shook his forehead as well as he could, saying no to our nonsense. A Red Cross nurse entered to call us back to order, reminding us that we were not supposed to wear him out. So we stood around him silently, like owls.

After a while, I placed a hand on the hand of my dying friend: he turned his eyes toward me and smiled, beckoning to squeeze my hand. "Did you confess yourself?" I asked him. He shook his head, even though it was difficult now in his state.

Again, we stayed there without words. Suddenly, he signaled to Captain Bevilacqua, his main competitor in the exchange of jibes and witty remarks during good times, who lowered his head all the way down to the front of his mouth so he could hear him.

"You're a big idiot," Captain Bevilacqua exclaimed, quickly raising his head, "you're the same big idiot."

"What did he say?" we asked.

"He said: 'It looks like the scene in the *Bohème:* all the friends around . . .'"

It was his last witty remark.

"You've always liked being funny, haven't you, Franco?" we said, our faces smiling forcefully, while anguish clutched our throats.

Then we went out in the hall to not wear him out any further, nearly driven out by the Red Cross nurse.

The new regiment's chaplain, Father Picchi, a young Franciscan with the round face of a recruit, was there in the hallway. I took him aside. "You haven't confessed him yet, right?"

"Not yet."

"What are you waiting for? He only has an ounce of breath left. Francescoli will be glad to confess himself."

I stayed lost in thought for a few minutes. "Listen, Father," I said, "I'm his friend: therefore, I know the world of his thoughts and feelings. Now, I'll paint you a picture so that it'll be easier for you to understand him, with the ounce of breath he has left."

The chaplain looked at me, surprised.

"You think that I'm brutishly ignorant on matters of religion, don't you? That's because you don't know me. On the contrary, I'm half-friar myself."

"So you'll know that God isn't a bureaucrat who . . ."

"Please, forget bureaucracy," I said. "He's about to depart, about to leap off this wall here into eternity, and you're talking about bureaucracy. What matters is that he depart joined with God. After his death, that's all that will matter: isn't that right?"

"Yes, that's right," Father Picchi admitted. (He would later prove to be an efficient chaplain, and would even have a leg cut off, but at that moment, he really seemed like a recruit.)

Without wasting any time, I painted him a picture of the dying man's soul. Certainly, it was something quite strange, but the only thing I could still do for him.

Part Four

1 BEFORE THE *CIL,* according to new orders, was to transfer itself to the south, a few dozen officers and noncommissioned officers were to precede it, to train under British instructors on equipment that would be assigned in the future. Later on, it would be their turn to train the units. It was a big nuisance; therefore, among us, the last men to arrive at the regiment were selected. As the last one to arrive in my unit, I was among those chosen.

Four trucks transported us along the roads of the Marches, which had been deserted back when we had climbed them during the fighting but were now invaded by endless ocher-colored British and Canadian columns. When we entered the Apennines, we found the mountain roads were traveled only by the occasional motor vehicle, ocher trucks alternating with a few American ones darker in color; they moved isolated in the rocky solitude, over which the clear sky loomed. From our seats we looked at our humble Italy stretching widely around us, permeated with poverty; here and there from the woods, wisps of smoke from charcoal kilns rose from the woods, a sign that carpenters had returned to the eternal struggle for their livelihood.

We entered Lazio after crossing a mountain road along the old Via Salaria. Occasionally, we could see wrecks of German tanks on its margins, their noses sunk in the ground, their black cross emblems almost wiped out. Even lifeless, they still weighed too much for us to remove them all from the area.

At times, brief stretches of consular road, built with blocks of stone, ran on the edges of the asphalt, where for centuries legions of world reformers had marched (we couldn't avoid the mortifying comparison: we had done this too). We felt a sense of dismay in front of that silent evidence of the past, but also a kind of determination not to yield; to endure, until less disgraceful days would return for Italy . . .

As we approached Rome, the convoys of motor vehicles—almost all American here—once again became endless on the roads.

The sun was setting when we entered the city. In the streets, military vehicles blended with awkward streetcars and other civilian vehicles, which were still far from finding an acceptable design during that era of unrefined mechanical aesthetics. This was noticeable in every city at the time, but much more so in Rome, because of the contrast with the splendor of the surroundings; in some way, this matter turned out to be comforting, because it clearly showed the provisional nature of our time.

The city streets were swarmed by soldiers: American, white and black, British, South African, Indian, Polish, French, Brazilian, New Zealander, Canadian, Philippine, whom the Roman population seemed to have literally wedded. There wasn't a street where one didn't see women beside or on the arms of foreigners, or wearing multicolored fluttering clothes on fast-moving American jeeps. We bitterly realized that what we had heard was true: Rome had become a huge house of prostitution.

Comments began among us: "Damned bitches!"

"They've all lost their heads."

"Look at them over there, it's incredible . . ."

"They say that it's even worse in Naples. In Naples there are even groups of kids who live by stealing."

"Here we are risking our lives for this world of whores and thieves."

"And there are still some of us who are surprised that foreigners treat us like losers."

"It's disgusting to be Italian!"

"Athens was like this too," one of them offered, "back when we occupied it."

"It's like this everywhere now," another one offered.

We raised these words like hands to shield our faces. But it was of little use.

At first, some insults were shouted from the orderlies' truck, lashing at the faces of women like whips; soon, though, even they fell silent.

Almost none of the Romans answered our few initial greetings, because almost no one was aware that Italian soldiers were at the front.

"Do you realize this? Then it's true that the Italian radio never spoke of us."

"The Italian radio? You mean the party's radio."

"It's only Radio Bari who remembers us sometimes, because the king still has some influence in Bari. These here, though, are waging war on the king: you know they want to take his place."

"It's disgusting to be Italian!" several men repeated.

The truck halted at the enclosure of the large barracks of Pretoria.

We made the orderlies lay out some tent-cloths between the trees of a yard—indignantly, because these almost weren't barracks but woods—and set up our pallets underneath them. Some orderly kept watch. The rest of us went to spend the last hours before nighttime in the city.

*

I walked alone along the streets through a city of contradictions, for millennia a teacher of justice and truth to the entire world, as well as, since the days of Peter the Apostle, a tragic Babylon of corruption: this world's focal point of alternating superimposition and fusion, always and never realized, between the Earthly City and the Heavenly City. Here it was, all around me, in its houses and streets and discouraging miseries, and also in its magnificent monuments; the City of Man, the mirror of all cities . . .

So much had happened in this circumscribed limb of land, so much history! But the past was the past. Because constant reasons for anguish kept passing under my eyes, I wondered what the Pontiff, the Vicar of Christ, was feeling at that moment. But I was unable to comfort him in any way . . .

The Polish bishop of Przemysl, to whom I had paid a visit during my journey on the Russian front two years earlier, insistently came back to mind . . . The dismal memory of the Bolsheviks, who had occupied that small city for twenty terrible months, still lingered in the air; the line of heavy cement casemates ran out of sight in the fields beyond its last houses by the sad bank of the San River, horribly spotted black where fierce German infantries had stormed them, one by one, with flame-throwers. Along the streets, I had run into two different groups of forced-labor Jews, women and men reduced to terrifying conditions; I also ran into German soldiers with hard backs and behinds who drove Poles onto sidewalks with long whips, in order to clear the way for one of their columns of baggage-wagons. This had been my first real encounter with Nazism.

I had been so full of indignation, just like my friends Zorzi and Antonini, two other second lieutenants destined for the same regiment, that we had decided to separate as much as we could the Italians' responsibility from that of the Bolshevik invaders and the Nazis. How? By declaring our intention to some Polish exponent: to the city's bishop, for instance, if he happened to exist . . . Yes, he existed, and we had bent one knee in front of him and, with involved Latin phrases, declared ourselves friends of his people. After listening to us paternally, the bishop had answered us in perfect Italian. He was an old intrepid Pole, similar to an oak tree, who made one happy by just looking at him.

"We came," we told him, "to declare to you that the hearts of Catholic Italians aren't with the Nazi allies, but with you Poles."

"We knew this," he had affirmed, "but I'll tell you that it's comforting for me to hear it coming from your mouths."

Then he had blessed us and lingered with us, asking about Italy and Rome, which he knew well.

Now, as I walked along the streets of Rome in solitude, I thought back to that episode with regret. It had been possible for us to offer some comfort to a bishop, even if he was a prisoner in his home. But here, in his city, it wasn't possible to offer the Pope comfort.

At Piazza Venezia (disgracefully occupied almost entirely by a parking area for the Allies' motor vehicles), an American soldier, clearly a ruffian of the lowest kind, broke away from a small group of fellow soldiers and cut me off wickedly, then, turning around, tried to trip me. I had to hold myself back from giving the foreign mob the spectacle it was looking for—adding this to other humiliations that everyone suffered—and keep the combination of it all from reaching its peak.

A short distance ahead I heard a Roman hoodlum covered with brilliantine say bitterly to another one, "Look at that paratrooper" (my uniform deceived him) "who still holds his head high! Like we didn't lose the war . . ." This was even worse than the American who tried to trip me.

*

I was tempted to shut myself in a cinema, so as not to see more of Rome in that state. But I resisted, and it turned out for the best because shortly after, on Via del Corso, I had a pleasant encounter. A Polish noncommissioned officer gave me a friendly greeting from the opposite sidewalk: I noticed that he had on his arm the badge of the Fifth Kressowa Division, the mermaid with the brandished sword.

I responded with equal friendliness, and he crossed the street to shake my hand. He had recognized me from the troops engaged in the Marches, he stated in fairly good Italian, from the jacket without a collar. Therefore, although my compatriots hadn't recognized us, the Pole recognized me and gave me a warm welcome.

We proceeded together. He was born near Lvov, and had been wounded in the Marches. A year and a half before, I had stayed in Lvov for a week at the transit Italian hospital: I told him that I had kept an excellent memory of his city.

He was clearly pleased by it; he asked me if I knew a song (he sang a few verses and translated them): "*If I were to be born again—I'd like to be born in Lvov.*" No, I didn't know the song. Then he asked me what it was that I remembered fondly. I answered him that it was the houses, and the streets, and the general atmosphere of Lvov, but mostly the humble nuns who worked in the laundry room of the asylum transformed into an Italian military hospital, and I explained why.

Realizing that this wasn't a conventional attraction, he asked me some questions on the current situation in the city, which I wasn't able to answer. However, I was able to give him an account of two pretty recent barbaric episodes that were unknown to him: that all the civilians locked up by the Bolsheviks in the city prison (hundreds, maybe thousands, among which were several women and many priests) had been murdered by the NKVD at the time of Lvov's evacuation, before the German advance; and that subsequently all the mental patients from the asylum (hundreds of them too) had been murdered by the Nazis, right after the occupation.

Both bits of news filled him with consternation, but he recovered immediately. Back then, he explained, he was already a prisoner in Russia. He wanted me to give him an account of the few details I knew.

Then he asked me if I knew about the desperate fight currently under way in Warsaw between the Polish partisans and the German army. I told him that I had heard about it. Did I know that the Russian command had forbidden the Allied airplanes supplying ammunition to the insurgents from landing inside its own lines? I told him that I knew of this too, and that the matter filled me with indignation. I asserted that the situation of civilian Poland, caught between the two countries of modern barbarity, was tragic beyond words. I told him about our visit to the bishop of Przemysl: as a civilian man and as a Catholic, I stressed with fervor, I was a friend of the Poles, to the point where before being called to arms, I had begun writing a poem to the glory of Poland. Yes, a real poem, in the old-fashioned way; those few pages of poetry were at my house right now: who knows if I still would find them upon my return?

He nodded with gratitude. "You've said it well: the countries of modern barbarity. That's just how it is! All of us Polish soldiers have experienced the reality of the Soviet Union, where deported Russian civilians die every day like flies inside thousands of *lagers*: just like we Polish prisoners died."

"You say that there are thousands of *lagers?*" I exclaimed, somewhat surprised.

He nodded again. "Yes, and when we arrived all of them were overflowing with common Russian people, and many continued arriving even during our departure. I only went by five *lagers,* so I can't give you a complete picture. But soon a book will come out with testimony gathered among all of us soldiers of the Corps: the title will be 'The Other Side of the Moon.' "

"Let's hope that they'll translate that book into Italian too," I said. "Who knows, though, how Stalin resolved himself to free you Polish prisoners. It must have been in exchange for British arms and equipment . . . Even now that action is incredible to me."

"How do you think it is for us?" the Pole exclaimed. He stopped for an instant. "Do you know what we all think, really all of us, beginning with General Anders? That it was a miracle, performed by our patron, the Madonna of Czestochowa. Remember to write it in your poem, if one day you continue it."

I agreed. (I still believe today, after so many years, that it had been a true supernatural intervention in history; I didn't see and don't see any other explanation.)

Completely consumed by our conversation, we walked for maybe an hour. I noticed that my companion wasn't troubled by all the misery around us: fighting, with its inevitable wealth of recession and misery, was the normal condition of his existence. As it was, the important thing for him was to continue to fight; after being with him for a while, the surrounding miseries ended up not affecting me either. For the first time I asked myself the question (it would present itself on other occasions in the coming years) of whether the authentic successor of Rome, that is, the true Romans, weren't the Poles.

Their steadfast determination suggested it to me, as well as the attitude of many of them who, seated here and there on church steps, no longer seemed tense like they usually were. They didn't seem like people in a foreign city; rather, they were like people who in the evening sit on the threshold of their homes.

2

LEAVING ROME the next day, our four trucks passed a massacred airport where lay the many carcasses of our airplanes, probably all destroyed on the ground.

A paratrooper lieutenant, wrapped up in his coat, indicated with his chin some melancholy wrecks sunk in the grass and told us what kind of planes they were. "Since they were the best existing models six years ago, during the Spanish War, they didn't bother to design new ones. Idiots. The new models are being manufactured only now, in time for the Germans to use them."

"We also ruined the Japanese, who had the bright idea to copy our tanks from Spain," someone else said.

"You call those things tanks? An anti-tank gun, not to mention a cannon, was enough to pierce through them from entry to exit . . ."

"In Gasfa, in the Tunisian interior," one of the infantrymen said, "one of those heavy British seventeen-pound anti-tank shells pierced through four of our M14s that were stopped side by side. Not only that, but then the shell kept going."

"Where did it happen?"

"In Gafsa, in Tunisia. I was there, and I saw the tanks pierced through."

"But do you know that we built a real tank too?" said a *Bersagliere* officer. "I mean a tank capable of competing with those of others: the P40, twenty-six tons. It's just that it was ready only a few months before the armistice."

"Right, like those new model airplanes, ready by the time the war was already lost . . ."

Everyone shook their heads.

"Of course, it had to be this way," an engineer lieutenant observed. "Once we entered the war, it was useless to change the series productions; anyway, we didn't have the first-grade materials necessary to produce adequately."

"Not on your life. It's our industry that isn't worth a thing. We're people who are only good at producing street women and shoeshines," angrily interrupted a paratrooper officer who was wearing a lot of blue—somewhat threadbare—on his chest.

No one retorted. It was the same old story: we didn't want to contribute to the Nazis' victory, and at the same time we didn't want to be defeated. But how? Meanwhile, we left behind the airport and its airplanes sunk in the ground.

The Roman countryside also remained behind, lined, back then, with long rows of ancient aqueducts with overlapping arches.

Once we crossed the countryside, we entered the areas where the battle for the Nettuno bridgehead had unfolded. There was Cisterna, dead, reduced to skeletal walls. The bell tower was still standing, but stripped to the bone by fire, and its once laminated gold spire—which, sparkling from afar, had guided my steps and Antonio's during the first day of our wanderings—was blackened. The viable lands of the Pontine marshes[1] were now completely flooded; the water stretched as far as the eye could see, isolating the white geometrical colonial houses, and thrashed without waves on the two low sides of our road. It was daunting to think of the manual labor that had been wasted.

The winter fighting had occurred on the lands of the bridgehead. Our four trucks crossed them, keeping close to the sea; it was frightfully deep. Little but debris remained of the cities of Velletri, Terracina, Capua, Formia, Gaeta. Only a few houses were still standing, with crowds of residents around them; our fast trucks sent waves of slow-fading dust clouds onto the residents and against the few houses.

Here and there, individuals in bad shape stood up on the sides of the road to point to uneven writing in English on the walls: "Wine," some said, or "Barber." They were trying to stop us in order to earn something.

"How will these people survive without any more resources, in an already poor land?" I wondered. "What do they live on? And other people from similar places?" They were questions that I had been asking myself for a while, but that now came back to me with a new immediacy.

Aside from the insufficient aid distributed mostly by the Americans and

1. The Pontine marshes are an area of central Italy between the Tyrrhenian Sea and the Apennine foothills. They were drained during the 1930s to produce fertile farmland.

the Pontiff—thanks to the help of Catholics in America (the Americans and the Pontiff almost kept from distributing it, in order to avoid propaganda, because of the execrations of Red demagogy, which did its best to render that aid unpopular)—there were loose initiatives by everyone to keep from dying of hunger. And among these, most of all, theft was multiplying out of proportion, and prostitution, not only for girls but also, and more so, for women who had children. The children themselves had united in gangs to get a little more food.

I thought back to the heavy silence of the front itself, of the places everyone had abandoned because of the war. "Sure, everything surrenders when faced with the mad violence of war; everyone withdraws. And yet, these civilians' sufferings must undoubtedly be greater than those we soldiers must endure in the front line . . ."

Now I understood my brother Achille better, and what he had written to me in his occasional letters: for months of "waiting leave for appointment" to lieutenant (an appointment that would not come for years, because already too many officers vegetated unused in the south), he had moved to Naples, intending to continue his engineering studies. There, after dignifiedly refusing a loan from our father's business agent, he imposed on himself the life of a student without resources; as a result, he had had to renounce all prospects of studies, and simply kept on living. On certain days, he had been able to pick up some soup from a convent that sold it at a very low price. Lately, he had decided to go to a port on the Adriatic where he hoped to devote himself to being an engineer on some fishing boat. He didn't intend on being privileged at a time of hard trials for everyone; on the contrary, he wanted to personally experience the hardships of those most poor. (An excellent sign, in my opinion: once he graduated, Achille would become a genuine industrialist, not a caricature like those that the Red culture already chattered about back then.)

The thick cloud of dust raised by the trucks knocked people to the sides of the road. As for me, in order to continue my own journey—it was mostly one of experience, which would allow me one day to truthfully restore the events of our time—I kept, particularly on difficult occasions, from letting myself become involved with those characters. I had to take action for them too, but as though they didn't exist, or I would have been immobilized.

Halfway through our journey, we came to a quiet olive grove on the solitary road that connected the towns of Piedimonte and Cerreto Sannita in

Beneventano. We pitched our tents under olive trees. All around us rose dark mountains, among which, it had been established, the *Corpo di Liberazione* would be spending the time necessary for its reequipment.

After a few days, however, the British command of the province made us take down our tents and return to the region of Rome, because that was where the British training school was located. But since that school had received orders in the meantime to transfer itself to Beneventano, we set out after it once more, and were back again among those mountains. This time, we quartered ourselves in the town of Cerreto.

"The Italian commands, with their usual inefficiency, would have behaved more or less like this," was the usual remark. "But who would have imagined that there were so many similarities in the way that the British commands and ours act?"

*

During our to-and-fro between Lazio and Campania, we crossed Cassino on a train. I had seen much destruction before, both in Italy and away, but none of it compared to this.

Not only had all buildings been reduced to debris but also every living creature, vegetation too, had been killed. Motionless water stagnated on the enclosed flat land between the mountains where the city once rose and flooded the large expanse of ruins; there wasn't a single tree or shrub as far as the eye could see. There was not a blade of grass on the slope, which climbed toward the square ruins of the monastery, furrowed by explosions; only a few broken-up and blackish tree trunks from the forest that had probably once covered the slope remained standing, looking like extinguished firebrands. Even the tanks with which the Poles—madly in love with their land—had attempted to exceed the limits of death for her lay abandoned here and there in the dismal swamp or on top of debris piles, like dead steel mastodons. The only vivid things were the ambiguous flowers that grow on top of flooded lands, which here appeared infrequently on the surface of the water.

"This doesn't look like other destroyed cities," a voice said suddenly from the car before us. "More like the ruins of Pompei."

The train proceeded slowly on the embankment between the waters and stopped where the Cassino station once stood, because someone on the ground had noticed a flame coming from a wheel hub. It was a strange flame, torpid; it started from the steel and it wasn't clear what it fed on.

"These cars have been out of service for months!" the voice noted.

"Look, I can't explain it," he insisted. "How does it sustain itself if it's coming from the steel?"

"It's so yellow!" he added further, after an oppressive pause.

His insistence on this kind of detail increased our discomfort. The silence was so great that it seemed as though we had entered the station during late night, not during the day. As a matter of fact, it seemed like our train had entered not a station, but an immense cemetery.

"They don't care at all about old railroad cars," the creepy voice insisted.

Unexpectedly, a brief procession of girls emerged from the flooded hovel of the station and came toward the train; most of them had small white roses in their violet-colored hair. They were real women, not ghosts; they carried wicker baskets of fruit that they offered to us when they reached the train. They were trying to sell the fruit and paid careful attention to the calls from the cars; in their presence we fell silent. "Don't be afraid," they began saying. "Buy. Buy, Americans," they said, smiling at the American soldiers who looked at them from their coaches. "Don't you understand that we too must survive?"

They looked around to see if anyone would buy from them, until the train departed with a long screech, leaving them behind.

3

THE TOWN OF CERRETO lay crouched out-
side the passage of time, on a crest between the mountains. It had been leveled to the ground by an earthquake ten years before, then incredibly resurrected, dreamlike, on geometrical roads. We traveled those roads now.

Since I had been in the service, I had always looked after my technical
preparation carefully. It was no different during the British course. I un-
dauntedly filled my days with practice and study. Only at sunset, when I
removed my overalls in front of my old, by now worn-out uniform set out
waiting on my cot, or in front of Morandi, who, with an unconvinced air,
wondered if I had orders for him, did I ask what it was that I was still preparing myself for with so much commitment.

The British instructors proved to be impersonally polite. It's true that
they didn't seem to think highly of us; nevertheless, they didn't burden us
with their opinions. Out of all other nations, the Americans seemed the
only ones back then to annoy the British—really annoy them. It was amusing to note how they regularly pointed out the meaningless, and at times
even nonexistent, deficiencies of the American equipment with which they
trained us. On several occasions an instructor went as far as to apologize
for those deficiencies; his attitude seemed to suggest that we couldn't reasonably expect more from the Americans.

I didn't feel like observing the British, even less studying them, tired as
I was of war and its experiences. Nevertheless, because they were continually in front of me, I inevitably noticed some of their peculiarities. For
starters, there was their tolerance of others' points of view, even when those
views were obviously unfounded; in this regard, after decades of democracy, I don't think that today there is much difference between British and
Italian young men, but back then there was a considerable contrast.

I also noticed, from the first days, how they didn't approach reality the same way we did. If we were shown a complex object—let's suppose a cannon—we would never begin with one of its secondary parts, for instance a tire, but would spontaneously begin with some of its main attributes. The British actually started with a screw or a bolt; one could say that for them all things were equally important.

On a different subject, I was under the impression that they were immune to Jacobinism, the obscene attitude that sometimes renders the Latin man similar to a dog whimpering against the sky. This discovery—or beginning of a discovery—seemed so important to me that I intended to examine it more closely, but then I dropped it.

Moreover, I noted that our moral sense and theirs weren't completely in harmony. I gradually concluded—to my surprise and disappointment—that, in certain spheres, they were undeniably more moral than us. In any case, it wasn't easy to gather this from the British in Italy in 1944; with the war having hastened a process already on its way, quite a few of them seemed to want to free themselves from moral ties. Turning a whim into a "right" seemed to be a big discovery for them; in short, sometimes they gave the painful impression of a nation that was beginning to get tired of its own virtue.

At times I happened to overhear what the other Italian "pupils" were saying about the British. Some of the other officers, completely mortified by the fact that foreigners were in command in our home, continuously reacted with remarks of the most trite nationalism, for instance, setting each of their merits against one of our larger merits.

There were also those who compared them with the Germans: "In spite of their rigid postures, they are weaker."

"Well, I think they're mostly more mediocre, without greatness."

"Maybe," another suggested, "their strength is precisely in their mediocrity. They've scuffled like ants for centuries, while other nations pursued ideals."

"Just think: they dare reproach us for the taking of Ethiopia, while they think it's normal for them to own a sixth of the globe."

"That's right: and the most incredible thing is that they think that they're honest and sincere."

"What a bunch of hypocrites!"

However, it should be said that most of the officers didn't look upon the British with a critical eye, but respected them without reservations because, in contrast with Italians, who had been so good at chatter, they had stood up firmly against Nazism at the time of its most frantic shove. They felt—actually, we felt, since I was among them—that their British resoluteness constituted an asset for all civilized people, ourselves included.

However, with the passing of days, I personally ended up appreciating something else more: the modesty of the British, and also their natural realism. I saw them almost always begin from how things were, instead of how they wished things were (something I was slowly realizing that we too often did). Seeing that objectively, in their practical nature, human beings are incapable of becoming enthusiastic, the British have resolved the problem of interpersonal relationships mostly through good manners, namely with limitations: by not disturbing, not speaking loudly, not making noise, etcetera, with undeniable results.

In later years, and after other experiences, I ended up being convinced that it was their patient objectivity toward each thing, starting with the screw and the bolt, that enabled them to create modern industry—one of the three or four greatest means that humanity has given itself in the entire course of history. I also noted that here too there were two sides to the coin: on account of their precise consideration for each thing, the British sometimes end up not giving importance to something that deserves special recognition. For instance, in their museums—among others, the National Gallery—they will line up some incredible daubs next to extraordinary masterpieces. In doing so, they miseducate the uninformed visitor in regard to artistic order; as a result, those places tend to deprive men of art, even though their intention is the opposite.

I cannot close this summarized list of my rudimentary, incomplete, and almost involuntary observations from that time without remembering that in Cerreto I was able to confirm one of my previous observations regarding nations on the whole: that there is not one attribute of one nation that is absent in any other. It is only that the same attributes appear, so to speak, in different stratifications and quotas. They produce, therefore, different effects. This is the case for sincerity, hypocrisy, loyalty, realism, steadiness, laxity, etcetera. Here too a single example is illustrative: back then, we found robbing our government almost moral, and a reason for pride. Although other nations were not like this, they, however, found it moral, and actually worthy (one thinks particularly of the Germans of that time) to ruthlessly rob other nations for their own advantage . . .

4

DURING THE British training course, I had the opportunity to see Naples again. Perhaps more deprived of its normal resources than any other city in Italy, Naples seemed to live only by underhanded cunning back then.

"A million human beings who live off schemes," I told myself during the trip on a truck from the British school. "It's a grand and tragic phenomenon." It was daunting, especially if one believed some of the messy and unrepeatable rumors regarding insanely obscene trades that were taking place in the city.

During my visit, however, I didn't encounter anything horrible.

We halted in the port area, which was devastated by bombardments, inside an irregular parking area of guns and materiel of every kind, supervised by numerous armed sentinels. The captain and British soldiers, who had come from Cerreto to collect some replacement parts, had to wait almost an hour for the corporal storekeeper to finish his tea (so, the British rear zone wasn't inferior to the Italian in its couldn't-care-less and selfish attitude).

After retrieving the parts, we went downtown. We climbed down from the truck in Piazza Plebiscito. While we were agreeing on the hour of departure, I became suspicious of some shuffling behind the vehicle. I moved to check on it; right under my nose, six or seven tomboys moved away a few steps with feigned disregard, then ran off. We noticed that the ropes of the back tarpaulin had already been cut . . . Without commenting, the British placed an armed sentinel in the body of the truck before we dispersed. I went looking for a dentist's office, having come to the city because of a painful tooth abscess.

Along a large dirty artery, I passed a ragged child who was sleeping on the sidewalk in the rush of the crowd; a piece of bread lay next to his finely chiseled head. After taking a few steps, I stopped, intrigued by another child. He approached the first child, studied him in silence, took the bread, split it in two parts, set one on the ground near the sleeping child, and left, nibbling on the other.

I resumed walking along dirty streets filled with Allied soldiers and civilians who were bustling about for unknown reasons. The city was animated in all directions by an immense mob, not only on the streets I traveled but also beyond the expanse of the ruins, on many other streets, even in the distance.

"What are they doing? How will these people survive?" I went back to asking myself. It was clear that not one Neapolitan had considered that it was necessary to discipline themselves, that even by organizing themselves it would have been difficult to overcome a situation like this one. "Will there be some who will die of hunger? Will there be many?" I asked myself, troubled.

In front of a bar, I lingered to listen to a little fellow reprimand a drunk American soldier. He pointed to himself for general admiration, and proclaimed: "American, American . . . Me American!" as he rocked back and forth on the threshold of the shop (who knows what brew they were selling . . .)

The little fellow—his hat was pulled down on his forehead like many Neapolitans used to wear them back then, to avoid the effort of occasionally adjusting them—both scolded and made fun of the American, and at times even insulted him vigorously. The simple fact that I had stopped led several other curious people to stop: some idle individuals, some kids, a matronly looking old woman, and others. Unfortunately, I wasn't able to stay long; I had to remove myself reluctantly from the small congregation.

Finally, there was a sign for a dentist's office, in the central area by the cathedral. The office turned out to be modern and well equipped. After a helpful medication (what suffering and what relief!) I resumed walking thoughtfully on the city streets. On one street I unexpectedly ran into a former fellow soldier, Mario Cicala, who seemed to have completely forgotten the military service and war. He pointed his long nose in my direction with great surprise and after a few moments of uncertainty, came toward me and hugged me with Neapolitan effusion.

I was sincerely glad to see him, and I told him so.

"Me too, me too," Cicala answered, and nodded with his eagle-nosed head.

After some polite greetings and a brief recalling of the fantastic time we had as recruits together in Piacenza, I said to him, "Listen. You have to tell me what really happened here in Naples during the days of the armistice. And also how things are now. Look, I'm really interested. I want a . . . detailed report."

"Detailed? You think that's not asking much? Ah, ah, ah!" He began laughing, very pleased for having run into me, and interpreting my request as a need for a distraction.

"No, please," I insisted. "I'd like to hear what really happened, from you who was here."

"You really want to dig up that sadness? Well, what can I tell you? At the time of the armistice, no one here was concerned about the Germans, who were more or less invaders . . ." He looked at me after this remark, arching his eyebrows, satisfied: his manners were decidedly more academic in his own environment than when he was in the service. "As for them," he resumed, "I mean the Germans . . ." He interrupted himself. "Of course, if I think about it, I'm still not convinced! They actually expected for us to return to the army to work for them . . . Can you believe it?"

"Indeed."

"Do you understand any of it? It wasn't enough for them to quarrel with the Americans, the British, the entire world. That wasn't enough. They also wanted it out with us, who didn't pay any attention to them."

"Maybe," I let out, pressing my cheek (which, because of the anesthetic, gave the sensation of being swollen as soon as I laughed), "maybe they thought that since Italy had lost the war, the Neapolitan had lost it too."

"Good one!" Mario Cicala exclaimed. "A real good one! I've always said that deep down you're a good wag."

"Well, go on," I urged him. "But, please, tell me what happened: the facts."

"The facts? I'll give them to you right away. First of all, the German General Scholl, commanding the square, had posters put up, ordering I don't know how many classes to present themselves for work immediately. According to rumors, around three hundred thousand of us should have presented ourselves. Do you know how many presented themselves? Thirty-two."

"Thirty-two thousand?"

"What thirty-two thousand? I said thirty-two."

"Notably less, a discount," I had to agree, pressing on my anesthetized cheek again. "Not even the Chinese who sell ties give such sensational discounts."

"But what do you think? The Germans were serious. They began searching houses one by one; the dodgers were to be shot on the spot. Then the women began crying, screaming something fierce . . ."

"I can imagine it."

"Well, I won't dwell on it. The end of it was that we revolted."

"Ah! So you too?" I said surprised.

"Me?" He looked at me almost as though he didn't understand. "Me?" Then he shook his right hand up and down, with the tips of his fingers gathered together, to mean, "What am I, stupid?"

"Whoever wanted to revolted, of course: many ex-soldiers, but also kids, actually especially kids, many of them, an infinity of them, a raging plague . . . I can't tell you who taught them to fire, especially to fire a machine gun, because they were doing that too, and how! The fact remains" (here his face rightfully assumed a challenging expression, as if to say: "Try to deny it if you can") "the fact remains that we drove the Germans out of Naples."

"Yes, in fact, that's what I heard. And later with the Allies?"

"With these other ones . . ." He was somewhat uncertain: "What can I tell you? More than anything, we must be patient. At first, they too were annoying, and not just a little bit. Most of all, the American generals. They wanted, I don't know, to organize us . . . They said that it was to help us get on . . . You understand? Poor guys!"

"But what did they want exactly?"

"What can I tell you? You know them, don't you? The usual stink . . . They were disappointed when they saw that no one gave a damn about their plans."

"I believe it."

"They even put those notices in English at the entries to Naples: 'Caution, city of thieves!' "

"I actually saw them."

"But then they let it go. Actually, because deep down they're not skunks, many of them tried to give us a hand; we must admit that too."

"In what way did they give you a hand?"

"What do you mean: in what way? In the only important way: they take food from where it is, from subsistence, and secretly get it to us."

"For free?"

"Well, you must thank them with something for their trouble. But all in all they don't take very much, and . . . Well, you know what? After they live in Naples for a little while, many Americans from all ranks—I'm not talking about deserters, because there are millions of them, you can't imagine—behave like true Neapolitans. With some things, they even overdo it."

"I understand," I said.

"All right," Mario Cicala concluded.

I saw more and more dirty streets, entire blocks leveled to the ground, and everywhere that immense mob.

On my way back to Piazza Plebiscito, I noticed with surprise that the Catholic Action was fighting here too its battle for morality, with posters on the walls. But that too was a Neapolitan battle: it was fought on its own account, without anyone taking notice of it, especially at that evening hour. I saw many women walk by on the arms of Allied soldiers between me and those few posters and didn't know if I should curse, or laugh, or begin to scream from the grief, like Neapolitans do.

Later on, 1944 Naples came to be described by other men who lived there. As for me, I didn't have enough facts during this visit and a few others to thoroughly and properly examine its reality. After all, I didn't even want to: what could I have done for Naples, me, a twenty-three-year-old second lieutenant? What was happening was so immeasurable, and urgent, and difficult, that just thinking about it took one's breath away; it was somewhat like the thought of our duty when we're on the line to move forward, always move forward, in order to liberate women and children from the torment of the front.

5

UPON RETURNING to Cerreto, I found my course mates irritated by the discovery (criticized with real anger by the many Nationalists) that the cigarettes passed on to us from British supplies were those for colored troops. I didn't know if it was true, but it didn't bother me. Like other "pupils," I had established a friendly relationship with some instructors, particularly with two specialists of anti-aircraft guns, Sergeant Clark and Captain Ingledew, whom I sometimes enjoyed teasing by praising, for instance, an American device or instrument; both of them smiled at my words and didn't react.

Somewhat less childlike, in those days I tried to talk to them about serious subjects, for instance of the great figure of Saint Thomas More, whom I already admired very much back then because of his incomparable diligence toward truth (today I consider him to be the greatest and most typical British man of all time). I wanted to find out his countrymen's opinion, but not much came of it. We also spoke of literature several times. Clark and Ingledew didn't have any specific training in British literature, and neither did I; therefore, we weren't able to say much about it. I had the feeling, though, that their sense of aesthetics didn't coincide with ours at all: for a few days I was truly taken by this problem and uselessly tried to clarify my ideas in this matter. I would have liked to submit my question to the colonel commanding the school, Roy A. Dehn, a philosophy teacher and an intelligent, cultured man who even spoke our language well. But I was an Italian second lieutenant wearing shoes that were by now in pieces, and he was a British colonel; I didn't find the opportunity.

I still had Margherita: she was the only one who didn't disappoint me, didn't make me weary. I increasingly held on to her memory, especially when at night solitude stretched out its cold mantle on the alpine town of Cerreto, and the voice of man or the plaintive voice of animal bewailing the coming of winter weren't enough to break through it. I liked picturing

Margherita bustling about in my future house, whose windows were golden in the evening.

Therefore, Margherita was no longer a guide and a Beatrice, but rather a digression, an escape from reality. But even as such, for me it is still the best memory of those distant days.

*

Meanwhile, all the units of the *Corpo di Liberazione* had poured into the towns of Piedimonte and Cerrato Sannita, and around the high, solitary road that connected them.

Many tent cities were raised among olive trees and rows of elms married to vines on the arable terrain scattered with stones; the hawks who took flight from some Lombard castle ruins on the surrounding mountain spurs looked at the tents from above and at the men in their midst and circled slowly around them, irritated. But the men were even more irritated than the slow-flying hawks, because in winter they would all have to find space in the miserable, already crammed houses of the area.

Once the British course ended, Morandi and I rejoined the anti-aircraft group that was being formed. It was no longer the unit that we had left: in fact, the regiment's command, in accordance with the Italian bad habit of improvisation, had decided to transform a field group that had been recently assigned to the regiment into anti-aircraft, while the old anti-aircraft battery, yielding few specialists, was now being transformed into a field group.

As fate would have it, our new group was the worst out of all those who participated in the *CIL* campaign: it was a unit that had not been cured of the exhaustion following the armistice, by either the beneficial training of the front or the enthusiasm of the advance.

We reached our group on a foggy afternoon: it was October, and the rainy fall had arrived. A truck let the two of us and our small gear off near a handful of poor houses on the side of the road. I began looking for the group's commander, leaving Morandi to watch over the gear.

The men who were to become my soldiers looked at me insolently, some of them seated on the ground, dressed in uniforms worn to the limit. They gave me the information I asked for without standing up. Then, by chance, I ran into an officer, who at first I didn't even recognize as an officer. He, however, was aware of my appointment to the group. "You are the new assigned man?" he asked me.

"Yes," I answered.

"In theory, I would be the 'quarters officer,'" he let out, "so I would have obtained a room for you, but I didn't even look for it. There aren't any in this sickening town. Those of us who are junior officers are all gathered in a kind of attic: if you want, we'll squeeze together and make some room for you . . . But," he added as we headed toward the attic, "I don't see how we can squeeze any more than we have already . . . We're already packed like sardines."

I didn't speak, but he immediately found a way to let me know that he was part of a subversive political group: clearly this was what was on his mind, not the lodging problem. "My father was persecuted by the Fascists," he declared with strange, irrepressible satisfaction, "very persecuted."

After climbing a disgraceful ladder, he pushed open a worm-eaten door. We entered the officers' quarters—maybe a barn with one small window—packed with cots and small improvised beds where the group's junior officers sat or lay down, nearly in the dark.

I introduced myself according to the rules, and they, somewhat surprised, stood up one by one to shake my hand. Then they offered me a stool. My escort didn't waste any time before igniting a political discussion: he was perfectly aware that the current disastrous situation was an ideal time for him, and others like him, to sow and harvest. The matter made a bad impression on me. "Here at the Nembo, we're used to respecting the duty that we as soldiers have not to discuss politics," I said aggressively.

He didn't care about my tone and my words. (A short time earlier, a soldier had even slapped him in public—I don't know over what quarrel—and it seemed that he hadn't cared about that either.)

I was getting increasingly irritated. I looked at him: instead of boots, he wore soldiers' straps; at first I thought, malevolently, that it was because of demagogy. Then I noticed that the straps, although worn out, were well taken care of: he must have rolled them meticulously every night. Maybe he was very poor. Maybe he truly unselfishly believed in the mistaken ideals of which he spoke. Maybe his uncared-for appearance concealed a real inner fire . . . I fought between conflicting feelings, and ended up by letting out my bad mood on the place: "Don't worry about making room for me. I won't come here," I declared. "It's an unworthy place."

From his cot, Second Lieutenant Laganà, older than most of us and who I would soon begin to respect, looked at me through his gold-rimmed eyeglasses. "Believe me," he said, "we weren't able to find anything better in this small town."

"In that case, I'd rather sleep in my tent," I declared.

"We're staying here all winter: how will you be able to spend it in your tent? Anyway, if you want to, the guns parking area is in a clearing beyond the road. At least there your tent will be watched over by guard duty."

"Thank you for the information. I'll get settled there."

I went out searching for the commander major, to introduce myself.

Major Valentini, a former partisan in Rome who had joined the anti-aircraft group only a few days earlier, was coming down a lane between the hovels, placing one bowlegged horse-rider leg in front of the other. He was short and sturdy. The captain adjutant, a taller fellow, walked at his side.

I introduced myself: "I am one of the two junior officers trained on anti-aircraft materials," I explained.

The major stretched out his hand. "I was waiting for you," he said. "We will be friends. The other instructor is from Rome, and I've given him a short leave. There will be much to do."

"Much to do," I agreed.

"How come you're wearing the Nembo uniform, and you ended up in the Sixth Group?"

"Because I was banished from the Second. I thought you were aware of it."

The captain adjutant's face grew dim; the major scrutinized me (he was considered, I would late discover, a good judge of character and, indeed, he was: he was a good commander). At the end of his examination, he stretched out his hand to me once more. "We will be friends," he repeated, then left down the lane, placing one bowleg in front of the other, followed by the captain adjutant, who was once again cheerful.

I crossed a sort of yard where soldiers were now lined up for the rations in a disorderly manner. But they were more interested in—and cackled over—the maneuvers of two turkeys spasmodically mating in the mud than they were in the rations.

Morandi was still waiting on the road at the edge of town, near our small stack of gear, with the barrel of our two submachine guns, his and mine, hanging down from one shoulder.

"We ended up in a nice pigsty," he said.

I nodded. "Come." We set out to pitch the tent where Laganà had suggested.

However, the rain had reduced the cart-road leading to the artillery parking into almost impassable mud, so I decided to make one last attempt at finding lodging in town. "Wait," I said to Morandi. "The house of the parish priest seemed less filthy than the others. I'll go see if I can find lodging there."

The house—one of the few with a plaster exterior—consisted of merely a single large room with bright floor tiles. The kitchen, the bedroom, and, in the middle, the office of the parish priest—a table with a few books—were all one.

The parish priest was also there, walking back and forth on the tiles; he was small, with his collar out of place, and with a bright face. I talked to him slowly, asking myself if I was talking to a mentally ill person. He answered me with prompt intelligence: "I am very sick, lieutenant. Nevertheless, even if I had only one other room, I would gladly put it at the disposal of the Italian officers: but I only have this one."

What places existed in Italy!

It rained throughout the night. The rain insistently beat against the roof of the tent, and I listened to it, dismayed.

I had experienced this once before, only a few years before. Then, life had seemed like a great game, and the sound of the rain on my tent, a song.

*

Every afternoon, after finishing the training, I used to leave our rotten quarters and walk in solitude among the deserted small paths of the olive groves. The sun painted them with uneven golden patches, where the last warmth of the year lingered.

October. These were the days when passing birds, full of wonder, came to rest on the leveled tops of fruit trees . . .

One evening on the road, returning from one of these quiet roamings, I encountered Captain Bevilacqua's car. He stopped to inform me that Francescoli had died several days ago, after he too had been transferred to another unit. He had been moved to the depot battery, among those useless; fortunately, however, he hadn't realized it.

"By now, no one even talks about Francescoli anymore," Bevilacqua reported. "The regiment is tripling; you know that it's gone from two to six groups. Even the colonel is different. Many new men are arriving. Everything is changing."

As he was speaking, I was thinking that no one would hear Francescoli sing anymore the sad song of the dress shaped by wind. And soon, who would remember his fair girlfriend, killed in Turin? In a few years, no one on earth would remember either of them . . . Their reality could not end in nothing; it could not be, and would not be. But, although unbearable, it was by now certain that their time on earth would end in such a way.

In the meantime, his mother, who had only him, probably continued to keep his bed made and his other things . . . Maybe mine would have too.

6

A SUPERIOR DISPOSITION unexpectedly transferred the Sixth Anti-Aircraft Group to the town of Cerreto, where I once again met Cèt, who had attended the course following mine at the British school. He offered to share his quarters: a large room whose only furnishings were two metal bedsprings on the floor.

The weather had become rainy; in front of our window, the water dripped down for hours from our roof's broken eaves, like a lace of sadness. The oppressive mountains were perpetually hidden by fog.

When the rain allowed, the square of Cerreto resounded with orders shouted by me and the other instructing officer and with the monotonous confirming shouts from noncommissioned officers and soldiers. The anti-aircraft 40-mm Bofors guns were quickly brought into position and placed in the battery. The long, slender barrels rose, lowered, turned to the shouted numbers; the guns were then once again prepared for hauling and returned in a hurry to a side of the square. We had no spectators, aside from the occasional stray dog who stopped to look at us, surprised that the town now had so much discipline.

Indeed, it took a lot of strength, and at times severity, to transform those men from the armistice back into soldiers again. Certainly at the end of the war, many of them would be forced to search for food, without any consideration for everything they had done for everyone. But could I leave them in their state of dissolution? Of course not. There was nothing left for me to do but be vigorous.

On a wet afternoon when a small group refused to leave their quarters because their shoes were in pieces, I took the main instigator and had him tied to iron bars. Italian regulations don't provide for such punishment, but our sanctioned punishments no longer had any effect on these kinds of soldiers. Shortly after, the punished man's companions untied him and began a mutiny. This occurred as we officers were gathered for a report in the company office; the noncommissioned officers, who had no authority over that group, came to tell us. The battery's commander, Captain Zuntini, a Florentine, more humanist philosopher than soldier, ordered me in front of the entire deployed battery to tie the man to the bars once again. No one dared to object. From that day forward, we realized that the troop had submitted to our will.

Some of the older officers were sent away by the commander major, unwillingly, because he was paternal and compassionate considering the times. The most insubordinate soldiers were transferred to the depots; the demagogue second lieutenant with worn-out straps was sent to another unit. Little by little discipline became normal.

With my hard way of directing the restoration of order, I ran the risk of being banished from that group too: I would have been if the old tendency for disorder, which lurked still in several officers, had prevailed.

"Can you tell me who's making you do it?" old Laganà asked me sometimes, observing me curiously through his gold-rimmed glasses. (He liked me in spite of everything; he too had been through many war experiences. On the Libyan front where, among other things, all his halftrack's companions had been killed by aerial machine-gunning, he had completed a long lap of the retreat, from dawn until dusk, carrying alone that load of dead. But he didn't speak much of his own experiences.) "Not that I disapprove of your actions," he said, "but don't you think you've been through enough?"

"Who's making me do it?" I answered him. "No one. That's my problem: it's me who can't stop myself. If it was someone who was imposing it, it would be easy to refuse."

*

When we weren't at training, Cèt and I stayed in our room without chairs, silently spread out on our pallets with our eyes closed. During those hours, no longer dazed by the action, I felt the dreadful decay of Italy, the weight that was sinking my country; it was a downfall in which, I realized, my personal problems were a minimal, microscopic reflection.

The minutes passed as slowly as the drops of water from the broken eaves in front of our window.

"There isn't even a bar we can turn to in this damned town," Cèt said at times.

At other moments he surfaced from his own thoughts to observe me with a kind of curiosity. "For you, it's not only the fatigue you accumulated this summer . . . The deadly fatigue from the Russian front is coming back to you. Or am I wrong?"

I shrugged.

"Well, the war can't be lasting much longer, let's think about that. The Russians on one side, and the Allies on the other are now on Germany's borders; by now they don't have much farther to go to put an end to it."

"Right. But when they meet, will it really be over? You know, the Poles hope that once the Germans are eliminated, the Allies will come to eliminate the Bolsheviks. Seeing the situation in Poland, it's understandable. On the other hand, it could be the Red Army who won't stop once it gets rid of the Germans . . . What a nice prospect, right? And aside from the Red Army, what are the Communists going to do now that they are gaining ground in all of Europe?" (Let's remember that in a few more months, at the beginning of December, the Greek Communists, who like the Italian Communists had been allies of democratic powers against the Nazis, would suddenly unleash their revolution. An exhausting civil war would come from it. My worries weren't unfounded.)

"For heaven's sake, let's not think of another war," Cèt argued. "This one is enough and then some . . . Listen, instead of being idle why don't we find some subject, a topic to rev us up a little, something really interesting? . . . For example, anticipating Italy's political reality after the war . . . better still, how the whole world will be once fascism and Nazism have disappeared."

As it turned out, we really tackled the prospects of the future, becoming impassioned and engaged. We talked about this several times, and from a certain point on it was as though the future depended, at least in small part, on the two of us as well. Youth's perpetual obsession with changing the world! But I won't relate those discussions, nor the intuitions that seemed then—and for years after—very important.

Once that topic had been exhausted, I became idle once again, for which Cèt reproached me, although in a playful manner. One time, I remembered fellows the same age as us who had paid with their lives. There had been Cederle, first of all, a student at the same university as me, who immediately after the armistice had dragged many student officers south to the battle of Montelungo, following which the Allies had decided to accept us as "cobelligerents." And Second Lieutenant Casati ("from Lesmo, in Brianza, therefore more or less your fellow townsman"): after persisting, he had managed to have his father, the new minister of war, transfer him from Sardegna, where he was vegetating, to the *Corpo di Liberazione.* Alfonso Casati had fallen after a few days while he was fighting in the zone of Belvedere Ostrense at the head of a platoon of the San Marco.

"Do you remember the uproar around Belvedere, the night that we were at Acquasanta making connection with the San Marco?" Cèt asked. "Who knows if Casati died then? I mean during that night, or the next day."

"Poor guy. He wasn't with the *CIL* even two weeks."

"In any case, he proved to be a clever fellow. Think about that other fellow too, Alfredo Di Dio, there in Piedmont."

It was a very recent episode that had come to a close just one or two weeks earlier. "Di Dio too was more or less our age," Cèt remembered, "and he was a junior officer too, and raised an entire republic on its feet."

"A small one, maybe."

Cèt had begun laughing in a youthful manner: "All right. But meanwhile . . ."

The Republic of Ossola, at the Swiss border . . . It would then remain the most famous enterprise accomplished by the partisans in Italy (in this case, it was finally the work of Christian partisans).

"Do you know the last radio message from those partisans?" Cèt continued. "It was a salute to us. Not to other partisans, not to the government, but to us, the soldiers of the *Corpo di Liberazione.*"

"Yes, I remember it well."

"Well, it's something that we're part of, it seems."

"We're part of it, all right."

At times, we discussed other recent events. We didn't have a radio, and the news reached us in an erratic manner, as though it were difficult for it to cross the awkward tree-trunk and earth bridges stacked on top of the ruins of other masonry bridges at the entrance of Cerreto.

During the month of October we heard the news of an unfortunate man, believed to be an accomplice to the German executioners in Rome, who was captured and assaulted by a crowd of men and women who became beasts. The unlucky man had succeeded in throwing himself into the Tiber and, although wounded, had desperately tried to save himself by swimming, but the crowd had battered him with stones and bottles, and had held him underwater with posts until he drowned. Later, it was learned that he was completely innocent.

"We have to admit that if the government and the magistrates don't decide to punish at least the greatest crimes committed during the German occupation, inevitably hot-headed people will begin carrying out justice. We'll see what kind of justice! It will come from the dregs of society."

"Who knows what will happen after the liberation of the north . . ."

"Yes, because, since Rome was liberated, some worthy politicians finally showed up on the scene. There aren't only the exploiters of the past anymore."

In spite of the fact that many politicians persisted in mistrusting us, we soldiers realized the tremendous difficulties involved in rebuilding, and the hidden anxiety of those politicians who, rolling up their sleeves, really tried to make a start. The means at their disposal were precarious; the scope of their power was uncertain and at the mercy of those dishonorable officials who continuously tried to exploit their offices. Earnest politicians were forced to spend most of their energy coping with such schemes; at the same time, they had to face the enormous problems the nation faced. We could see their distress: they risked everything and were sustained by almost nothing other than good intentions, and they were even poorly dressed.

"With things being as they are, why don't they see us soldiers as potential allies?" Cèt and I asked ourselves. "Why do almost all of them continue to oppose us?"

"You know they consider us supporters of the king."

"How is it possible that they don't realize that there are also some republicans among us, and maybe even many? After all, on no account would all those of us who favor monarchy accept being transformed into Praetorians. The king wouldn't want Praetorians either."

"Right. But try to get them to understand that."

7

THE RAINY, dreary days continued in Cerreto, monotonous, uniform on our shoulders.

November and the sad days of the dead passed. The olive trees surrounding the town drank in the last of the sun, as they already had the water and fog, with their ancient patience; the houses along the straight streets welcomed the sunlight on their damp facades, which became bright again for a few days. Then the water came back to darken them, and the rain began falling once more on the olive trees and foggy mountains.

In December, I met Anna during a dance organized by the group's command.

I wasn't enjoying it very much (a dance at that time!), but as I was leaning on a wall of the room, I noticed that one of the girls dancing—the most unrestrained dancer of them all—occasionally glanced at me. Suddenly, she was in front of me, without escort, somewhat out of breath: her hair, oddly pressed against one side of her head, reminded me of a short mane. She stared at me for an instant with sparkling eyes. "You're not dancing, lieutenant?" she asked. "You haven't danced once until now."

"I'll confess quietly: the reason is that I don't know how to dance."

"You don't know how to dance?" Anna widened her bright eyes.

"All right, maybe I shouldn't have come to the dance. But, you see, we have so few opportunities to . . . socialize."

She shook her head disapprovingly; it seemed that I was on the wrong track.

"I'm very surprised that you, especially you, look down on dancing, which still is a form of art," she said slowly. "Or am I wrong?"

I remained uncertain.

"Am I wrong?" she repeated, with a sudden relaxed smile.

"Why do you speak of . . . art, Miss?"

"Because a little while ago while the British Captain Ingledew was danc-ing with me, he told me that among themselves the British call you 'Lord Byron.'"

"Ah! I wasn't aware that that nickname was so fashionable."

"I hope that you're flattered by it." She stared at me once again with her strange eyes, full of light, her lioness head slanted a little.

"Miss, the British are very good at using nicknames to make fun of peo-ple. Even if sometimes they repeat themselves; for instance, they call the worst student in each course Montgomery."

"But you . . . I don't think that they mean to make fun of you. At least, not maliciously."

"It might not be malicious. But you can bet it's with some irony."

"No, maybe you're mistaken," Anna said. "Ingledew told me that they call you that because you're more interested in their art than in their weapons. That you've asked him and others quite a few questions about it. Do you understand? And it seems like it pleases them."

"Ah," I murmured, surprised. "So that's where the nickname comes from?"

"You didn't know?"

"No. I must confess that I didn't consider that."

I had attributed that nickname—which I had happened to hear only a few times—to the fact that I had walked around with my old broken shoes, even after the beginning of the distribution of new shoes; I had not replaced them until no soldier in the battery was left with broken shoes. I didn't want to be more privileged than anyone else during our practice in the mud. Viewed sarcastically, it was the romanticism of a strolling player . . . But in-stead here it was: the British were, with their *humor,* giving me a lesson in generosity, nothing more. And also in class.

"What do you know," I concluded, tottering my head.

Anna observed me in silence. I had to admit that posing or not, whether her manners were practiced or spontaneous, she was attractive, very attrac-tive.

Maybe she realized it. "I'd like to know," she said, pointing at my fore-head, "what you're thinking. What thoughts are in there right now?"

She was a woman! That is why, from the start, I had been more taken than the conversation itself allowed. She had the face of a woman, and her eyes—so strange—were the eyes of a woman. While we talked, our ideas, I thought uncertainly, and the same timber of our very different voices seemed to fit together, as though forming new creatures . . . unstable, of course, "with winged feet," but creatures nonetheless . . .

I wondered if by chance this stranger was someone who could truly understand me. How could I assure myself of it? As I was asking myself this, Anna made a nice bow and, laughing, left me to return to the dance.

I shrugged and moved to the side, to a window opening. I moved the drapes a little aside; beyond the glass, it was raining in the dark streets. Suddenly returning to an adolescent's state of mind, I felt the need to be outside, cast out in the cold, as though that was the place best suited for me.

Some young and old British officers went by one after the other, they too with their emotions, and maybe their weariness, inside. The very young Second Lieutenant Guidi, from the same battery as me, recently commissioned an officer and therefore full of hope in spite of the times, said, "It's great, huh, being with girls?" He said it without removing his eyes from them. "It makes you realize that when they're not around you're a . . . poor fellow."

I agreed, smiling.

The other junior officer of the battery, old Second Lieutenant Laganà with the gold-rimmed eyeglasses, came after him.

"What are you doing here by yourself, angel?" he asked me.

"Call me wretch instead," I answered him. "I've just been betrayed."

Laganà nodded and, with a vague gesture of solidarity, moved on.

Shortly after, the gramophone struck up Francescoli's song, the one about the dress shaped by wind; it was a pretty popular song at the time, normal to play at a dance. But what was I doing there?

I headed toward the door. I was about to reach it when Anna unexpectedly sprang in front of me; she held on to her new partner with one hand only. "I take part in gatherings at Captain Zuntini's house. We read poetry. Will you come?" As she was talking, she sketched dance movements with her feet. She was, I was forced to notice once again in spite of myself, very attractive: "Circe the sorceress." The idea presented itself suddenly. "Hey, didn't the sorceress Circe live somewhere around here?"

"I'll come," I answered, nonetheless. "Thank you."

*

I went to it. A few Italian officers, some of the town's notables, and five or six women and young ladies, among them Anna, were gathered in an elegant old house—not that much different on the exterior from other houses. They were seated in front of a marble fireplace, where a chaste fire burned and made reflections on the marble. A very southern clock, large, gold-plated, and drowsy, beat out the rhythm of the minutes in the cold house, which was usually inhabited only during the summer.

I would have liked to participate in those gatherings silently, listening to others, in order to enrich myself a little. But from the very first time, my battery commander, Captain Zuntini, did not allow it. A civilian had started the reading of some poems by our hedonist poets from the beginning of the century such as D'Annunzio and Gozzano (at times they delighted, I learned, in reading to the British, to amaze them with the musical power of our language). "I fear," the captain said during a pause, "that Lieutenant Corti does not like this kind of poetry."

I spread my arms, asking to be neutral. But the captain-philosopher insisted, returning later to the subject, forcing me to explain my ideas bearing on art. Back then—I mean, before I began writing—I tried, during certain slow periods, to anticipate my future poetics; at times, I even summarized the fruits of such reflections in messy notes that I later did not keep because I always found them unbearably inadequate. Thus, urged by the captain, I began explaining, as well as I could, the thread of my young ideas.

But Anna began interrupting me right away, sometimes on the subject ("Ah no, lieutenant, absolutely not: you've made a big assertion, and you must justify it . . ."), other times for the simple pleasure of cutting me off, as though it were a game.

In the wake of one of those interruptions, I remember that an honest-to-goodness debate about Classical art, which I prefer and still consider not only current but more powerful than all others, ignited the room. Even the older gentleman who owned the house participated in it (a gentleman of manners, not of possessions). "You should see, lieutenant, the horrors produced in London and even worse in Germany, by those who claimed to be Classical during the eighteenth and nineteenth centuries," he said. I declared that I agreed with him because "one cannot be Classical in form, if one isn't so in substance."

"But . . . but . . . but . . ." Anna continued to argue, and shook her beautiful head, then tilted it to one side, staring at me reproachfully. Despite the seriousness of the discussion, that strange behavior and her manners of a tame lioness ended up distracting me from my thoughts, and almost influencing me. Although at times I tried to snap out of it ("Be careful, it's probably with this kind of ploy that Circe brought everyone to their knees . . ."), I wasn't really apprehensive; therefore, I too underwent some sort of enchantment, like the old and unprepared companions of Ulysses.

I was released from it by the discovery that four officers—both Italian and British—were courting Anna, and she was pleased by it. Her objective was to add me to her collection. I wanted to reproach her for it then and there; I found it more convenient to stop seeing her.

8

OCCASIONALLY, indecently muddying my new British shoes, I went to visit the two Antonios in San Lorenzello, a village downstream from Cerreto Sannita.

Here, Antonio Moroni had kindled the love ("Now look how miracles repeat themselves!") of the young landlady. However, he didn't requite it.

"See how many other men today wouldn't court that girl?" Castelli said. "It's clear that there's something that's not working, or is working backwards in this world."

"Here's the proof," I told him, "that our definitive existence isn't this. Here is the proof for the hundredth time, my dear agnostic soldier. But that's enough, I don't feel like preaching right now."

"Meanwhile, though, you're preaching," he noted.

"What's going on? You wouldn't be feeling down only because they've banished you from the Second Group too?" Moroni said. "By now you should be used to being banished from groups."

"In fact, that's not what's depressing me. It's your company, the simple fact of being with you." I considered Castelli again. "You surely are something, staying a nonbeliever after everything we've seen!"

He raised his eyes to the sky impatiently and grumbled, "Stop your rubbish, please. Cut it out."

Instead I kept going. "Honor and duty . . . You build your life, all your actions, on that. Right. But explain something to me: if God doesn't exist, what is the meaning of honor and duty? Today, a man can consider it honorable and his bound duty to slaughter the man next to him: like Hitler and Stalin and the millions and millions who follow them," I concluded, raising my voice a little. "Isn't that right?"

Castelli looked at me for a moment with hard eyes; then he remembered that he was my friend, snorted, and let it go.

"Enough. You can keep living as long as you want," I pressed on. "But you have no way out: when you find God in front of you, you'll have to believe in him."

"Be a good chap," he let out. "At least abstain from making predictions. You know how they get on people's nerves."

The house's landlady would walk in the room while we carried on like this about theology. Although she was southern, she had light skin and hair of an almost transparent blonde, reminiscent of a tenuous watercolor. Sometimes she brought us pleasant portions of chicken on small plates, exotically prepared. But she always sat off to the side, and she didn't eat with us.

"Susanna," Castelli told her, eating heartily, "your boneless chicken surely is good."

"Fit and ready to enlist," I agreed also, joking in the jargon of soldiers. In truth, her name wasn't Susanna; I imagine that Castelli called her this to make it less dramatic. He had recovered the name of our good-luck-charm goose, which the paratroopers had ended up eating some time ago.

"Thank you," Susanna answered, smiling indulgently.

"Thank goodness that you're here to remind us that civil manners still exist in the world," Moroni said to her, very opportunely.

Susanna smiled again and after a while, when civility allowed, she left; perhaps she was satisfied to have harvested, in Antonio Moroni's proximity, a small crop of things to daydream about, known to her only.

*

At times, a very old priest leaning on a long walking stick, wearing torn clothes splashed with mud—my two friends promptly requested a mess tin of rations for him—came to the place where we carried on our theological discussions. He ate with extraordinary voracity and conversed with us at the same time, as much as he could.

Retired for many years, he lived in poverty with an aged niece near a small deconsecrated church in the middle of the countryside. "I'm canonical, from the Cerreto Cathedral," he informed me each time, as though that made everything all right. He always spoke very loudly because he was deaf. The goal of his visits was that small ration and a military coat still in good shape that Moroni had promised him as soon as it was available. The old man spoke of the coat openly, with extraordinary satisfaction; he even dreamed out loud about it: "I'll dye it black," he would say, "and it will look good on me, really good." During those particular moments, his gestures and his voice resembled those of other Neapolitans when they talk about a woman.

At other times he spoke that little bit of Latin that he still remembered, using with us a pleased tone of fellowship (we were officers, and therefore—according to him—learned people). To increase our connection, he also described several times a quarrel that he had had with the Germans. In their savagery, they had stacked a large mine deposit inside the deconsecrated church and against the outside walls of his residence, far away from towns. He had tolerated it out of necessity, but when a sergeant and two soldiers appeared to inspect the inside of his house, he hadn't allowed it. He had scolded them with vehement words, which he now repeated for us, filling the premises with Neapolitan shouts from a window overlooking the entrance, until—it wasn't clear whether it had been intentional or accidental—a vase of geraniums had fallen on the head of one of the Germans. The German had remained dazed, so that his two comrades had had to support him, while the old man waved his stick around—like he was doing now as he recalled his tale—and yelled out to them "Serge . . . Serge . . . leave me alone, or I'll make you feel this too. Leave, Serge . . . " "And the sergeant," the old man concluded, "left without saying a word." Finally, he too would leave, limping and full of misery, shaking his head with some residual grumbling.

Afterward, I returned to my alpine town, again indecently muddying my new British shoes.

9

IN DECEMBER the mountains around Cerreto became dusted with snow.

During training, the faces of the soldiers were purple; when dealing with steel, their frozen hands produced sores at the smallest scratch. By now, I was fond of those soldiers, and they were fond of me; many were grateful for my vigor in making them become soldiers, and told me so openly.

During the days that preceded Christmas, the wind blew for hours and hours through the straight and deserted streets of the town. The icy wind licked the few leaves that remained on the trees, and the leaves shrieked; they seemed to weep in front of us, reproaching us for having brought sorrow to all beings.

Most of the soldiers from central and southern Italy had gone on leave with makeshift transports; those remaining, almost all northern, frequently drank until they were inebriated enough to get their families out of their minds.

On Christmas Eve a brawl took place in Cerreto between paratroopers, artillerymen, and sappers, with eight wounded by hand grenades; unfortunately, all the artillerymen involved belonged to my section. This is how the events unfolded: Valentini, commander of our Sixth Anti-Aircraft Artillery Group, had had a dinner prepared, as comforting as possible, that officers and soldiers would share in the instruction hall. While they convened for the dinner, the soldiers from my section decided to stop in a tavern. One of the two artillery chiefs preceded them, Corporal Major Sciaini, a stern fellow and farmer from the mountain of Como who had been an artillery chief of the Second Alpine Artillery Regiment on the Russian front. Once inside the room, he hadn't been able to tolerate the obscenities that the paratroopers were directing toward a servant girl. He had turned to the paratrooper most to blame and ordered him to apologize "because soldiers and hooligans are two different things." Unfortunately, the paratrooper was a very quarrelsome character; an amateur boxer from the suburbs of Rome, he was short, thickset, with slicked-back hair and a head that only allowed for half an idea at a time. His idea this time had been to scurrilously insult Sciaini. Violence became inevitable: Sciaini, of imposing stature, had thrown a punch straight into his opponent's face that "would have knocked down an ox," I was told; the paratrooper, though, had remained standing. A free-for-all ensued between the remaining paratroopers and the other artillerymen, at first in the tavern and then outside in the street. The two sides were about equal in number, but the paratroopers were more skilled in boxing; the fight probably would have ended badly for the artillerymen, despite Sciaini and Morandi, solid towers.

I was walking at my own pace—heading to the Christmas Eve dinner— along the street of the boxing match, thinking about Anna and her wicked enchantments, shaking my head once in awhile with disapproval, when suddenly I heard an uproar and saw the turmoil. I could tell from the voices that men from my section were involved. I hastened toward the rival parties and let out a tremendous shout, powerful enough to immobilize the artillerymen. The paratroopers, although it wasn't their habit, stopped, unsure. I furiously ordered my men to come to attention, about turn, and forward march, without allowing them to utter a word, while I shouted at them (how the world can be unjust!) that they weren't soldiers, but damned hooligans, and made them march up to the hall of the Christmas dinner. The paratroopers set out, puzzled, in the opposite direction toward their quarters. Later, however, they reconsidered and, undoubtedly, thought their taking of orders from an officer who wasn't even a paratrooper had been inexplicable; therefore, stocking up on hand grenades, they returned to the place of the fight, where some completely unaware sappers were now flocking. Unaware, but not without tongues: they answered the insults thrown at them without cause from a distance by the paratroopers with more insults. The paratroopers, half-drunk, ended up throwing several hand grenades in the midst of the sappers, wounding eight of them.

Major Valentini's unrestrained wrath was all focused on me, since I had been the only one able to report anything when the news reached him (how the world can be unjust!). His order to me and to the officer commanding the paratroopers had been to "immediately" capture the ringleaders. We were able to immobilize the boxer with the slicked-back hair without serious complications, only because, thank heaven, the paratrooper officer was also a boxer, and of superior caliber. We delivered the boxer and his accomplices to the *carabinieri* sent by the division's command, who took them away handcuffed in two jeeps.

As a result of so much disorder, I wasn't able to participate in the Christmas Eve dinner and ended up letting the group's lieutenant doctor, Simonelli, already tipsy, persuade me to engage in a challenge as to which of us could withstand drinking the most alcohol. A native of the Marches and a doctor in Port San Giorgio on the Adriatic, Simonelli was short, but with a Homeric spirit. He very much liked Homeric citations, so that he often enjoyed exchanging some with me. That night he insisted on forecasting my collapse from alcohol, comparing it to the collapse of Sarpedon: "*Sarpedon collapsed / like an oak, or a poplar, or a pine falls / that the forger, for his navigational need / cuts on the mountain with a sharp two-edged ax.*" I argued proudly that I would withstand more than him and, because of his nonsense, proclaimed him "*similar to a bird with long feathers / the owl, the sparrow hawk, or the white-crested laughingthrush / who on the sea shore befriends the crow*" (here the connection with Port San Giorgio seemed apparent). At times, however, I also called him "*tawny lion*" because his face was very flushed from the libations. All this on Christmas Eve, exactly two years after the most terrible night of my life, the night I left the "valley of death" of Arbuzov . . .

The next morning, I still felt somewhat sick when Morandi, who cunningly feigned a look of surprise, came into my large room to wake me up. As I got up, he shot a hand in his pocket and, somewhat embarrassed, pulled out a new fountain pen: it was from the town's stationery shop. "It's a Christmas present from the section, lieutenant," he said. I later kept its remains for years.

I thanked him and told him to thank the others and, given that it was Christmas, I indulged in a few remarks with some difficult words that he liked, and he was satisfied.

*

In January, completely reequipped by the British, we left Cerreto Sannita. Our headgear and badges were the only things remaining from our uniform. But even without looking at these, the Italians were immediately distinguishable from the others, just as before it had been easy to distinguish the British from the Poles, the Poles from the Indians. In fact, on us the British uniform acquired an inconceivable liveliness, and even seemed, without anyone introducing changes, to be breaking up into as many types of uniform as there were soldiers.

We left aboard our new Bedford motor vehicles for the Marches, where we were to finish one last month of training before returning to the line.

So the mountain town with its symmetrical streets stayed behind too. With the passing of the years, its memory would dissolve for us, and Cerreto would become almost an imaginary place, like the places sung about ("*when it snows in my town, the church's bell tower turns white . . .*") in the beloved Neapolitan songs of long ago.

Part Five

1

ON THE THIRD DAY of our journey in the Marches, we crossed Lanciano and the areas of our first battles. The Allies had laid Bailey military bridges on top of the stumps of destroyed bridges, which allowed adequate traffic.

The people in the towns no longer paid attention to us; they were all consumed by their everyday worries. Even the streets and houses, under repair everywhere, were barely recognizable. We felt that the towns, the countryside, the hills, the land for which we had risked our lives, were by now a stage where our performance had ended.

Captain Zuntini gave me a week's leave to spend in Giulianova near Abruzzi, where my brother Achille had been staying with some college friends after his attempts to find work as an engineer by the Adriatic had proved useless.

The villa where Achille was staying—very beautiful, with frescoed vaults, surrounded by an old garden—swept from above onto the peaceful sea, which stretched out like a seagull in flight.

When I got down from the truck, Morandi handed me my submachine gun; if I remained unarmed some Fascist or Communist could have attacked me. We were surprised when the head of the family, the Baron Don Carlo Ciafardoni, half smiling, half concerned, asked that I not keep the weapon. Such peaceful places still existed on earth?

In this house of nobility, Abruzzese hospitality reached its peak: everyone, regardless of the times, seemed to live for us, the guests. Don Carlo had been like this with Achille for months, and also with one of his fellow soldiers, another engineering student who had gone with him to Naples to find work on the Adriatic. He undoubtedly would have been like this for several more months, even years if the war were to last years, and both men, as the hosts begged, would have stayed for the entire length of the war.

I was fascinated with the family, particularly the mother, of classic composure but every moment aware of the needs of others. Just like my mother, she felt that every well-bred person was her child.

The little grandmother, Donna Maria, dressed in a style from the turn of the century and always with a shiny brass warmer between her blue hands, seemed to be living on the hidden poetry that is part of everyone's daily life. Somewhat deaf, she seemed in search of that poetry; her face brightened and she almost clapped when she found it. I spent a few hours conversing with her, amazed that each phrase that came out of my mouth was transformed into poetry.

"These people, the nobles from here, who don't work in the same way we do," my brother noted to me, "at one time we would have considered them with a critical eye. But we shouldn't. Their refined manners, their extraordinary courtesy, the tolerance that they have accumulated in the course of many generations could one day be useful to all people. And after all, these are the things, much more than material goods, that distinguished the civilized man from the caveman. So, if you think about it, these people's contribution to civilization might not be inferior, but superior, to the contribution of our friends, industrial workers and laborers."

Later on, the grandmother with the blue hands died. If in the eternal world God, who concedes so many human things, reserves some inconceivable place for poets, she would be there. If I keep my faith in God, I will find her there.

At the end of the war the head of the house, Don Carlo, also died. As we grieved, my brother and I rushed back to escort that unique shepherd king, whose biggest joy had been in giving, to his burial. Now he lies in the cemetery of Giulianova, joined by the everlasting fickle voice of the sea, which laments or rejoices or speaks or accuses or sings or moans, surrounding the tearful lands of men, and so, like a loyal dog, brings back to the shepherd king the sufferings of life, as though he had not died.

*

Lavished with gifts, including a medal of the Holy Protector, Virgin Mary, around my neck, I was about to get onto the truck that would take me back to the regiment when Achille appeared in front of me. "I've decided to join the service again," he said. "I'm not going to wait any longer for an officer's appointment. You have to help me."

"But . . ." I protested, caught by surprise. "But . . . what kind of nonsense is this?" I tried to object with common-sense arguments such as my father would have made. But evidently neither my objections, nor those of our dismayed host, did any good. I had to take it upon myself to find him a position in the regiment of Captain Adjutant Bevilacqua. It wasn't standard procedure, but back then many things weren't standard in the army. "If we must accept the reality of arbitrary absences," Bevilacqua pronounced, "why not also accept arbitrary appearances?"

A few days later, Achille was able to pick up a uniform and sergeant ranks, as well as the beret that made us stand out, from the regiment's depot. At my request, he had been assigned to the Second Group, which Pelaformiche had left while many of my friends remained. Since Achille wanted to take part in the war, it wouldn't have made any sense to have him join my "shirking" anti-aircraft artillery group.

2

ON MARCH 1, 1945, we moved in a very long
column from the Marches to Tuscany and to the "Gothic Line," which, between La Spezia and Rimini, cut off central Italy from northern Italy.

An incident occurred immediately, during the first hours of travel, to remind us of something that had happened during the journey to the front
the previous year. Back then, a few British soldiers had made the First
Group remove the tents we had just pitched in a playing field so that
they could play soccer. This time a British noncommissioned officer had
brought his platoon to carry out maneuvers on the street where we were
marching. It was clearly done out of scorn for us. After coming to a stop,
our trucks began moving again. "The British were falling like skittles," the
soldiers of the first truck, all paratroopers, later reported joyfully.

During the course of the night, in Foligno, a second incident occurred:
a paratrooper who had been bludgeoned by a British policeman turned
around and killed him with a dagger. His companions promptly disarmed
the other policemen on the scene; with the word out, the officers were barely able to stop the men from attacking the British stationed in Foligno.
Many even emerged from the trucks gripping light machine guns and the
new Piat trench mortars. Here and there, the assault cry: "Nembo! Nembo!" and also "San Marco! San Marco!" rose in the dark. The scornful behavior of the British soldiers was threatening to cause what years of war and
air raids hadn't been able to accomplish: Italian hatred of the British.

The entire division, which now included thirteen hundred motor vehicles, was in transfer. The two meager paratrooper regiments had become
one. The San Marco sailors formed the other infantry regiment. Our artillery regiment now included six groups and at least fifty-six guns. Nevertheless, to my disappointment, the units were still organized in the cen-
tralized system from before the armistice, even though our soldiers would
have been better suited with the decentralization established de facto

among the alpine troops. But no changes had been brought about in this respect: either the commands had not understood its necessity, or there had not been enough time. "In the army," the soldiers kept grumbling, "everything's crooked, except the handles of shovels, which should be."

Another reason for complaint was that the division name had been removed from our units, which now had the staff of regular divisions, and had been replaced by the term "combat group." "To hide from the peace table that at the end of the war six Italian divisions will be in line against the Germans," someone asserted.

In columns, the Folgore Combat Group crossed an Umbria carved in silver.

Before dawn, Francis's small land was held by darkness, so we could not see mystical Assisi on the mountain, nor its peaceful stone walls, nor the slopes that surround it, enraptured by olive trees. Nor could we see at the foot of the mountain beneath Assisi the humble church of the San Damiano poets and the row of cypresses, always full of praising sparrows, which descends from the city to the church among the olive trees.

On the side of the road where we marched, I was able to recognize with some difficulty, by the light of the fire in a bucket that had been lit beneath it by a British sentinel, the beautiful worn-down portico of Santa Maria of Angels. That slight halo of sanguine light around the shivering man was the only thing I was able to see of the places where Francis had taught docility to wolves.

Very shortly after, with early dawn, we crossed Perugia.

Under a violet sky, the tall walls, the fortress, the houses, the paved streets of the aristocratic city had the eminent beauty of twilight and moonlit nights. It is then, in the dim light, that the works of men show only the essential creation. Small miseries and ugliness, inheritance of original sin, are not discernable; the works seem pure, as though they've passed through their own purgatory.

"What a beautiful city!" Fiandrino, the Piedmontese driver, murmured at my side with each new silent sight. "Perugia is such a beautiful city!"

In the medieval churches, the warriors lay with their heads resting on pillows of stone, their hands closed on their chests around the hilt of their heavy swords that resembled crosses. Their faces, their bodies, their coats of mail and other clothes were made of stone. Their axes tied to their sides, so feared in field duels, were of stone. But it is said that their hearts were not of stone, and were condemned to suffer while the factions that first divided our people continued to divide us. In fact, it is said that at times, before dawn, when the earth under the Umbrian sky is similar to paradise, those people of stone awake while men are still sleeping. Maybe it is a concession that God made to St. Francis. At that moment, the warriors leave the church and lament loudly, marching through the hills; by now, it isn't up to them to make amends. After studying the tracks left behind in the dew, the Umbrian peasants will perhaps mistake them for those of a stealthy hare. But ancient women hear their lament and descend from the frescoes and from painted tablets, and the angels follow them bearing lilies, and the medieval nuns rise from their nameless tombs, and the modest friars dressed in gray come out of the earth. Santa Chiara, born from a hateful family, leaves her own urn, a bright plant from St. Francis's garden, and the angels, warriors, monks, women and nuns, all the people, gather behind her in procession. She carries in her hands the basin with the blonde braids that she one day sacrificed to God, and she sings. "Oh God," she says, "Loving God of our Father Francis, listen to us, your ancient Italic people, who find no peace in paradise while the factions that have divided us since our time continue to divide us. Give these people unity, oh God."

The celestial procession, passing through the slopes of an Umbria carved in silver, moves toward *Santa Maria degli Angeli;* the praising sparrows join the chorus, and the Franciscan swallows, and the lark of the Umbrian plains dressed in gray, and they all echo: "Give unity back to these people, oh God."

It is said that the small procession stops when it reaches the cathedral, and each time three saints move forward. Santa Chiara places the basin with the blonde braids on the same altar in front of which they were one day cut off. "Here," she sings, "oh God, if once is not enough, I again sacrifice my hair, so that you may remove hatred from our earth, so that the hearts of the brothers who first ignited it can find peace." And Agnese, her sister, holding out her head obediently like a dove, sings, "Oh God, let me be beaten and trampled upon as I was before the tonsure, but remove the hatred that divides this earth." And the third, Rita, the great Umbrian saint, with a hand on her own son, prays, troubled, "Here, oh God, is my son: I offer him to you again like before, during the tragic days of his mortal life, when I asked you for his death before he could hatefully kill. But prevent today's children from continuing to kill one another."

Then all the people shout, "Oh God, remove factions from Italy. Alas! It began in our time, and since then we no longer have a people. We will continue to implore you until you remove them, oh God."

The warriors then raise their long cross-like swords, holding them by the tip, and shout, "Forgive us, oh God!"

And the angels each raise their heavy lily, and say, "So be it."

It is said that when God accepts their prayers, the rose bushes will suddenly bloom again, and from then on the warriors will sleep peacefully. But until now the bronze sound of the bells of daybreak has brought the restless spirits back to the grave.

*

We passed from Umbria to Tuscany, where I was left disconcerted by the exasperation on people's faces: those unmistakable Tuscan faces, with their sharp cheekbones, which I had known through paintings and statues even before seeing them in real life.

Long lines of ancient cypresses went up the sides of many hills, and severe garlands—the only ones worthy of that land which taught beauty to the whole world—surrounded their summits. Even the buildings, in spite of the war's attacks, had not lost their perfection; often, in that area, even the houses of peasants could be astonishing.

But how could one look at such things after seeing those human faces? Everything seemed to lose its identity when men were transformed into wolves.

During our two brief stops we were dismayed to learn that there had been a terrifying run of hatred here. The partisans, almost all Communists, had killed many people, including unarmed individuals in the streets or inside their residences, in order to provoke increasingly savage responses from the Nazi-Fascists and, as a result, fierce reactions from all the people. Like a beast without a glimmer of intelligence that responds to every challenge in the same manner, the German SS had answered with massacres never before seen in Italy. As for the Fascists, swayed by events much larger than themselves, they had ended up by torturing and murdering in ways that were worthy of their Nazi allies and the Communist rivals against whom they were fighting. None of the soldiers, from that point on, would utter another word in their defense.

By now, it seemed as though in this region man was left with nothing but hatred and new murders.

"Who knows if the civil war will reduce all of northern Italy to this state?" I asked myself. And I answered sorrowfully that it wouldn't; it wasn't possible. After all, I argued, except for the bordering Emilia, there weren't only the Communist partisans up north . . .

Above Florence, which we skirted, the streets of the rear zone were re-duced to icy dust, covered by very intense Allied traffic. Ruins appeared everywhere, frequently along with sad piles of materiel and ammunition of the usual khaki color. But we knew that even the British didn't want to be wasteful, and, contrary to the previous year, they wanted now to lead a thrifty war.

When it was dark, we halted at the foot of the Apennines, where the front was traveling. The soldiers gathered, covered in their new overcoats, to take rations; like many other times, they made the trucks into shields against the frigid wind. Each one felt alone, whatever common suffering there was locked in his pack.

The flash of artillery continued to break swiftly through the darkness, as it had for years.

3

THE FOLGORE Combat Group replaced one of the most renowned British divisions, the Sixth Armored, relieving its positions in the parallel Santerno and Senio Valleys; as anti-aircraft artillery, we positioned our guns, now practically unused, in the rear zone, in Ronta, as protection.

For the division, this second operative cycle, which climaxed with the battle that broke through the Gothic Line, was bloodier than the one the year before. But as second formation, we would only learn of this at the end of the war from the stories of others, and from statistics that would surprise us.

Because the anti-aircraft group did not grasp the frightening gravity of the civil war in progress, a certain pattern of indolence and petty behavior typical of the rear zone began to take root among the soldiers. Everyone became more selfish, demanding, and intolerant of whatever didn't go his way. As for the front—since it was at a fair distance, no one thought of it.

I had the opportunity to see the front—maybe I was the only one from the group—when I paid Achille a visit on the line. From a grassy ridge, I could see that below and in front of us the ruins of the villages of Fontanelice and Borgo Tossignano were in our hands, and the terribly devastated other side, opposite Tossignano, was in the enemy's hands. We were on the slope of the last Apennine range toward the Po Valley.

A very long stratus of cinereous overhanging rock rose before us parallel to our mountain, as far as the eye could see, as though an immense wave had sprung from the plain, thrown itself against the Apennines, and become petrified the moment it was about to overturn. The invisible German line ran along its crest. The tiny puffs of smoke that occasionally rose here and there from our stray shells or from the enemy's mortars were almost without sound and did not disturb the vast stillness. But we could see a barge moving out of range on the pale blue mirror of water, down where the Santerno River, interrupting the overhanging rock, showed an edge of blue flatland with the whitish spot of the city of Imola. This warned us that the enemy was still busy blocking us from that flatland, the long roads and grass of which reached all the way to the thresholds of our homes.

The return trip on the jeep along the steep road made me retch, something that hadn't happened in many years, not since I had been a boy.

The soldiers, always satiated, only gathered for the anti-aircraft deployment during the hours of rations, or at night to sleep, when those most drunk came down with uncertain steps from the town to the tents, supported by some companion, rambling loudly, singing, or even crying between resonant belches. Those who stayed true to themselves were increasingly fewer in number; sometimes I gathered with them on the grass near our guns, uselessly brandished upwards. At a short distance from us columns of Indian trains would march along the country road headed for the line. We would watch the men with their noble and lean figures (they were Sikhs, very different from Gurkhas) and the mules with slender legs that lowered their heads rhythmically as they walked, as though they asserted their goodwill with each step.

Aside from Morandi, Lance Corporal Freddi was also present now from the old patrol, having succeeded in getting transferred to anti-aircraft artillery (others too had tried, but without success; only after the war did I realize the rare loyalty of those soldiers. Back then I had so much of youth's thoughtfulness in me that I found it natural). It was in fact Freddi who usually requested our meetings on the grass: "Lieutenant, let's not waste our time. This is why I came to the Sixth Group: to hear you speak like you did on the Musone, and like when you talked about Dante. You discuss difficult things in a way that regular people can understand."

Artilleryman Leonardo, a Puglian fellow of modest education but intelligent and eager to learn, and Chief of Artillery Sciaini, who at Cerreto on Christmas Eve had for moral reasons started the big boxing match with the paratroopers, were among the new soldiers who always attended. "I don't understand," Sciaini would occasionally say, "how they can be reduced to this: seeing that now they no longer are in danger of dying, they only worry about eating, just like pigs."

"Well, let's not forget that this is the state of all rear zones and generally of rear commands," I reminded them a little absentmindedly.

They asked me: "What will happen in Italy after the war? In whose hands will we end up?" Or also: "Do you think that democracy will be able to remain standing here?"

"England and America have it, but in Italy?"

"You've seen what happened to the democracy that we had before fascism, and even now, just hearing the uproar of these politicians . . ."

I ended up reminding them that, after all, we Italians lived with democracy long before the British and Americans—many centuries before.

"When?" Lance Corporal Freddi asked, smiling. "It wouldn't be in the age of . . . chivalry?"

"Exactly," I answered him. I couldn't keep from smiling too. "I must seem like I'm obsessed with that era, uh? Anyway, it's a fact that it was in that era, and in no others, that Italy had an extraordinary blossoming of democracy: of free medieval communes."

"But look, lieutenant," Leonardo intervened, "are we sure that democracy is a good thing in itself? Since the Americans have won now, everyone glorifies it. But if we think back to the mess of 1920, 1921, 1922—which my father talks about all the time, even though he isn't a Fascist—when it was almost impossible to have a normal life in many areas of Italy . . ."

"Listen, Leonardo: if democracy is the political system that allows for the most freedom—and it is—for everyone, we must also recognize that it is the most humane. And that is to say, the political system most suitable for man, the one that is most suited not only to his dignity, but to his very nature. Of course, democracy can only work under one condition: that all citizens be willing to make serious sacrifices. Democracy can't hold up in towns that lack this one condition, in which case I agree that it's senseless to take on democracy. Undoubtedly, in that case any structure is better, even if very flawed, than a permanent state of disorder; if nothing else, it generates a lot fewer deaths."

Freddi once again got back on the track of his previous remarks: "Please . . . could you tell us about the democracy of the Middle Ages? You said an . . . extraordinary blossoming?"

I nodded. "Our medieval democracy was much greater than what we have today: that's right, greater, more appealing. I found a great proof of it, better than in other books, in the account of the German chronicler that I spoke of on the Musone, do you remember?" I turned to those who hadn't been there. "*Ottone of Frisinga:* someone who came to Italy in the twelfth century after Federico 'Barbarossa.' I know many of his words by heart, from having reread them so many times because they seemed so important.

He wrote '*the rulers of the community*,' namely the governors and administrators, were replaced more or less every year in Italy '*so that they may not be overcome by the desire of power.*' Is that clear? And the population of our free communes, to his surprise, since evidently in Germany things were different, '*did not refuse to elect young men of low lineage to all ranks of authority, even workers of mechanical arts that other people keep away, like the plague, from the more noble and liberal tasks.*'"

Morandi intervened: "Mechanical arts? Like Freddi who's a contemptible carpenter?"

The others nodded, smiling.

"Let me finish," I said. "That chronicler also wrote, '*You can hardly find a noble or great man with so much power that he escapes obeying the laws of his city. Therefore, they*'—meaning the citizens of Italian communes—'*can all move forward in the world of wealth and power.*' There, that's the state of affairs that Ottone of Frisinga encountered when he arrived in Italy around eight hundred years ago—the year of the battle of Legnano. We have to understand that the type of democracy that we know today has a different origin: it comes mostly from the English and French Revolutions. But, as you can see, Christians had found a way to live with democracy many centuries earlier. And without a need for revolution, meaning without needing to kill anyone: they found it here, in Italy. After all, we must remember that much earlier, the ancient Greeks also lived with democracy: the word actually comes from them, a Greek word."

Once again I happened to catch some hope in the eyes of some of the men, as I had during our discussions on the Musone, that we might finally be able to find a way out of the stifling troubles of our time.

"But why did democracy disappear from Italy?" Leonardo wanted to know.

"Because a regression of morals took place—just as it did among the Greeks—and gradually people were no longer willing to sacrifice some of their own points of view to make room for those of others. Dante described well the state of affairs that came about in Italy in the fourteenth century: to put an end to the continuous fights and arrogant behavior, it became indispensable for someone to impose order by using force. So lordships and principalities began to form everywhere, and democracy disappeared."

We were once again dealing with great arguments and life's great questions. I must admit, however, that we lacked our previous eagerness, since the gigantic Sergeant Canèr with his thoughtful words was missing among us, as were too many others from the old patrol. We couldn't behave as though they were present.

4

ONE DAY, quite unexpectedly, a contingent of a few hundred Communist partisans arrived in Ronta, assigned as reserves for the Folgore by the Ministry of War. Only their blasphemies left an impression on me, maybe because they especially offended me: they were different from the outbursts of the common soldier, as they were filled with hatred. In their speech, the Tuscan coarseness was nothing but an ingredient. Trapped by a sort of permanent exasperation, those fellows poured out from the apartment house where they were quartered, plaguing the air, the paths, and the low branches of trees with their cursing; rarely did they mix with us.

Nevertheless, I managed to speak with some of them. They referred to the future Communist revolution as something obvious and inevitable; not only that, but they also seemed actually to have a physical need for it.

They had brought along with them a few prostitutes. Although one of them didn't seem older than a child, it was impossible to determine her age: deformed all the way to her bones and cross-eyed, she was so thin that she seemed molded from fog. A large rock was on the side of the cart road that came down from the town to our artillery; when the partisans left her alone, she crouched on it, beneath the sun, and remained bent over, without ever raising her eyes to those walking by.

Fortunately, a few days after their arrival, after the division's command rejected some of their preemptory conditions (they wanted most of all to remain united, and did not accept being divided in various units), the provisionary alliance with the royal army was canceled. They returned home, loaded up on our trucks. The soldiers of the group, who had run up to attend the departure, laughed with relief and slapped their knees in approval; from the moving trucks, the Communists reacted as always by shouting blasphemies and more blasphemies.

*　　*　　*

After their departure, however, the petty frame of mind of the rear zone once again overtook the soldiers, like a storm that becomes more oppressive after an initial clearing.

Gradually, the atmosphere of slacking swallowed almost everyone. Now the men kept very busy organizing dances with the girls of the half-destroyed town; if by chance some of them were seen arguing, it was over such matters as the better rations that our men on the line enjoyed with the Americans. Since their contempt grew stronger every day, they considered themselves increasingly more authorized to talk rubbish.

Because of my obvious disapproval, many secretly began to oppose me. In addition, I fell ill; my nerves were rebelling under the strain to which I had been subjected for years. I had heart palpitations and stomach contractions, and at times I had difficulty breathing. The doctors prescribed rest. But what kind? We already had physical rest, even too much of it, and the other kind, spiritual rest, how could that have been possible?

At times, in an attempt to relax, I left my tent and began walking slowly through the countryside.

But I couldn't help thinking unrestful thoughts. Among other things, I lingered over our institutional problem. Besides the Red partisans' subversive plan, I realized that by now most of the people had gone from the 1943 hosanna for the monarchy to an attitude of aversion toward it. The fact that I personally was for the republic didn't keep me from sometimes considering the tragedy of those people involved at the top. Aside from the king and the prince, I thought about our unhappy queen.

She had come to us from another land, placing her trust in the king and in Italy, only to be awarded her current fate. At one time, poets were only interested in the tragedies of queens, I thought, overlooking those of common women. Now, on the contrary, they seemed to be interested only in the tragedies of common women. This wasn't fair either, I told myself. And for me, an Italian, the plight of the queen of Italy (as of someone who is already dead, who no longer has any way to be heard) was especially bitter.

May this remain, when encountered, my canto *pro rege*.

A large prison tent, permanently guarded by the *carabinieri* of the divisional command, was at a few hundred meters from our deployment, beneath some oak trees. I approached it once and, seeing that the *carabiniere* on guard didn't object, looked through the only open window.

I could make out a single prisoner inside, lying down on a pallet: I recognized the boxer from the suburbs of Rome who had provoked the big brawl in Cerreto on Christmas Eve. He too recognized me, and greeted me in an almost joyful manner.

"You're still in here for that great feat in Cerreto?" I asked him.

He got up and, shaking his head, pleased, came to the small window. "No. What are you saying? Who still remembers that? It's old news," he answered me. And without me asking, he informed me of the following. The eve of the Folgore's departure for the front, he had been sent back to his unit. However, in Foligno during his trip, he had happened to kill "with a dagger stab" a British policeman (he had been the one, then, who was the source of this other nice deed). "He thought that he could take me down with his club . . . Me? Me? I'll take on ten of those British grave-diggers." Therefore, he had been imprisoned once again, and now they had to put him on trial. He could get the death penalty; I didn't know if he was aware of it. He told me that what he regretted the most about the brawl was being unable to finish "with blows" his fight with Sciaini, whose strong punch in the face he remembered perfectly, even if he minimized it as "nonsense." His words also held a halfhearted reproach for me, for interrupting such a noble fight for petty reasons of discipline.

During those contemplative walks, I also asked myself what my duty would be after the war, at least until the outbreak of the Communist revolution, which seemed to me inevitable after my encounter with the Tuscan partisans. Sure, as soon as possible, I would begin writing, working in the field of ideas: is it or isn't it important? It is, agreed. But it's also too orderly, I told myself, like participating only in the battles of war and not in the daily grime and weakening exhaustion that are a soldier's heaviest burden. Did I have to also directly participate in the political fight? Maybe in its most unrewarding forms, like square assemblies? Just the prospect of it made my stomach turn; my entire spirit rebelled. Nevertheless, I realized that, given the times, I had no way out: it was my duty as a Christian; these are not empty words. I didn't imagine then that my future companions in simple political action would take care to keep me from this embarrassment, especially certain workers who, sensing my aversion to the politics of the square, would take it upon themselves to do my part with charity: "Let's share: you've already gone through enough."

5

AROUND APRIL 10, the Eighth Army launched its final offensive.

The main effort to break through the German line was carried out by the tireless Poles, as in Cassino in breaking through the winter line. Closing their eyes to the obvious, the Poles continued to hope absurdly that their advance would continue until Poland was liberated. They attacked on the plain with their armored units and opened a breach. Simultaneously, the Folgore Combat Group broke through in the Santerno Valley, opening a new route to the plain; after this its sector was urgently broadened to include another valley closer to Bologna, the Sillaro, where it attacked again. To our left, in front of Bologna, the Americans were attacking, and farther on was the Combat Group Legnano, which had incorporated all the other units of the old *CIL*. The Germans resisted tenaciously and counterattacked again and again. Their last great battle was the one on the Gothic Line; already most of Germany had been invaded, but they continued fighting as they had their first day, although they now lacked many essential supplies: they were truly great soldiers.

When we were least expecting it, our shirking anti-aircraft group was transferred to the line. The shameful frame of mind of the rear zone left us as soon as we found ourselves in the midst of the threadbare and dust-covered knolls, surrounded by the sudden uproar of artillery. We went back to dedicating ourselves to the task at hand; we went back briefly to being soldiers. After an arduous battle with the German paratroopers, our paratroopers succeeded in opening in the Sillaro Valley another access to the Po Valley.

On the morning of April 21 all artillery of the sector fell silent, with the exception of the British 90 long-range guns, which, positioned a few hundred meters behind us, once in a while fired a few piercing volleys. During the breaks in the fire, the tall artillerymen from the Gold Coast would hang hand and foot from the barrels, insisting on polishing them in this hanging manner; theirs was the only visible movement in the dust-covered hills. The barrels sparkled like mirrors in the sun.

Suddenly, the news reached us that Poles from the Carpathian Division, Italian grenadiers from the Legnano group, and American troops were entering Bologna from three different directions; first, even if not by much, went the Poles.

The Germans finally abandoned the Gothic Line and began folding toward the Po, hammered without truce by the frightfully powerful air force and attacked by masses of partisans. In this region, in fact, the guerrilla warfare had greatly intensified after the SS, responding to partisan attacks with savage exasperation, burned people in their houses and exterminated the entire population of Marzabotto, a town in the mountains.

Maybe, I thought, all the soldiers who were withdrawing inside that hell looked like the lieutenant that I had seen dead on the dirt road after the battle of Musone.

Two halftrack drivers who lived around Imola, on the closest side of the bluish plain, were the first two from the Sixth Group to reach their homes, just liberated. They returned and announced that their parents were alive and their houses untouched. We congratulated them, asking questions that might have seemed strange but that reflected those that each of us had carried in our hearts for some time.

Within a few days, the Folgore Combat Group was transferred to rest in the Emilian Plains, where there were rumors of Fascists and killings of innocents. I don't know if the Folgore was relocated in that area to control the people; at any rate, no one told us, perhaps because many politicians would have interpreted an explicit judgment regarding our command as the army's illicit interference in their field.

*

As soon as I had the opportunity, I went to visit the two Antonios encamped in the countryside not far from us; I hadn't seen them since our time in Cerreto.

I found Moroni very tired. "Come see Castelli," he said. "He was at Grizzano."

"Where?"

"Grizzano. Where there was that damned mess."

"What are you talking about?"

"How could you possibly not have heard of it?"

"You know that now I'm a shirker," I said.

"It was maybe the nastiest battle of the whole campaign, worse than at Filottrano. Castelli was a patrolman there."

The encampment of the First Group was set up near a green alfalfa stretch; Castelli sat in that grass, with only his head and shoulders sticking out. His receding hairline brought to mind a skull. He was reading very slowly from a book and didn't notice us.

"Antonio," I called out to him.

He looked at us and didn't recognize us at first because the sun was in his eyes. Then: "Ah, it's you? Come here, sit down. I'm letting the sun warm me up a bit."

We sat in the tall grass in front of him.

"Well, this time, it's really over," I said. "Soon, we'll be home."

Castelli nodded. We said a few more words in order to feel at ease again.

Then: "What's this story about Grizzano?" I asked him. "Come on, tell me everything properly."

"An ugly story," he answered. "It began the morning of the nineteenth. Three days ago, while it was still dark. The Second Paratroopers Division had arrived in a hurry, almost by surprise, on the Grizzano hill; it actually was the cornerstone of Bologna's defense, but we didn't know it. An entire battalion of the German First Paratroopers Regiment was on the summit: those from Cassino, among the best German soldiers. Well, in short, we found ourselves up there, isolated, us and them: two battalions."

"What fun . . ."

Castelli nodded. "Grizzano is nothing more than a bald hill with a few houses on top; neither we nor they could withdraw anymore, because both the artillery and mortars had immediately started a brutal barrage behind both sides. That fire lasted all day, from morning until night: a hell." He was quiet for a while. "We all ended up inside houses: there were only a few dozen meters between us and them. You could say that we each dismantled the houses on our backs, with anti-tank projectiles. I tried and tried, with the radio, to get a gun to fire on them, but you can't fire on a target that's twenty meters in front of you: we were also directly in the shooting path, and I had to give it up. Five times during the day (those were the worst times!) we went outside to attack each other with daggers, still with the battalion's commander in the lead."

"Who is it? Do I know him?"

"It's Colonel Izzo, that Puglian with white hair. He's alive, even though he's wounded."

"Ah!"

"They were those heavy soldiers. You can see them, can't you? With camouflage uniforms full of weapons, something scary. Our people, though, were magnificent! You know what, before then I didn't know the paratroopers well enough. In short, we're the ones who came through: at night, those who were still alive abandoned their position, taking advantage of the darkness. If you had seen how many dead were on the ground . . . One of our sergeant majors and a German marshal were hugging each other, each with his hand on the handle of the dagger plunged in the back of the other. What faces! Starting in the afternoon, though, they began dragging and sheltering our wounded men near their houses. And finally, when they departed, they left their doctor there to take care of them: 'As a sign of admiration,' the doctor declared himself."

After a while, he added: "Many of them were volunteers and had sworn to die rather than return to an invaded Germany. You understand?"

"Yesterday," Antonio Moroni said, "General Alexander, the one who commands the Mediterranean forces, came to visit the Second Battalion. He decorated Izzo with the Distinguished Service Cross and, one by one, shook the hands of the battalion's paratroopers. I wonder how many photographs will be in the next issue of the divisional newspaper."

"Well, I'm glad you came to see us so I was able to give you an account of it while I'm still deeply affected by it," Castelli said after a pause. Some of his old liveliness began to brighten him up. "It must have a good impact! Too bad you feel that you're a writer and not a painter: you could have painted my portrait. Couldn't you, just this once, be a painter?"

"Ah, no, I can't, because even if I hadn't started writing, by now I consider myself in the union, you understand? But it doesn't matter, I'll describe you in a book. You'll see. I'll say 'his nostrils quivered.'"

Both of them agreed: "That's it, quivering nostrils."

"So," I said then, as a way to conclude, "at the end, not only did the Germans not hang our prisoners, but they left their doctor to take care of them? My thoughts aren't entirely sharp yet, but this seems to me like something important, definitely important."

"You want to draft one of your concatenations, huh?" Castelli said. "What an obsession!" and he shook his head.

"More than an obsession; by now it's become a real bad habit," Moroni pointed out.

Suddenly, the air filled with explosions. All three of us jumped to our feet, our hearts in our throats: above Via Emilia the sky was filling with small red anti-aircraft clouds, among which two German airplanes darted acrobatically. They were the only enemy airplanes to appear since I had been part of the anti-aircraft artillery. I ran toward my guns.

When I reached the group, the airplanes had disappeared; the soldiers, each in his combat post with a helmet on his head, were talking about it animatedly.

"Shot down?" I asked.

"No, they left."

"Thank goodness," I said.

6

WE FOLLOWED the last war operations on the radio. We were especially worried about what was happening on the Yugoslav border. With a triumphant voice, the announcer from London gave report after report concerning the entrance of Tito's Communist bands into Istria and their spread toward Trieste, trying to pass them off as successes. He didn't say that up there the last afflicted units of the Fascist Republic continued fighting, some after the Germans' retreat, on that border where the previous war had cost so many deaths; now they completely sacrificed themselves by uselessly waiting for us or the Americans or the British to come relieve them. May these painful pages honor those good soldiers who in the end certainly did not die for fascism, but to defend Italy's borders. Meanwhile, we stayed idly under our tents while Communist bands raged through Istria like a flood and did nothing but kill and rape and kill some more.

We received some rumors of Communist exploits: three or four Italian women had been hung and cut to pieces in the butcher shop of Villa del Nevoso; near Fiume several men had been shoed with horseshoes, with the nails hammered at the bottom of their feet, and forced to walk until they died. Many others, it was said, were being thrown, dead or even alive and tied, into pits.

My stomach spasms began again; those women's pieces dangled in my mind, now showing their white and smooth part covered with miserable woman's skin, then their bleeding flesh. In the afternoon, even the haunting smell of freshly cut-up flesh surrounded me in the sultry tent, and entered my mouth.

But Communist partisans were everywhere in northern Italy . . . fortunately not as many as in Tuscany and Emilia, but still they were fairly numerous, especially in the cities. What was really happening in our north where a general insurrection was now under way?

And what was happening in the rest of Europe? In Germany, Czecho-slovakia, Hungary, and anywhere Red anti-Christs had replaced the brown Communists? Undoubtedly, while they executed the offenders, the Communists were also killing, or deporting, many innocent people. How many? And who? Maybe all of those who could have been, in one way or another, obstacles to their future dictatorship?

The Allies did nothing, at least nothing that was apparent, in the face of such a tragic reality. And neither did we; actually, we Italian soldiers only wanted to return home.

What was I doing? I suffered for the dead who day after day accumulated in the pits of Istria (altogether they would reach around ten thousand!). They might have been relatives of Cèt and others who lived in that area. For me at the moment, it was enough to know that it wasn't my family . . .

On April 28 "Free Radio Milan" announced that Mussolini, *Il Duce* of fascism and Italy's dictator for more than twenty years, had been captured by Communist partisans while he was fleeing along Lake Como and shot. He too, then, in the decisive moment had tried to save his own life, after having tried for so long to impose on everyone a disregard for their lives (*'If I retreat, kill me!'*). He was dressed like a German soldier, he who imposingly enforced the worship of the Roman spirit.

Always full of contradictions, he was no longer theatrical in the hour of death; in fact, toward his end he hung dreadfully onto the mark of Dante's law of retaliation. Even the insulting crowd, which inevitably challenged him after so many years of senseless acclamations, was there. And yet, shame on you, Milan, for those corpses hanging upside down above your crowd of rejoicing citizens!

In any case, we tired men only wanted to return home.

At the beginning of May, the regiment initiated a plan, studied for some time, that would enable each northern soldier to spend a day at home. By that time, the German and Fascist resistance had ceased in all of Italy.

7

ON THE NIGHT OF May 4 the first three slow, teetering trucks with the Sixth Group left the fields where we were encamped. They traveled two or three kilometers of country roads between dust-covered hedges, emerged on the still nicely asphalted strip of Via Emilia and, after our own hearts, began speeding along.

At first we rode in the dark, then in the uncertain early light. The prosperous Emilian towns of brick and terra-cotta were left behind one after the other; given the hour, they were still deserted, with all windows shut.

The engine of the truck on which I had been assigned, a three-ton Bedford, suddenly crackled, picked up again, and went back to crackling. I looked at the driver questioningly. "Do you know anything about engines?"

"Yes, I'm also a mechanic. There must be some water in the gas."

The engine stopped. The soldiers' worried faces emerged from behind the tarpaulin, the collars of their British overcoats raised around their necks. "What's going on?"

"Nothing," the driver answered, having promptly climbed down to open the trunk. "We're leaving at once."

The other two trucks (each under an officer's command) slowed down and finally stopped. The second began to slowly back up; worried faces looked at us from its body.

A truck on the move passed us; we were surrounded by a chorus of greetings, immediately carried into the distance. "The First Group," the driver told me, raising his head from the engine.

After the water was removed from the carburetor, the engine started again.

We drove through Bologna, whose long paved streets were deserted at this hour. Perhaps new troubles for Italy were being plotted here. In any case, I didn't feel like dwelling on such thoughts: be it weariness or cowardice, I preferred to tell myself that, after all, this too was a city like any other, with the same kind of people.

Once we crossed Bologna, it began to be morning. The streets of pros-

305

perous towns were becoming animated; occasionally we noticed, here and there, squads of armed civilians, whose appearance wasn't in the least re-assuring. The sight of them gradually filled me with anxiety: what were those armed partisans doing, ten days after the end of the war? We could also see them entering a few houses. There had been word already that they were murdering offenders and innocent people that they didn't like. Later on, we would learn that the reality was worse than our suppositions: in fact, more than two thousand people in Emilia alone were murdered, some in ways no less barbaric than in Istria. In upper Bologna, for instance, in or-der to avenge the Fascists' brutal execution of the seven Cervi brothers, sev-en other brothers and sisters, the Govoni, only two of whom were Fascists, were executed even more brutally.

The trip continued. Some places were devastated from air raids; in the countryside were parking areas of American tanks and large gray masses of German prisoners. On Via Emilia, two convoys, mostly Americans, fol-lowed one another in both directions. On its margins many soldiers from our "workers' groups" trudged, heading north, most of them dressed in the shameful British coffee-colored uniforms for prisoners; undoubtedly, they had deserted the southern ports in order to return home. They moved along, perspiring, some bent under their packs, which may have been full of loot. We carried as many of them as the truck could hold.

Piacenza.

It was the place where I had begun my military service more than four years earlier: the circle of my soldier's experience was closing.

There it was, in the outskirts, the new church of *Corpus Domini,* its bell tower with its sharp cross, the perpetual false target of our practice. Mem-ories of those days came back to me quickly in the truck, even the sense of adventure and the heroic dreams of twenty-year-old men . . . Those dreams had been followed by the reality of decay and blood, because war, win or lose, is mostly decay and blood.

In many areas, Piacenza appeared devastated by air raids; most of the massacres were in the neighborhoods around Via Emilia and the train sta-tion. There it was, the roof of our old headquarters, broken through. And, not far in the distance, the two pillars holding the Roman wolf had been unhinged. From those sidewalks, prostitutes with their red mouths had let out their slippery night calls when we came out of our quarters, our twenty-year-old blood already throbbing in our bodies.

I had prayed as I walked by those red-mouthed sinners who had tempt-ed us; perhaps now they only had mouthfuls of dirt between their teeth and the curved bones of their palate. Who knows if anyone had ever been truly available to take interest in them, if they had had mothers to raise them with love . . . Maybe no one. Christ had been the only one who had loved them, and he had sacrificed himself also for them, the prostitutes of Piacenza.

Since the large Po bridge had been cut off, our three trucks crossed the river—very slowly and bumpily—on a long boat bridge. As we reached the other bank, I found myself on my Lombard land: mine for millennia. My mother's heart was made of that land. I blessed my land, covered with poplars, after twenty months of absence and war.

Once more the tires sped on asphalt, and their dirge quickly lulled us again. (How could I forget it? It's the cadence that modulated our thoughts throughout the years in which we participated, through good and bad, in the history of the world.) Crossing some famous village or another, or the view of some large dairy farm nested in the plain, distracted us sometimes from that fated sense of travel. Meanwhile, around us, the characteristics of Lombardy increasingly took shape: earnestness and omnipresent life; there wasn't a piece of earth here without its blade of grass. And there was no turmoil here, but calm.

The names of locations began to inform us that Milan was close. The foreign motor vehicles were once again becoming more frequent on the road. Occasionally, I watched the American and British soldiers who traveled on them. The tide of organized anti-Christianity was rising in all of Europe; would these men—half-Christians—be able to stand up to it, as seemed to be their assigned task? They appeared to struggle when confronting the Red revolution in a small country like Greece . . . But it's also true, I told myself, that they had applied themselves diligently, that they hadn't avoided the task.

Finally, from a crossing on the city's outskirts we saw in the distance the small Madonna on the main spire of the dome, which emerged alone from the uneven surge of roofs (there were no skyscrapers back then): *La Madonnina del Duomo*, for us Lombards a symbol of our land. But that joyful sight immediately turned to grief, because for a while the statue of the Madonna was hidden by a red flag hoisted on the pediment of a tall factory. Once again the Reds had punctured the enchantment of our return. Then came the streets of the city, not cordial that day: in fact, on the walls were too many Red posters furiously calling for hate. I remembered some of the irresponsible, lustful posters from peacetime, which our era alone since pagan times had tolerated. If we chose paganism because of its delights, we also had to accept its sufferings.

At first, even though I looked around, I wasn't able to capture the deep moral countenance that is characteristic of Lombard people, or that at least had been until recently. Yet the color blue also appeared on the walls—still tough, much tougher than anywhere else—alternating with the red color of hate, to remind us that the forces of good were still deep-rooted and great in Milan. Those forces—uplifting, nourishing, inspired by the breath of God—had molded me since childhood, and many times, horrified by barbarity, I had turned my thoughts to them in order to regain my strength.

*

We stopped for ten minutes near the San Vittore prison to allow our driver to make sure that one of his relatives, who had worked there during the armistice, was still there, or at least to see if someone had news of him.

As we were waiting, a young Liberal partisan with a tricolor scarf who was escorting a long column of French SS prisoners (headed to the prison, those soldiers walked slowly, looking around them as though stupefied, oddly patient in their blue hybrid uniforms) broke away and came beneath the window of the truck to amicably shake my hand. He asked for news of the army, then he began his own reporting, saying that, among other things, he had seen with his own eyes the Fascist leaders' corpses hung by their feet in Loreto Square above a rejoicing crowd.

"Rejoicing around the corpses?" I observed, without beating around the bush. "How should we define it? A crowd of savages?" The fellow looked at me uncertainly. "Sure, that's true. But it's not that simple. Not everyone was enraged . . . There were also many people who were curious." He thought it over for a moment: "Not everyone. One person—he seemed like a worker—stuck his bike between my hands: 'Only for a minute,' he said, excited. 'I want to see those dead people close up.' When he came out of the crowd, I told him that in times like these he shouldn't have entrusted his bicycle to a stranger; I could have been a thief. 'By now, there aren't any more thieves!' he started shouting, and widened his arms like this: 'Now, we've all become honest!' You understand? It wasn't only a crowd of enraged people," he repeated, while I turned to look away.

*

According to my instructions (of the three car leaders, I was the only one who knew the city), the other two trucks went to park in the nearby square of Santa Maria delle Grazie, bordered by the main road for Piedmont.

When we joined them (a half-hour stop had been appointed for Milan),

I realized that only the outer walls remained from Leonardo's greatly renowned *Cenacolo*. Someone had placed some railroad tarpaulins on the marvelous fresco, which had become completely bare, to at least protect it from the rain. Troubled by such a sight, I headed almost in a hurry toward the nearby house of one of my mother's sisters, but as I was about to go up to it, I was called back: none of my people lived anymore in that house, which had been requisitioned for months. I tried then, with increasing haste, to establish telephone contact from the porter's lodge with other relatives who lived in the city, but without success.

Lastly, I dialed the number of a priest who was a friend of the family; since he wasn't home, I went from phone number to phone number. In the south, we northerners complained about the lack of telephones, but here it seemed like there were too many . . . I reached the priest when our half-hour halt was about to run out. "Be reassured," he said to me, "all your family is alive, everything is undamaged. Your older brothers who stayed home, Giovanni and Piero, lately became partisans . . ."

Piero too, then, a boy and a medical student, out of his compassion toward men. With the wards deserted, he had started playing with war like an enthusiast; in his kindness, he couldn't have imagined how brutal the game was. At the moment of the uprising against the Germans, everyone's enthusiasm must have been huge here.

"Where is Achille? Why isn't he with you?" the priest asked me.

"He'll arrive in a few days, with the Lombards' shifts. Because we're doing shifts. I'm passing through Milan on duty."

"Are you hiding something from me? Is he maybe wounded?"

"No, I'm not hiding anything. Thank God for . . . for everything I just learned from you." As I was talking, I went back and forth excitedly over the few steps that the telephone cable allowed.

"I'll take care to let your family know right away. In the meantime, don't worry about all the red that you see around you. The archbishop did a lot in Milan, and on the mountains too there were some great Christian forces. Of course, unfortunately now the Communists are taking revenge . . . Is it true that there's an inert government in Rome that hasn't even punished one offender until now?"

The soldiers had already taken their places on the trucks and were waiting for me. As I came out running in the square of Santa Maria, Morandi leaned out and shouted, "Lieutenant, good or bad news?" Everyone was looking at me.

"Good," I shouted.

Everyone was relieved, for themselves too. The sun was shining against the terra-cotta facade of the old Bramante church and on the stretched-out tarpaulins that protected the marvelous painting.

For once, then, the news had been good! Deeply moved, I thanked the Madonna of our people, the Madonna of the Forest, while the trucks slowly began moving again.

*

Magenta; the Ticino River with its wide gravelly shore: the bridge on the river was intact. We crossed it and found ourselves in Piedmont. After a few kilometers our truck separated from the other two and headed toward the Alps.

At the house of a soldier, the gigantic corporal of the First Group, his joyful acquaintances gathered around. As he shook their hands, I saw him suddenly burst into tears and shake his head convulsively. I came down from the cabin. "Some of my family was killed by the bombardments," he said. "I thought I'd find them here, instead . . ." He smiled. "But my mother is fine."

"Good luck!" he finally yelled out to the other soldiers, and moved away between laughter and tears, followed by a swarm of people and children. Before going inside his house, he turned his large torso around again and awkwardly waved.

*

The soldiers arrived at their houses one after the other; some sorrowful scenes were alternated with many of exultation. One of them, however, was barely interested in his family: "Where's my motorcycle? Did you keep it hidden?" Even during the war, he always talked about his motorcycle.

So, in one way or another, everyone met their family.

*

Morandi was the second to last we took home; the last that day.

The sun was setting as we began going up his steep valley; at its entrance we could see several ruins of burned houses. In spite of the season, some snow was falling. Although in the larger Ossola Valley, from which this one branched out, we had met mostly blue partisans, here the few towns swarmed with partisans wearing red scarves around their necks.

We halted at a handful of houses because an old man was tied to an iron gate on the side of the road. The thin rope around his purple neck forced him to stay on the tips of his toes against the bars, like a badly tied-up beast.

Six or seven partisans moved away from him to come closer to the truck. We exchanged a few uncertain words; two or three recognized Morandi.

A partisan girl in men's clothes, decked in red, came beneath my window and, without wasting any time, winked at me.

"What formation are you?" I asked her uncertainly.

"We're *Garibaldini*."

It was like saying that they were Communist partisans, although I did not interpret it this way quite yet, because I still hadn't resolved myself to accept their stance—in my opinion, inadmissible—between nineteenth-century patriotism and Communist internationalism.

"*Garibaldini?* Not Communist, then," I tested her.

"Not Communists," she lied.

"Thank goodness," I said stupidly. "You sure do have a lot of red around though!"

Maybe the death of that unlucky man tied to the gate resulted from these words (I become agitated still today, after so many years, just thinking of it!).

"Who's that wretch?" I asked. "What did he do?"

"He's a Fascist spy."

A young man who seemed to be the leader came forward. "What do we do with him?" he asked. "Can we kill him?"

"Kill him without a trial? But . . . what's got into your head?" I exclaimed, feigning astonishment, as though such an action were inconceivable outside this valley.

Unexpectedly, an old civilian who was witnessing the scene a few steps away came forward too. "Enough," he said, turning to the partisans. "He's nothing more than a poor devil; you've mistreated him enough, let him go."

Since our truck had stopped, everything had been happening as though on stage: we were like tiny marionettes against the rough backdrop of mountains. I realized this somehow, and I tried to also recite my part, but foolishly I didn't fully understand my role and what was at stake: the life of a man, who could probably have been saved by a few words, by my behaving in a well-chosen manner. The old man's intervention was very brave, I later realized, but useless because of my foolishness.

"Go away!" the partisan leader yelled at him. "Get out of here immediately! And be very careful: I know that you don't have a clean conscience either. You be careful too!"

The civilian took a few steps backward and no longer spoke; he limited himself to gesturing no with his head.

The prisoner didn't even try to speak: his neck was clenched and purplish, his eyes closed, his hands tied one on top of the other on his stomach with a string, like in children's games.

Undoubtedly, the best solution would have been to take him away . . . But would the partisans have let him go? There were only four of us soldiers left on the truck and we were armed with only two pistols, mine and the driver's.

"All right, we agree," the partisan leader decided finally, turning to me again. "We won't kill him. Do you know what we'll do with him? We'll give him another sound beating, then we'll take him to the partisans' command of Domodossola."

Domodossola was in the larger valley from which this one branched out, where there were also Christian partisans with blue scarves; as I mentioned, we had met several already (among others, a large formation busy moving a captured column of German trucks). They weren't people who killed prisoners or let them be killed. I remembered the burned houses at the entrance of the valley; they were almost certainly the work of the Fascists. This man, perhaps, could have been one of their friends too. After all, if these fellows were *Garibaldini,* in short Mazzinians, why would they deceive an Italian officer? But they were Communists instead, and I let them outwit me.

"Yes," I decided, "it seems like the best solution: bring him to the Domodossola command." Turning to the driver, I said, "Come on, let's keep going."

*

We kept going and dropped off Morandi in his small town, which was the highest one of the valley, at the end of the road.

No family came to meet him because he didn't have any; even his grandmother, who had brought him up since birth and raised him instead of his parents—often beating him with her knotted fist—had died years before. One last time, Morandi invited us to spend the night with him; then he left, with his everlasting swinging bear walk, toward his log house, refined by the geraniums on its windows.

Each time that I had seen him arrive somewhere during the war, I reflected, it had been an allusion to this arrival. But did this one really have a taste of finality? Maybe this didn't have it either; maybe it also was only a reflection of the only true arrival that each man makes, unaware, his whole life.

"Get to the plain before it's dark," the people told us, "because there are still some Germans and some Fascists on the mountains." So we did.

We didn't know when we left the steep valley that the unlucky prisoner, against whom rested only very vague evidence, had already been murdered by the Communists. Morandi informed me a few days later.

8

THE NEXT MORNING, after dropping off the last soldier in front of his house, I directed the truck toward the capital of the province; here, according to orders, the trucks would have to stop until traveling again the following dawn to retrieve the soldiers. But I had decided otherwise: first of all, since Margherita lived in the capital, I would see her again "according to our destiny." After that I would go and spend the rest of the break at my home, which was only sixty kilometers away.

Margherita! Every other thing, every other thought faded into the background. As we drew closer to her city and the countryside once again became level and lined with rows of poplars, I struggled to keep calm, awaiting this great event that I was about to experience.

I won't relate the details of what transpired. I'll only mention that I met a beautiful, nineteen-year-old girl, whose appearance was very similar to the one I had idealized and dreamed about day after day for twenty long months. This other Margherita—meaning the real Margherita—behaved politely, with native courtesy, even though she was very surprised by my visit. Trapped by very strong emotions, I listened to her speak like one would listen to an oracle and answered her clumsily. But after a certain amount of time, as the minutes passed, a glimmer of doubt began creeping into my mind: perhaps this beautiful girl wasn't the one who, along with my angel, had escorted me on my long journey. Instinctively, I tried to chase away this insidious gnawing; I was in trouble if that was the case.

When after maybe an hour I came out of her residence, I was mostly confused. In any case, I told myself, determination and will count greatly; well, then, with my will I would have . . . I would be . . . Meanwhile, Shakespeare's words on the love of love, bitterly troublesome, crossed my mind. Was it possible that I too happened to love love itself, the idea of love, but not a real woman? If that's the way it was, if the Margherita I had longed for had existed only in my imagination . . . I sensed, at least partially, heavy consequences: in this case, I would find myself alone! I would find myself as alone as the man that God had seen so alone that he had had pity on him and had created a woman for him. My woman, in fact, would uncreate herself, dissolve into nothing . . . Well then, it absolutely couldn't and wouldn't be like this!

Before returning to the truck, I walked uncertainly back and forth in the nearby streets, trying to chase away the beginning of that disastrous perception. I had to be especially careful not to hasten things! That's it: I needed to take time, study the situation carefully, to find a way, for example, to overcome the inevitable changes in both her and me during our separation . . . But of course, clearly, the small inevitable changes . . . In any case, a single visit couldn't be enough. There would need to be several visits before reaching a conclusion. Indeed. In the meantime, nothing was compromised. Was it true that nothing was compromised? For a moment, the question brushed past me like a sneer: from now on, which Margherita would I project in my mind, this one or the one from before?

As I climbed back up in the truck, I tried to snap out of it. "You're a wretch," I told myself, "making such a fuss over this girl when so many people are suffering everywhere."

Nonetheless, I wasn't the least successful in turning my mind to anything else.

This thing, this other thing, the itinerary, the kilometers . . . I had to pay attention. Here we were on the road to Milan. American armored columns were coming with great uproar from the opposite direction and spreading out all over Piedmont: magnificently efficient columns. They would make the Communists uneasy. Suddenly, I wondered if I still cared . . . If I had been wrong, if my wonderful, vital wait was over, irremediably over, why should I care about everything else?

"Hey, calm down. Try to control yourself!"

*

Once again I saw the streets of Milan, the houses and house fronts bound together without relief, the swarm of Italian cars (all running with gas generators, that is, with charcoal), after so many years of not seeing almost any civilian cars, and our women with their embittered and hollowed faces.

Beyond the city, the large road that headed north was almost unrecognizable because the old plane trees that had covered it with their gigantic green shade since the Austrian occupation had been knocked down the winter before by the poorest people in town for firewood. Only a few remained standing, alone, with their trunks meticulously gnawed by bill hooks and blades; their large dead branches seemed oddly bewildered now that they no longer fit with the others.

We arrived at my town in a little over half an hour. The roads among the hills of Brianza had gradually become smaller than what I remembered, exactly like the poets teach us. I firmly resolved myself to hide my recent distress, in order not to disappoint my family after such a long wait.

Here was my father's factory. As a boy, that sight filled me with pride when I came home from school; I remembered asking myself vaguely, in the previous months, if this return would bring a sense of guilt (therefore, to some extent, I too had resented that stupid Communist demagogy). In any case, I felt nothing, as though I was dazed, unable to feel those kinds of emotions.

The truck stopped in front of the railings of our old garden; on the other side, some of my family was in front of the house. I jumped to the ground and waved an arm: "Hi!" I shouted. Everyone came running toward me; after twenty months, I embraced my family.

A small crowd of workers and peasants, who kindly broke out into applause, immediately formed near the truck. I turned and, very seriously, made the military salute; I must have looked funny.

In order to hide my emotions when I went inside the house, I pointed to a large porcelain vase that my sister Caterina had finely worked with gold: "That one," I said, carrying on an old joke, "I was really hoping not to see it again, hoping the bombardments would have succeeded in getting rid of it."

Everyone laughed. Shortly afterwards, the kids joked around noisily, staying around me with their eyes like stars.

Everything in the house was as it should have been. My father, the patriarch, didn't take his eyes off of me; undoubtedly, he thanked God in his heart for returning the eldest of his ten children to him after many terrible dangers (first on the Russian front, then during this war in Italy that had involved such a long separation). He rejoiced to find me able to walk, talk, gesticulate: God had not only returned his son, but returned him whole, without disabilities; he realized that this was a deep grace.

My brothers and sisters, so dear to me, did their best, according to their ages and their individual personalities, to give me a warm welcome: they wanted me to feel at home, in this home that was ours, always awaited and now welcomed, and surrounded by the fullness of life, our home's leading trait during those years.

Seated in a corner, my mother didn't stop from gazing at me, smiling, like my father, but with her eyes full of tears. Maybe she already sensed the new sorrow—at the moment, unknown to her—that hid itself inside me and, therefore, she resolved to help me (as she always had before, and as she always would afterwards during the course of her life).

*

The next day, the driver and I departed before dawn in the dark. The truck retraced the trip in the opposite direction and, having gradually picked up the soldiers, left Emilia after twenty hours of driving and advanced, jerking slowly, on the uneven road between the hedges. We arrived at the encampment of the Sixth Group again in the thick of night.

The men came down from the body of the truck, saluted half-asleep, and set out, initially with uncertain steps, toward the encampments of their respective groups. Each one carried his bundle of novelty, already old, on his shoulders.

A sentinel came forward and informed me that Achille had left a few hours before, with a shift of Lombards; I thanked him and set out alone (I hadn't been able to pick up Morandi because the snow had made his valley inaccessible) toward the tents of my battery.

At my shuffle, one of the useless dogs that the soldiers adopted during the rear-zone war gave a few barks and immediately fell silent. The British halftracks with their ancient profiles towered motionless over the morbid silence, and all the tents slept in peace. The elms, which held the grapevines in rows in the middle of wheat, barely moved their downy leaves, as though to better drink in the moonlight. I gropingly entered the officers' tent. Since it was British, it was therefore different from the ones we had been used to before. I looked for the lantern along the central pole; when I turned it on, the light pointed out the sleeping outline of Captain Zuntini. Laganà's and Guidi's cots were empty; undoubtedly, the two of them were traveling somewhere in trucks, in order to take other soldiers home where their lengthy yearning would come to an end.

After undressing, I turned off the light and lay down on my pallet.

From outside came the insistent call of an owl that pitifully roamed the moon-whitened countryside seeking a little bit of love. His lamenting request continued endlessly.

Who would have kept me from thinking, like I used to, about Margherita's curly blonde hair before falling asleep? No one would have noticed. But I understood that I couldn't lie to myself, and all I could do was cry.

9

THE DAYS CONTINUED to move forward.

The Poles from Anders's Army Corps were quartered nearby, in the small cities along Via Emilia. When we drove there we saw them wandering the streets of the outskirts, usually alone or in small groups, their hands in their pockets, without talking.

They now realized that they wouldn't be able to return to their country, for which they had fought so hard. For some of us, our return home had been a source of sorrow as well as joy; yet there had been some joy, sensed rather than experienced, and without whose occasional encounter we no longer wanted to continue along life's path. For the Poles, there was no joy.

Originally, in Poland, there had been the terror of attacks by much stronger nations and the desperate defense on two fronts against the terrible hordes of modern barbarians, then wagons of deportation to the East, where each day corpses piled up (and the living in those collective coffins screamed for hours and hours, asking for water, and eating the flesh of the dead in order to survive). Then, in the Russia *lagers,* more death, more death, more death, like a pendulum with always the same stroke. Afterwards, after the miraculous release from the *lagers,* there had been Cassino (more death!) and the rest of the war. Now there was a void.

For each soldier who was still alive, how many fellow soldiers were dead? Six, maybe seven, for each one, it was said.

We knew from experience that to keep going during the deportation and the war, all of them must have had in their hearts their return to their families as their goal. But now it was certain that such a return would be followed by another deportation. They were in an exhausting situation, even just thinking of it . . .

The Emilian Communists, mostly former Fascists—and, therefore, accessories to the Polish tragedy—sensed the Poles' inevitable aversion to communism, and found nothing better than to accuse them of being Fascists . . . We could see it written here and there in red paint on the walls of Via Emilia.

The Poles didn't react. The only time of day when they seemed to stir was early morning, when they sang the prayer of exile deployed in front of their flag. Several of them would cry as they sang, because in the morning that brings hope to all men, that prayer, composed in another century by one of their refugee poets, was enough to truly break one's heart.

I wasn't able to say good-bye to you one by one, you were so many, proud Poles, friends, people like few others—honest and free of complicity—when you left Italian soil. With these pages, if they ever reach you, accept my grateful salute.

A few weeks after the end of hostilities, the Folgore Combat Group was transferred to Veneto, near the city of Verona, which Shakespeare, setting in it his most beautiful love story, defined as gracious. But those were different times, and Shakespeare's opinion had not been able to prevent aerial divisions from reducing entire neighborhoods of the city into plains of debris. We were moved from Verona to the blue mountains of Belluno; our group encamped near the small city of Agordo. After a few weeks came another transfer, this time to Trentino; my section was sent to a small town with the strange name of Roveré della Luna, with the task of guarding some German depots.

As soon as we left Agordo, Communist partisans resumed their executions, which they had unwillingly suspended while we were present; by now lacking Fascists, they murdered, on top of it all, some fellow citizens who had proved to be friendly with the army during our stay.

It is said that as Italy was liberated, murders continued everywhere, and every morning people discovered new corpses in the streets, and rivers and canals transported corpses daily. The Communists weren't the only ones killing (although it was mostly them: in fact, it would be several months before Togliatti firmly took the party in his own hands). Others continued committing murders as well, lacking any real political goal and stirred only by the lust to kill. In addition to Communists and to those whose road was greatly facilitated by abstract violence, "laic" extremists were organizing themselves into the "action party," which more than actually killing continued to obstinately demonize fascism and Fascists, maliciously wishing their elimination. This made stemming the killings very difficult for other democratic parties, especially for the Christians.

Among these, many who had fought against dictatorship tried to save innocent people as much as they could, but had to do so secretly and at their own risk. They too would have been unable to save themselves in those days if someone, seizing the right moment, had assaulted them, screaming "Fascist," just as no one would have been able to save themselves in other historical eras if accused of spreading the plague. Some soldiers and officers of the liberation army were also murdered in this brutal manner.

Alarming news continued to arrive from Greece: the Communists who had unchained their revolution in December 1944 seemed again to be expanding. In truth, it was only the beginning of the tragedy; it would take Democratic Greeks three years of harsh fighting, and the help of first the British and then the Americans, to expel Communists from their borders and achieve free elections.

However, there was no hope of freedom for the people of Eastern Europe, almost one hundred million human beings, who were pressured by the Red Army. And still, even they were less harried than the people enclosed within the new borders of the Soviet Union: in fact, due to their complicated theories, the Bolsheviks at first left some semblance of independence in Eastern Europe. However, they immediately began to deport the people inside their new borders and turn them to Bolshevism. We knew that many people were again hiding in the woods in Lithuania, Estonia, Latvia, and eastern Poland. But with what hope? We came to know their name: they were called "brothers of the woods."

Sometimes I remembered those peasants with large heads and kind faces, present in great numbers in the Red Army, who were left dead in the snow where the Germans had passed. They had been the ones to save Russia, not the Bolsheviks. The Bolsheviks, however, continued without constraint to use them as instruments toward their own domination. Those peasants must have entered devastated German cities with astonishment; who knows how they felt when they had seen their women again, being deported by the millions for forced labor in factories . . . Now they saw them loaded up again on trains and deported ruthlessly to Siberia, branded with the prostitute mark; in fact, per Stalin's decree, anyone who had experienced in some way (even in that way!) European life could no longer return home in the Soviet Union. There was a sad Russian song about these tragic circumstances. Who would ever help these Russian peasants with their endless sorrows?

During those months the best-known Allied commanders began leaving the units in order to assume civilian assignments in their countries (precisely as partisan leaders were doing in Italy). Occasionally, a printed circular letter was distributed in which one general or another took his leave and, according to Anglo-Saxon custom, wished us happiness; the word happiness reoccurred frequently in those messages.

Morandi shook his head. "Look at what's written here: happiness. Who would have thought? People in the command!"

And yet, they weren't foolish people. On the contrary, just thinking of them is exalting, especially the Americans, whose task in those days was to begin confronting the terrible problems of the world. They were realists, and precisely because of this, in my opinion, they unfailingly ended up by choosing Christian solutions. This is how the splendid system of assistance, not only for Allied nations but also for enemies that the war had prostrated, was born. People in some way had become brothers once again . . . Nothing like it had been seen since the Middle Ages and the knightly wars.

In the following years, envy—present everywhere—hostility toward whomever fate favors, and more hatred disguised everywhere as Christianity would sow in the entire world the seeds of aversion toward America (of course, not toward all of America, not for pagans, but instead for this missionary and Christian America). The phenomenon assumed such a dimension that in many nations even many Christians no longer knew what to think, and still don't know even today. In truth, that nation, and those men who in the face of the terrifying problems of the postwar era willingly worked hard to resolve them, remain an example for us all, no less so than other major examples from the past of a man's sense of duty.

10

COLUMNS OF American soldiers who were bringing back to Italy former prisoners from Germany, and also Italian civilians (these latter organized by a special Pontifical Commission) marched frequently not far from Roveré della Luna, on the federal highway of Brennero. This march, with half the large internment camp of Pescantina, near Verona, would continue for months.

One day, a former prisoner who had come down from a stopped truck approached as, by chance, I happened to be on the road. He looked at me doubtfully. Usually we didn't look at each other, those of us who were stylishly dressed in a British manner and those who wore the old, very worn, gray-green uniform, as though it was, for opposite reasons, embarrassing for us to recognize one another.

I addressed him jokingly. "Up there in Germany," I said, "you even saw Neapolitans work like Germans, didn't you? It must have been an enjoyable display."

He didn't pursue my joke. "You have stars," he murmured. "Are you Italian? An officer?"

"Yes. This area is garrisoned by our army."

"I don't want to hear any more talk about the internal army." His bristly beard stuck out from the hollow cheeks around his mouth.

"I understand. Well, in a few days you'll be home. You'll finally be able to live in peace."

"Since you're Italian," he asked me, "why aren't you beating these Germans from Alto Adige? While we were being deported, if one of us succeeded in escaping from the trains, they would capture and confine us immediately; don't you know?"

"Yes, we know," I answered him. "But it's time to stop retaliations, don't you think? We have orders to avoid all quarrels with these people, and it seems like a good order to me."

He nodded. "The Germans are a wretched nation," he said. "Even now that they've been defeated, they all hold themselves quietly like before, and we can't give them their due, if we don't hit them."

My interlocutor was called away; after having given me, somewhat unexpectedly, the military salute, he moved his rags back to the truck, which he struggled to climb.

Units of defeated Germans were present in our area also: soldiers, but mostly workers of the Todt organization in military uniforms who worked in large squads along the interrupted railroad of Brennero.

Sometimes I stopped to watch them.

They had given us Nazism; half and half with that other nation, the Jews, who in the vanguard of modernity refused Christ, they had given us Marxism as well: the two doctrines most laden with death in our time and certainly in the time to come, at least as far as I could see.

Now here they were plainly, Germans, heavy in their bodies and in their ways, all soiled in blood up to their elbows, and yet with an air of large blameless dogs, unjustly beaten.

They had no excuses, I told myself. And yet they had not been the only slaughterers of our time, and probably not the worst ones either; besides, the main difference between them and the other great slaughterers, those from the East, was in the great consistency with which they applied death doctrines. They had behaved, one by one, with the anti-Christianity of those doctrines, without the nineteenth-century hypocrisy of the Communists. We had to give them this to their merit—their only merit: they had never hidden their own methods and intentions under humanitarian disguises.

All the misshapen trucks of the Pontifical Commission that drove on the federal highway, sometimes in short columns, sometimes in long ones, hoisted the Vatican's white and yellow flag, which waved cheerfully.

I compared it to our humiliated *Tricolore*. Back then I was still in the dark regarding several misfortunes relating to the birth of the flag of Italy. Sure, I knew, like everyone, that our flag derived from the French, but I wasn't aware that the green in ours had replaced the blue in order to satisfy Freemasonry; furthermore, in 1797 it had been a defrocked and quarrelsome priest, Giuseppe Compagnoni, who had suggested and gotten the constituent assembly of the Cispadana Republic to accept the *Tricolore* (all of them gathered in Reggio Emilia in a room shaded by the Torre del Bordello; everything planned!). Nearing his death, he would once again seek shelter under the wings of the church (thus implicitly rejecting even his suggestion of adopting the *Tricolore*).

I wasn't aware of these founding details, but it was clear that if Italy chose to transform itself into a republic (as I myself wanted), the Savoy coat of arms would necessarily disappear from its flag. With its shape of a cross and medieval origins, the coat of arms was the only component that dignified the flag in some way. In fact, without this modest coat of arms, the flag of a nation with a history as great as ours would obviously end like the French; not only that, but it would even fall to the lower level of some Central American or African flags (and, in fact, today it does not distinguish itself from the Ivory Coast flag).

It was a time for drastic ideas; therefore, I asked myself if it wouldn't have been appropriate to change the flag completely, adopting, for instance, Dante's coat of arms (an eagle's wing on a bicolored background), which is nobler by far and, if nothing else, ours. As the days passed, I slowly became convinced of this opportunity. It was the postwar experience that would change my mind, when, with almost all Liberals and generally those of the *Risorgimento* nearly silenced, mostly Christian politicians ended up defending the *Tricolore* against the threat of Red flags. Afterwards, when the Red threat lessened, it was the *Alpini* and their fellowships, who for decades also tried to introduce the *Tricolore* to youths by distributing it in schools. Who could have been more qualified than they to deserve the flag? The extraordinary heroism of the *Alpini* on the battlefields and their sacrifice, along with other loyal soldiers, has redeemed their humble origins: that is how they felt. Later on, something new happened, which incites me today to make a suggestion: it seems as though it is the cross, in fact, the crosses of medieval naval republics returned in the navy's *Tricolore,* whose memory summarizes our civilization and greatness well: Genoa (with Columbus and the discovery of America), Venice and its extraordinary charm, Pisa (and, therefore, Tuscany, with its great art), finally the lovely Amalfi, which gave birth to the "perpetual" philosophy on which rests the rationality of the Christian world. Those coats of arms are, above all, very beautiful, so that—placed in its center—they've made the navy flag perhaps more beautiful than any other. Why, then, don't we adopt it as our national flag?

11

AT THE END, the Folgore Combat Group was transferred to Alto Adige, between mountains with colors as beautiful as the most beautiful paintings. As we traveled among them with the trucks, I thought about the one I had lost, and I wanted—amidst so much of the Creator's splendor—to fool myself into thinking that she still existed, to return to look for her at the end of every road.

At Vandoies in the Pusteria Valley in July I received a letter from Cèt: after months of silence, he informed me that the Yugoslav Communists who occupied the island of Cherso had deported his mother without any explanation. (In truth, they had shot her, along with one of her brothers and other members of the Italian community of Cherso, but he wouldn't learn this for years, until he turned to a Communist member of parliament for information.) Now he was alone, his father fallen in Greece, his mother deported, homeless. He asked me if I would be willing to look for her with him: we would go around Yugoslavia in civilian clothes.

I remembered his generosity and nobility under every circumstance, but especially during the weeks we spent in Cerreto. Why did God torment him like this? There was an answer, of course: God was putting entire innocent nations to the test, like Poland and Lithuania. And this was the height of Christianity. But now that my friend was being put to the test, I found it very difficult to accept.

After considering my thoughts carefully, I wrote to him that neither he nor I were entitled to commit suicide. At the time, I felt as though I was answering him as a friend, and I felt relieved; but later on, I began wondering if I didn't feel relieved simply because I had refused his reckless suggestion and if after all I hadn't been a coward. I was greatly afflicted.

There were also other worries: back then, a fifteen-day leave was granted in turns to each soldier, from which the few Communist soldiers almost systematically failed to return. I began to wonder—and I wasn't the only one—if at this point an insurrection like the Greek one wasn't imminent in Italy. We all knew that the Communist partisans, far from obeying the call to turn in arms, were now, thanks to the Fascist and German surrender, much more armed than before. A reoccurrence of the events in Greece seemed more probable each day (even afterwards, once discharged, I awaited the revolution for a long time, my heart skipping a beat with every distant explosion I heard . . .). Still, in those days, after so many exhausting years of fighting, the prospect of another war, and this time a civil war, seemed especially unbearable. "When will we stop fighting?" I wondered. "And why do we still fight, since it's clear, understood, that war doesn't solve anything? These new problems that are beginning are in themselves proof . . . War only makes matters worse: period."

Some days, I didn't feel like talking. I subtly moved away from the others; at times in the afternoon, after duty, as I was walking along the paths of firs that surrounded Vandoies, I would think back to my past from the start, just like the Molisan peasants, I remembered, in the farm dominated by the Fortore River, when the war with its threat of death was about to run them over.

I was very stirred by distant and close memories: all the good things from my past stirred in me and, at times, I felt an unrestrained nostalgia. I wanted again my childhood days filled with sunshine, and the thrush that I kept in a cage when I was a boy, who seemed to hold in his dark eyes all the depth and mystery of the forest; when he sang, I would listen to him without being seen, and I felt as though I was being transported to fantastic distances. I loved all over again: the pure expectations of adolescence, the trusting serenity of my twenties, the bright wall of San Ginesio, Margherita, Margherita; for my friend Cèt to find his mother; for my dead soldiers, one by one, to be no longer dead, to be able to speak with them again on the grass like we used to. And since all of this was impossible, I was torn with sorrow.

Although during duty I treated my soldiers like I had before, many of them began to stand against me, even those who had been the most loyal. This included Morandi, who, from one day to the next, asked to be exempt from his orderly duty. They were bothered by the strict discipline that I still expected, and even more by the training that I imposed on them—almost forcing the captain's hand—during a period of general release.

*

Achille was discharged in August. I too had asked for a discharge, to return to school with books under my arm . . . But I would be ready to defend my home when the Red revolution broke out. There was no retreat beyond my home: the idea of being far from it and, therefore, not anxious was almost comforting.

My last day of military life was in mid-September; once again summer was drawing to a close, making way for the advent of fall.

Captain Zuntini, conscientious as he was, had distributed the sugar saved in the kitchen during leaves to the soldiers who were being discharged. My new orderly brought the bag and cut it: "This is the payment for whoever is discharged. Five hectograms:[1] so, if I'm not mistaken, it's one hectogram for each year of your military life. You've spent five years in the army. Isn't that right?"

"No, only four and a half years."

"And they're giving you five hectograms! You realize that this generosity can only mean that your military life is really over."

The next morning, very sunny, with the perfectly blue sky of the Pusteria Valley above us, I deployed the men in my section in a clearing between the firs in order to take my leave. While I spoke, I remembered other speeches, or "sermons," for the soldiers; the farewell at the last position on the Don, for instance, to the "old men" of the *CSIR (Corpo di Spedizione Italiano in Russia)*[2] about to be repatriated in rotation: what true words came to my lips that day! The soldiers had suddenly begun to cheer, many with tears in their eyes . . . And that other address, very different, during the tragic encirclement in Arbuzov, among the burning *isbas*. If providence hadn't prevented it, that night in my lucid delirium I would have brought them all to their deaths . . . And the melancholy farewell of the Marches platoon, with Canèr present for the last time. At twenty-four, my memories tore me to pieces. "Enough," I tried to tell myself, "forget it. Stop caring. The past is the past."

The soldiers looked at me without emotion. Now that I was leaving, no one would trouble them with training and other nuisances (the captain was skeptical about the possibility of a Communist revolution; he wasn't wrong, after all).

Not even Morandi showed any sadness. Nonetheless, maybe he was holding it in. He too was about to be discharged; maybe, later on, when he no longer felt me to be a burden, he would mention me like he sometimes

1. Five hectograms are equivalent to one pound.
2. Italian Expeditionary Corps in Russia.

mentioned some of his old officers: "Lieutenant Corti used to say . . . If Lieutenant Corti were here he would . . ." Probably that wasn't me anymore. Maybe sometimes it still would have been: "I was sleeping during the battle of Filottrano: the lieutenant shook me and I said to him: 'I want to eat 149 grenades . . .' You understand? I was drunk as a skunk. What did the lieutenant say to me? Nothing."

Freddi was the only one at the departure with tears in his eyes.

When the others broke ranks, he came forward and took a revolver out of his pocket and handed it to me. "It wasn't easy finding it. It's a 7.65 caliber, which civilians can also carry. I'm giving it to you as a keepsake." He spoke with his usual unassuming manner, with his good, keen face turned away. "You might need it to defend yourself once you're home."

I took the revolver and examined it; it must have cost him a lot. "It's a good weapon," I said. "Thank you." We shook hands.

"At this point, it's all military life," Lance Corporal Freddi said with half a sigh and, after having raised his right hand to his beret in salute, he about-turned.

I then remembered Antonio Morandi's words, the ones he had spoken one night among the mountains when our peasant hosts had deprived themselves of their dinner in order to feed us: "One feels a need to fight for people like this."

"If we don't fight with weapons, we'll fight with ideas, with civil action, maybe." Indeed: that's it! At that moment, I felt the Spirit inside me, and understood that there was no escape.

About the Author

Eugenio Corti was born in Besana Brianza, Italy, in 1921. He marked his debut as a writer with *Few Returned* and went on to write major works of historical fiction. One of his most recent books has been published in English as *The Red Horse*.